Recent Indian English Fiction

Winner All the Way

Recent Indian English Fiction

Winners All the Way

N. Sharada Iyer

ADHYAYAN

ADHYAYAN PUBLISHERS & DISTRIBUTORS

New Delhi-110002

Published by
ADHYAYAN PUBLISHERS & DISTRIBUTORS
4378/4B, 105, J.M.D. House, Murari Lal Street
Ansari Road Darya Ganj, New Delhi - 110002
Ph.: 011-23263018, 011-23277156, Fax: 23280028
Email: adhyayanpublishers@yahoo.com

Recent Indian English Fiction
Winner All the Way

Edition 2011
ISBN 978-81-8435-280-1

Printed in India

Published by Harish Chandra Yadav for Adhyayan Publishers & Distributors, Delhi. Laser Typesetting at Jain Computers and Printed at Tarun Offset Printers, Delhi

To my Parents

Meenakshi & Natesa Iyer

Acknowledgements

Gautam, my nephew a rare combination of computer science and ancient history for helping me retrieve my lost treasures. And to Mr. Harish Yadav, Managing Director Adhyayan Publishers and Distributors, Delhi, not only a good publisher but a good PRO too.

Preface

After the first flush—Mulk Raj Anand, R.K. Narayan and Raja Rao the 1980s marked a turning point with writers like, G.V. Desani, Kamala Markandaya, Attai Hossain, Ruth Pawar Jhabvala, Manohar Malgoankar and Khushwant Singh. But the real mark was made by Salman Rushdie with his *Midnight's Children,* the book was quiet unlike anything that had happened earlier except, Desani's *All About Hatter,* which was exceptional in the way Desani had used English and the reality of India was a revelation. Salman Rushdie extended it and expanded it to bewitch the whole world. He delivered his vision of a place, time character—a vision that was Indian. It freed the Indian writers to do what they wanted, and not sit around writing the sort of fiction that was called 'the heat and dust' fiction, where the exoticism of India was stressed. The flies, the dirt, the dust and the quaint custom of this country it has all that, but it also has that particular reality which is part of the inner cities of the West. It also gave a cadence to the fact that English is now an Indian language not necessarily hued to rules set by the BBC or VOA. But it is distinctive, organic and an integral part of India. A language that is valid as any other English one that we use as anyone else in the world.

After this flood gate opened the trio were, Vikram Seth, Salman Rushdie and Arundhati Roy whose names were cited around the world. Vikram Seth has proved that when it comes to virtuosity his genius is unmatched-a comic verse, a big saga in verse, 19th century novel travelogue and his exquisite meditation on music. The fourth to join the trio is Rohinton Mistry who began with a collection of short stories and furthered it up with much acclaimed novels such as *A Fine Balance, Such A Long Journey and Family Matters,* Others who are enormously talented are - Vikram Chandra, Bharati Mukerjee, Amit Chaudhuri, Alan Sealy, Amitav Ghosh, Upamanyu Chatterjee, Shashi Tharoor and David Davidar. All have established major following. All this has happened between 1980s and 1990s. The closing decades of the last century and the first decade of the 21st has promising talents like Jhumpa Lahari, Kiran Desai, Pankaj Misra, Ameen Merchant, Arvind Adiga and the commercial market dominated by Shobha De, Namita Ghokale, Chitra Divakaruni who have done well despite mixed responses.

The future holds a much assured place, Indian Writing in English is being taken seriously. One may hope to see more romantic, scientific mysteries all well developed, when India can say 'we have the writers we deserve, the publishers we deserve and the readers we deserve.

N. Sharada Iyer

Contents

Introduction

Indian English Fiction was for a long time a one tall hill and R. K. Narayan's was a lonely reign. There was Mulk Raj Anand writing with great intensity and the fair voice represented by Kamala Markandaya, Nayantara Sahgal, Ruth Pawar Jhabvala. Shanta Rama Rau writing a prose of great refinement and dignity. Erudite minds Raja Rao and Nirad Chaudhuri cultivated an exclusive clientele, while Khushwant Singh steamed powerfully into public consciousness with *Train To Pakistan.* But seen from the readers extended perception, the hills of Indian Fiction in English had one tree silhouetted prominently the strong root shade giving *Tamirindus indica* of Malgudi. Today five or six decades later the position is different. The rock is covered with rich and variegated flowers

The 1930's saw the 'foundling fathers' of Indian English Fiction-Mulk Raj Anand, R. K. Narayan and Raja Rao, the 1940's Ahmed Ali, G.V. Desani, the 1950s a crop that included Kamala Markandaya Ruth Pawar Jhabvala Khushwant Singh Attai Hossain, Babani Bhattacharya. Dom Moraes, Nissim Ezekiel , Kamala Das in the field of poetry. Nirad Chaudhuri and Ved Mehta in non-fictional but very creative prose. The 1960's novelists like Nayantara Sahgal, Anita Desai, Arun Joshi, Manohar Malgoankar and out standing poets like Parthasarathy, Ramanujan. The late 60s and 70s also saw the emergence of gifted group of poets and novelists, good translators of poetry, fiction and plays from Indian languages to English and vice versa.

During the 1980s in the wake of Salman Rusdie's *Midnight's Children* there appeared a cluster of new novelists-Amitav Ghosh, Alan Sealy Upamanyu Chatterjee and Shashi Taroor, who were students of St. Stephen, Delhi, in the '70s, and a fifth Vikram Seth. Because of his brilliant school leaving results Vikram Seth walked into an Oxford college, instead of its Indian counterpart.

Within the subcontinent's literary history Rushdie and his epic novel seemed symbols of a significantly different way of experiencing life and writing about it. Followers of de-construction jargons would label this difference from earlier ways of perceptions and expressions 'a-post partition-ontology' which meant that the post Rushdie writers had no direct oe livid experience of colonization or the national movement.

On account of the post-colonial existence the new generation had little to do with English as a people, or as a presence, or as an oppressive race, and everything to do with the nicest legacy of colonization-the English Language. If 1947 was a political watershed Rushdie's novel marked it with an aesthetic force that seems stupendous and unlikely to be matched. And also as a cultural and literary break Rushdie's stature as a light house to the new Pharoahs of partition subcontinent fiction only complements the position of *Midnight*'s *Children*. Within Indian English literary history Rushdie is the Colossus, who strides across and fuses diverse worlds, most specifically the Anglo-Saxon and the Indian, displaying a vocabulary and syntax drawn from both- a necessarily hybridized and native variety English. The sort of linguistic advance reflected in Post Partition Indian English Fiction was a fictional fraction the works of Rushdie and Ghosh was an extension of what had been started in English Indian Poetry. Kamala Das, Nissim Ezekiel, Parthsarathy, and Ramanajum refused to toe the lines drawn by the British vocabulary and syntax, and began the process of unshackling it and Indianising it. Irreverence, hedonism, iconoclasm and witty form of subversion, fossilized and dominant form of thought and power characterizes Rushdie's fiction that contributed to the making of some of the new fictions that appeared in the 1980s.

The sudden realization of the reality of history in which the individual has to play an important role is reflected in the novels of 1980s. The experience of having been so close to losing one's freedom, democracy and idealism had been an intense and poignant one. The feeling of having been given a new lease of life, with which to make a second beginning with renewed pledges was quiet pervasive.

If the 70s in India affected the way the novelists were to use their material, it was because the late 70s for the first time since 1947 threatened the security of the pan- Indian middle class intelligentsia.

For there had been terror before the emergency, terrors about unpredictable and repressive police action as in Telangana during the Naxal phase, the period of the 'white terror' in West Bengal following the Bangladesh war in 1971. But these were confined to pockets of which the rest of India remained unaware or chose to feel self righteous about. The Emergency only awoke the middle class to the infinite possibilities of state repression. It mobilized the Indian middle class as never before, and naturally affected the creative sensibilities. Rushdie's *Midnight's Children* and a short story *'The Free Radio* 'imaginatively exploits the national scenario of the late 70s. To the noted historian C.H.Carr" History is a social process in which individuals are engaged as social beings.....what I have called the dialogue between the past and the present is a dialogue not between abstract and isolated individuals but the society of today and the society of yesterday. The past is intelligible to us only in the light of the present and we can understand the present only in the light of the past. To enable man to understand the society of the past, and to increase his mastery over the society of the present is the dual function of history".[2]

It was perhaps this need , variously felt in culture throughout the world, that led to the upsurge in the 60s and 70s of creativity that tried to interpret man in terms of his social historical past. The multiple search for new dimension of reality which would combine past and present could hardly have been without its impact on the Indian intellectual scene coming down to the newer generation of Indian writers.

The new directions were to prove full of exploits, the early philosophical inventiveness that had made Raja Rao such an event on the Indian English literary scene was not along the highways bye-lanes of such jaded piffles." The artist in our time is more overtly concerned with the apprehensions of reality than the philosopher is and the image of violence seems often an appropriate way of his mode of perception.[3] Trilling speaks in a special context that of Isaac Babel's involvement with Cossack ethos. Trilling says we aught to be aware of the powerful obsessive significance that violence has for the intellectual.

Extending Trilling's observation one can see what the Indian English novelists of the 1980s did was to violate the predictable pattern .The image of violence as a fitting one for language, structure, world outlook were all pulled apart. It was Inqalab Zindabad so far as the formal writing of the novel writing was concerned, and raising the curtain was Rushdie's *Midnight's Children*.

The potential of the Indian mythology has been commented upon by R.K. Narayan "with the impact of modern literature, we began to look at the Gods, demons , sages and kings of our mythology and epics not as some remote concoction but as types of symbols possessing some psychological validity even when viewed against contemporary background."[4] And it is this that *The Great Indian Novel* by Shashi Tharoor written at the end of the decades explores. As a saga of Indian polity Tharoor's adaption of *Mahabharata* succeeds. The self deprecatory tone of its narrator Ved Vyas, later abbreviated as 'Vvj' spares nobody from his own Brahmanic ancestors to the British Resident Aeons of history are comfortably sandwiched into the first forty pages and it requires no elaborate straining to identify the drift of the events. While a one to one equation would have stretched one's credibility and diminished the satire, Tharoor's selectiveness keeps the basic narrative intact, falsifying neither its potential nor its metaphoric application. Even the title in the book carry their own story, though these begin to read like jokes at an Anglo Indian tea party 'The Twice Born Tale' 'The Duel With Crown' 'A Raj Quartet' 'The Power of Silence' 'Midnight's Parents' 'The Man Who Could Not Be King" 'The Bungle Book' or 'The Reign of Error' These incestuous literary references rather overshadow the more imaginative ones like 'The Rigged Veda' *The Great Indian Novel* is an attempt to retell the political history of 20th century India through a fictional recasting of events, episodes and characters from the *Mahabharata.* The issues it raises and the values it seeks to promote are central to what makes India, India. To take characters and situations that are so laden with resonance, and to alter and shape them to tell a contemporary story, was a challenge which Tharoor has done so admirably.

An important theme of the book is Tharoor's response as a novelist to British attempts to depict the same period in fiction-the Empire striking back. The theme is signaled in chapter headlines like 'The Duel with the Crown' and 'The Bungle Book' and in the names of several British characters. The deliberate caricatures to which the British characters are reduced mirror the two- dimensional Indians in E.M. Forster's *A Passage to India* and a host of lesser books.

The narrative technique of *The Great Indian Novel* is varied in tone, form and scansion as the epic itself with its numerous interpolations and digressions. Jokes, puns, wordplay are integral to the satirical spirit of the enterprise a spirit captured in the title itself. Tharoor's aim as expressed by him "was to reclaim the story of India for Indians. My fiction is infused in this sense with the 'greatness' of India of *Mahabharata,* a greatness that emerges from the fusion of its myths with the aspiration of the country" Belonging to the same club as *Midnight's Children* and *The Great Indian Novel* is Alan Sealy's *The Trotter Nama* dedicated to the other Anglo Indians. It has a family tree like Shashi Tharoor's but it is more cleverly conceived and goes a step further providing maps.

Categories such as "Legends' 'Chivalry' 'Romance' 'Prose History' 'Decadent' 'Diaspora' and 'New Promise' distinguishes the different generation of Trotters, and the narrator belong to the last.

Nama chronicles the entire history of the Anglo Indians by drawing metaphoric parallels between general destinies of the Trotter family and the public history of an alienated minority to which Sealy belongs

Rushdie has repeatedly asserted his closeness to the Indian narrative tradition. A tradition with its tremendous elasticity, its capacity for absorption, transformation, realism and exaggeration which however primarily oral tuned into the needs of the audience. It was this awareness of their audience and the pulse of their age as not mutually exclusive that gave these narratives their power to quote Sartre" What is the literature of an epoch , but the epoch appropriated by its literature"

All three appear to chronicle in as much the same direction that the other writers of the 70sand 80s tried to do. All the three were concerned with national history which is not homogeneously but heterogeneously catalysed and bounded.

Amitav Ghosh made waves with his very first novel *The Circle of Reason(1986)and* with his second *The Shadow* Lines(1998)established himself at the forefront of the fleet of Indian English novelists flying the Indian Flag, but plying international waters with eased zest. He belonged to the brash urban generation that regards all the cities as one. The post- colonial world has given the post-colonial cosmopolitan generation the linguistic and cultural access to not now so distant shores which can presumably be visited with a feeling of equality and familiarity. The generation had easy access and so feels international and perceives no boundaries. It finds it impossible to hold on to the traditional distinction -East is West and West is East entwined the two shall remain. The problem of East West encounter that agitated earlier generation just do not exist. The generation belongs to the united urban world-moving with ease from hamburger at the Golden Gate to ice-cream at India Gate. They are no longer content to ply the backwaters of native shores sending out status reports -tabulating exotica to Western publishing houses or even to visit foreign part to list with awe the differences or to write home about the problem faced by them there. They are world citizens at home in every city. Amitav Ghosh represents and writes for this generation which feels boundaries exist only in other people's mind, the problems were constructed and the difference lay in people's perception.

Vikram Seth came to people's notice in 1983with his engaging travelogue *From Heaven's Lake* A gripping account not because it takes us to' Lands unknown and clymes untryed' but almost because of the opposite. It shows the exclusiveness of much that is taken to be commonplace and the ordinariness of much that is supposed to be exotic. Seth has brought with him the structured fluency of Pushkin and the controlled effervescence of Frost. And both these are accompanied by the alert balance of Zen. With these rare gifts Vikram Seth arrived. It is the distinctness of his writing that his works are compared with one another than with those of any other poet or novelist. Seth's books touch plentitude and poverty, desire and deprivation. They are inclusive enough to accept the unlovely as much as the truly beautiful, the exciting and the mundane no less than the strirring for all those arc at the 'heart of life'.

The 80s have been a remarkable decade in terms of literary output. While on the one hand there have been formidable volumes of new publications and new names, it has also seen an equally formidable vulgarization of the printed world, selecting feminine writing out of this muddle has been an interesting experience. This has forced one to read and ponder over a whole new range of fiction- from Namita Gokhale's *Paro-Dream of Passion* to Bharati Mukerjee's *Jasmine* the journey has been circular.

In an incisive phrase Romesh Thapar once described Rajiv Gandhi's government as the government of 'baba-log'. Baba-log was meant to describe those children, products of a privileged childhood who were brought up by ayahs, perambulated in parks whose only contact with poverty was what they saw in their servant's quarters. The writings of women writers can be called 'baby-log' which would include generally those convent educated genteel young ladies whose 'tussors' and diamonds proclaim their twin worship of Gandhi and mammon.

Behind their growth is the growth of Indian democracy and behind the debased, sordid and common worlds of their texts a large matrix of squalor. Their fictions were filled with listless lust and witless dialogues. The roots of this fictional world lie in a sub-culture spawned by the Bombay film and the pulp fiction popular in the late 60s The idealism and self denial of earlier faded before the glitz of high living and simple thinking. This simplification of life's problems and replacement of quality by quantity was slowly to overwhelm a whole generation, shape their minds and consequently their language. Added to this was the scandal reporting in film magazines like 'Stardust" and one has the key to understanding these novelists

Both Shobha De and Namita had their roots strengthened in the culture of film journalism. Shobha De was the editor of 'Stardust'. She is credited with having introduced that element of juicy tintillation that was out of the range of old fashioned film magazines like 'Filmfare' . Intimate details of the personal lives of film stars were discussed in column like "All you wanted to know about but you were afraid to ask[1] In fact between. Shobha De and Devyani Chaubal of 'Star & Style' there was nothing that remained a secret in Bombay's film industry.

Interesting as this is in the context of the novel that emerged from this was another and more pernicious factor that was introduced by this -a new language that was a mixture of convent cliches and bazaar Hindi. Hindi verbs were made into English adverbs, and the alliance of the two became an index not only to the yoking of two cultures violently together, but the basis of that raucous, vulgar and hideous lingo that the collegians throughout the country was to adopt as their own.

Like Shobha De, Namita Gokhale started to edit clone of 'Stardust' 'Super' It is thus no mere coincidence that the plots of both *Paro* and *Socialite Evening* are based around a 'bitch goddess' heroine. Namita has no literary pretensions. She was neither a Jhabavala nor an Anita Desia and hence liberated from the literary heritage. Her novels combined Mills & Boons romance with 'Stardust' style Beneath the structure of their 'masala curry prose' lies the state of flux these women sensed within the new bourgeois society they were members of. They write to describe the process that proclaim "we are different notice us. We have a secret life and longing, we must speak about".

The study of the gynecology of these novelists is to understand that these are women in the process of becoming. Their narrative, their character, their language are part of a pattern that emerges when suppressed voices find utterances and a new world opens. The text of these novels is about the bad and dangerous woman who is battling with the troika of father-husband-mother-in-law, and their context the rising urban middle class. However, inadequately it is put across there are the first stirring of a novel of protest.

Narration on the same theme of the problem of affluence and neurosis are provided by other novelists as well. The narrative is usually in the first person, has stray autobiographical strains of self confession and is used by these women to construct new selves in new structure. The coarse and vulgar language of the earlier two novels is tempered to polite hushed tones. The world of these novels is a suffocating one with masked question and unspoken pain. Torn between loyalty to one's roots and an anger, at this loyalty, these novels are neither conformists- like Mills and Boon- nor wholly critical. The neurosis are like those nagging headaches that are neither strong enough for a pill, nor piffling enough to ignore.

Enter into the neurotic world is the exile and one finds another perspective. In the writing of the exile, the fine inter-relationship between the mother culture and the acquired citizenship gives rise to stray feelings of ambivalence which then form the dialectics of this fiction. This genre was shaped equally by the sensibility-of the emotional exile and by the mode of narrative adopted. The popular narrative mode adopted here is the saga adapted from the *Katha* which is episodic and autobiographical with touches of magic realism and the picaresque.

Two novels, Nina Sibal's *Yatra* and Leena Dhingra's *Amritvela* are two notable novels in this sphere. Both come from affluent Indian background which makes them more at home abroad. The result is a residual guilt and a feeling of treachery which colours their narrative texts. The title of both the books proclaim a 'dil hai hindustani' loyalty but behind this loyal claim lies a mass of discomfort and loathing. These novels fail to impress because of the lack of imagination and a failure of language, their upbringing and education has only made them unable to express themselves coherently in any language. They have sacrificed their relationship with the motherland to an extent that their loathing is sublimated not by laughter but by a false posturing.

The hollowness of these novels is made more evident when placed against the regional novels. They expose themselves as dilettante dabbling of vapid minds that have remained so remote from the changes in India that they have become pathetic. Shobha De's soft porn has always succeeded in any booming middle class environment. It is a natural byproduct of both the 1970 money boom and the burgeoning urban middle class. Indeed it has been a publishing staple since the advent of Victorian penny dreadful and every succeeding generation has had its quota of celebrated women writers churning out sexual fantasies in the name of female exploitation. Just as Danielle Steel and Jackie Collins are descended from Charlote Yonge and Marie Corelli, but no one remembers them now. Therefore, it is an accepted rule of the market that instant amnesia is likely to follow an instant success.

References

1. Vinay Kripal (ed) *The New Indian Novel in English-A Study of the 80s,* Allied Pub. Delhi, 1990, XXI.
2. C. H. Carr: *What is History*. Penguin Books, 1973, p. 73.
3. Lionel Trilling: *'Isaac Babel' in 'Beyond Culture' Essays on Literature and Learning,* Penguin, 1967, p. 127.
4. R. K. Naiayan; English in India: *The Process of Transmission.*

1

V. S. Naipaul – *Magic Seeds*

Approaching more than half a century mark of a literary career, V.S. Naipaul has entered 'his last phase'- as scholars and biographers euphemistically refer to the production of old age. Now reaching his 80s, he has published fourteen works of fiction and an identical number of non-fiction, a tidy congruence, winner of the Nobel Prize for Literature (2001), he is after a life time of heroic labour, home free.

Naipaul seems to concur with T. S. Eliot, who glumly described after winning the Nobel Prize 'as a ticket to one's, own funeral', when in a speech on his new novel *Magic Seeds*, made a public announcement that *Magic Seeds* may be his last, "I am really quite old now", turning his biblical span into premature senescence. "Books require an immense amount of energy, it is just notpages - it is ideas, observations, many narrative lines, and because Naipaul will no longer write the genre must die. I have no faith in the survival of the novel. The world has changed and people do not have the time to give that a book requires". It is almost over for him.

True, few novelists have achieved new breath at the end of a long career. Thomas Mann published *The Confessions of Felix Krull Confidence Man* when he was 79; Saul Bellow his masterpiece *Ravelstein* when 85; Henry James published no novel after *The Golden Bowl,* which he wrote when 61.

Though writers continue to write and publish even late in life, but add nothing to their reputation.

Naipaul, on the basis of *Magic Seeds,* seems not prepared to go quietly. The sequel to *Half a Life* (2001) is subtle if slender book, a novel that revisits the theme-exile, identity, the precariousness of civilization-that he has been grappling over with the past several decades.

In *Half a Life* and its sequel *Magic Seeds* he has returned to fiction after forays into travel writings, reportage and autobiography. It is a strange kind of fiction sifted through a life time of engagement with an abandonment of various literary forms. From early novels like *House of Mr. Biswas* (1959), in which Naipaul joyously recreated the Trinidad of his childhood, his vision darkened and deepened. The theme of cultural displacement became central, and he gradually evolved into one of the greatest pessimists of the age, witty, disdainful and often mocking. He once said, "I think literature should be read privately; it is not for the young, it is for the old and the damaged who require balm of certain sort. Tribal societies do not need literature. They have their yarns".

Willie Chandran asks his father one day, "Why is my middle name Somerset". So began *Half a Life* (2001) thirty years or so after he had first pronounced the novel a dying form. The story begins in 1930 in a South Indian princely state where Willie's father embarks on a half hearted rebellion against the 'servility' he sees all round him, against the false security of the maharaja's little state, against the pieties of his Brahmin family- 'foolish foreign ruled starveling priests'. He resolves to follow the Mahatma's call, and chooses some unorthodox varieties of Gandhian sacrifices and civil disobedience. He decides to strike a blow against the evils of caste system by taking a young woman from the backward caste, whose dark skin, 'coarse tribal features and terrible rough voice' both repel and fascinate him. He wages a low level campaign of civil disobedience, in the law office where he works, and destroying evidences of a fraud. The consequence is he finds himself miserable in his marriage, reviled by his family and faces prosecution for destroying evidences. His reaction is to fall 'as if by instinct into the old ways'. He walks barefooted and barebacked to the temple and declares himself a mendicant.

Somerset Maugham comes to India to research *The Razor's-Edge,* his proto-hippie novel about the search for spiritually. He is shown around the temple by one of Willie's father's enemy, a man who knew what a scoundrel he was but still "a good servant of the Maharaja's tourist department" he tells Maugham - the story of a high caste man, high in Maharaja's revenue service, from a line of people who performed sacred rituals for the ruler, of turning his back on his glittering career, living as a mendicant on the alms of the poorest of the poor. Maugham writes admiringly about his great man in his travel books and describes him as a great 'spiritual force'. Respect from abroad changes everything, now he is seen in his own place as a holy man and the fraud case against him is dropped. Willie's father sets up an ashram which attracts many visitors from the West. Like Gandhi he takes a vow of sexual abstinence, but fails. The result is, Willie is named after Maugham as Willie Somerset Chandran and his sister Sarojini.

This tale constitutes the foundling myth of Willie Somerset Chandran, whose adventures form the subject of *Half a Life* and *Magic Seeds,* conveying in a compressed form various Naipaul's long standing themes. Like the earlier novel, *Magic Seeds,* al least in parts, is autobiographical. Willie, like so many of Naipaul's protagonists, is a writer. As a student he writes stories and fables in his note book, that depict in an allegorical form, the shameful history of his family-his father's marriage to a low caste woman, not for love, but as an act of social defiance, the birth of the two children, Willie and Sarojini, the torments of life ruined by loss of status. To escape, Willie goes off to London. It is a journey that will prove 'transformative', just as it did in '*A way of the World*' and '*The Enigma of Arrival*", two earlier novels in which Naipaul obsessively traced his own classic journey from the provinces to the great cosmopolitan world. Just as often it's a journey, he traces in the reverse direction. Naipaul, more than most novelists, is driven back, again and again, to his origin. However, unlike William Faulkner or Saul Bellow and many regional writers, the territory he covers is not particular region but global.

Half a Life followed Willie Chandran from his birth place in India to a college in London and then to Africa. His name suggests a man of little will. In *Half a Life,* Willie moved neither with friction nor intent from one identity to another, a trajectory that added up to less than half a life. His sister wrote a letter that planted a seed, "You will see how much there is to do in the world and how selfish you are. Wasting your life in London doing this little thing or that little thing and not knowing why you are doing anything". *Magic Seeds* begins in Cold War Berlin in a 'bubble' not just the Walled city. Willie has escaped from an eighteen year stretch in the mad stream and is persuaded by his sister to return to India to undertake a sort of renunciation "submerging all the paths of his nondescript past in the ennobling new ideal"

Willie comes to India, where he means to join up a revolutionary group, but inadvertently joins a splinter organization, opposed to the leader who inspired it. He writes to his sister. "I must tell you I feel T am lost. I don't know what cause I am serving and why I am doing what I do". When its time to fight he feels he has "lived too long now with his disconnected landscapes, his disconnected duties with no true idea of the result of his action". He merely still follows the movement, giving Willie a fleeting purpose, as if he is living a whole life.

The long terrifying episode that follows is as powerful an account of murderous political idealism Naipaul has ever written. Unlike the overwhelming middle section in *Free State,* it is written from within the movement. Willie is lost to the world, living among the poorest of the poor. As the movement progresses, the members despair of success. "We must give up the idea of remaking everybody".

"How terrible it would have been to have lived without even attempting to lay claim to one's portion of the earth, to have lived as one had been born, unnecessary unaccounted.

Stripped of any sympathy, the same idea reoccurs in '*A Bend in the River*'. The world is what it is; men who are nothing and who allow themselves to become nothing, have no place in it. Willie threatens to become just such another person, a 'Casualty of freedom', the ironic phrase used by Naipaul in '*Free State*' When we catch up with him at the beginning of *Magic Seeds*, Willie has left Africa and is living in Cold War Berlin, with his sister Sarojini in a temporary 'half and halfway'. His search for a place in the world for wholeness starts again, as if from a scratch. Encouraged by his sister, he joins a movement in India.

In an interview Naipaul talked about the genesis of the first half of the Magic Seed, "I went to India and met some people who had been involved in this guerilla business-middle class people who were rather vain and foolish. There was no revolutionary grandeur in it Nothing. And then I put the whole thing out of my head. And then, as is often the case, I found a way of using that material as it should be used". The reference is to the Bengali communists whom he had interviewed in India for a *Million Mutinies* (1990) who had now joined the Naxalite Movement. By the time Willie becomes a guerilla, the whole course of the Movement had changed from peasant hunger to killing class enemies. He had gone with the intention of joining Kandapalli (Kandapalli Seetaramaiah, founder of the People's War Group in Andhra). After a torturous recruitment process, he arrives at the rebel training camp in a teak forest, only to realize that he had fallen among the wrong people and wrong revolution. It is confirmed by his sister that there has been a mistake, the Movement has split and that he was among psychopaths. Willie spends seven years among them. He lives a boring, violent and pointless life. The section follows Naipaul's line very closely- dream of Utopia becoming a living hell. The novel reserves the fiercest criticism for the deeply compromised men of the Left who justify their obscene acts with reference to the class struggle. "No revolution can be a movement of love" concludes Willie. The corruption of causes is complimented by Conradian grotesques-Willie consoles himself by concentrating on the yoga of his hour to hour life, looking on each hour, each action as challenging and important. But eventually Willie, naive and unanchored as he is, realizes that he must leave. This too is bungled. He confuses surrender with amnesty and is surprised to find himself in prison. After the yoga of the Movement comes the yoga of the prison. In an abrupt semi comic change of scene and mood that characterizes these two novels, he is saved by English literary friend Roger, a lawyer, who persuades them to release him on the ground that a long forgotten book of stories had established Willie as a pioneer of modern Indian writing. Saved from a purgatory in prison, Willie finds himself back in his own London stamping ground, confused still, lost on way to what Naipaul in *The Mimic Man* (1957) calls the greater disorder, the final emptiness in London and the Have Countries The final effect is a nightmarish chaos of opinion, a vision of world spinning in darkness, with everyone in it lost and association within abstracted from creation, as Willie puts it.

The Britain, to which he returns, is in its own way part of the jungle, another backward looking place, another world of slowly crumbling privilege that no one entirely seems to want to overthrow. Even with most to gain, appear to prefer the narrow round. In the West there is caste/class, which West has always known, but with much resistance to change. Naipaul shows that we all dream of change, we look to leaders, spiritual or political hoping for fresh ideas, we continue to cheat ourselves-as if by a packet of magic seeds - with visions of transformation. "We are like paupers who take their meager goods to market in the hope of getting magic seeds in exchange" observes a character.

The London Chapter formed a sustained and depressing meditation on a civilization that had apparently unraveled itself. The Notting Hill Willie knew in 1950 is changed to a Yobbish, proletarian London. The city has changed. Willie's experience of class resentment and poverty in India and Africa inform his judgment of England, which is presented as being rich in nothing except vulgarity.

Mapping the decline of London, a country which had become the most horrible kind of socialist parody, the novel seeks to place the blame entirely on the pernicious effect of Council Housing State benefits. "London's Council Estate are full of plebian" artful dodgers, an underclass of calculating scoundrels who are all living on benefits. The working-class who do not work are "growing fat, eating chocolate, pizzas and burgers". They feed off general taxes. They give nothing back. "We now have a full socialist revolution and the bizarre thing is that it does not mean high culture becomes available to everybody. It is terrible this aggressively plebian culture that celebrates itself being plebian" Naipaul said in 2000,

Surrounded by zealots, blood thirsty maniacs, Willie tries to preserve his sanity by living in his own memories and finds literature a possible way out. Rejecting the ideology of Marx and Lenin he recollects the works of Rudyard Kipling, whom he had read at the Mission School which had led him to become a writer later.

The solution to these modern ills in *Magic Seeds* is return to the old days: a return to the days when everybody knew their place. Roger complains, "There was a time when a substantial portion of the population was in domestic service. There was no problem". Willie too agrees. In his earlier novels Naipaul would have taken care to interrogate such inflammatory statement. Now he seems to be content merely to rage about cultural annihilation in an unfocused apocalyptic way. There is a glimmer of optimism in the closing pages, when Willie moves himself from the vulgar and vulgarizing city, to attend a wedding in the country.

"His mouth stopped increasingly on the winding main road there were Indians and Pakistan and Bangladesis... Willie knew about the great immigration from the subcontinent but (same ideas often exist in compartments) he hadn't imagined that London could have been so repeopled in thirty years". In this short passage there is so much, not only the claims of solidarity with the immigrants but also the claim to the literary tradition of the colonial power. T.S. Eliot following Dante, had seen the streets of London crowded with the walking dead. "So many/ I had not thought death had undone so many" to which Naipaul's answer is "All right for these streets are being repeopled (wonderful world) by my country men".

Ideas and beliefs being passed, as a result of population change, between different cultures were becoming meaningless or worse and demeaning both cultures in the process. The sense that India's spirituality is a con, form of institutionalized poverty, institutionalized servility- 'a religious response to worldly defeat' as he wrote in India: *A Wounded Civilization* (1977). It expresses a complex form of rage (a key term of Naipaul) towards India and Hindu culture; its disorders, its squalor, its indifference, its humbling rituals, its aping of foreign ways, contradictions and confusions of its political movements. This rage sustained his two famous travelogues about India. *India: A Wounded Civilization* (1977) and *India: Area of Darkness,* whose brilliance is matched only by their capacity to provoke and offend. This rage is still there in *Magic Seeds* when Willie joins the Maoist Movement.

By now Willie had traveled the paradigmatic journey-from home, father, family, a world colonial, circumscribed insecure-to London, moving from the margin to the centre of the imperial world. Like many of his heroes, Willie experiences the immigrants dislocated life, he studies, he writes, publishes, endures the traditional Naipaulian tussles with prostitutes and loose women. He loves, marries a Portuguese African women and returns with her to her country. But, after 18 years, suddenly decides to leave. Thus, abruptly the first book ends in *Half a Life* in Half and half worlds and probably half a novel too. It is a tale of restless India. Naipaul continues his chronicle of the dispossessed.

For several decades, Naipaul has put before the world, his unsparing scenario of the post colonial dissolution. In most of his novels, including *Guerrillas, A Bend in the River,* as well as the documentary reportage of books like *Among the Believers* and *"India"*, he has given the fragmented cultures and the unhooked population, as well as the ad hoc political initiation and the consequences they inflict on individuals bereft of viable traditions. At the same time, he has refused consolation of victim psychology, looking as remorselessly at the disinherited as at those who have done the disinheriting. Though, after he has made himself difficult to be liked, but is also equally more difficult to be ignored. Since then he has been working *Half a Life* and *Magic Seeds* recounting the life of Willie Chandran through his many journeys from India to London and thence to Africa where he witnesses at first hand a culture falling apart. Willie is brought face to face with his own passivity and at the end of the novel, when deciding to leave he tells his wife Ana, "I am forty one and I am tired of living your life. Now the best part of my life has gone and I've done nothing".

Magic Seeds describes the saga of Willie, the modern man who has lost-worse who has never found-the sense of self. He is like a die, ready to be cast; and, when his sister, Sarojini, an outspoken, politically enjoyed, film maker suggests, he is ready to join a revolution back in India. He allows himself to be led slowly, stage by stage, into the nomadic back country life of the insurgent cadre. Any sense of mission he has acquired is turned inside out when he learns from his sister's letter that he may be fighting on the wrong side. His hard won sense of purpose collapses; and, when he moves to leave, he surrenders, only to be imprisoned.

Willie's story is told with a ruthless economy of means and an almost brutal simplicity. Although the novel has full panoply of characters, it is Willie Chandran, a middle aged man, whose is the dominant voice. A nomadic soul, who drifts from India to England to Africa to India and back to England, in pursuit of his own identity, a man who feels himself, trapped with 'half a life and half word', neither one thing nor the other. He is a semi internal ruminating kind; forever in restless pursuit of his own elusive essence.

The life Willie leads and the reality he observes is painfully bleak tense, accurate, concrete, it offers a brutally claustrophobic image of existence. Willie searches continents for a glimpse of valid conviction, which is always missing.

This reminds one of the fictional musings of Camus and Satre, that pursuit existential of the ever unknowable and unreachable essence. Nothing counts but that. The reality is nothing other than the reality of the self emerging into faithless confusion and dubiety. At the very moment when Naipaul was starting out as a relatively conventional writer in England, just across the seas the French existentialists just finished doing what Naipaul was striving to do half a century later. Naipaul's conclusion is he seems to find in all cultures the same sadness of soul, much the same to delusions.

Behind the story of Willie Chandran is an old sleight of hand. The young Naipaul saw himself as escaping from a culturally insignificant world- coming home to a European society, grounded in a classical culture, which he thought he understood better than the most. Since then his writing has waged war against inferior cultures and individuals. Naipaul held that he belonged to a superior tradition and in his fiction the voice was that of the unmoved mover, a godlike narration from the upper regions who knows all and sees all.

However, *Magic Seeds* introduces a curiously chastened commentary. Willie realizes that there are two worlds, but unlike the young Naipaul protagonist, Willie sees something else as well. The two worlds co-existed. It was foolish to pretend otherwise. He was clear in his own mind now to which world he belonged. It had seemed natural to him 20 years ago, at home, to want to hide. Now, all that followed from that wish, seemed shameful.

As though to make certain that one does not miss the point, Willie follows this up with a reference to an earlier book-*India: An Area of Darkness*-where the author watches some low caste Indian sweeper and notes that they are simply spreading dirt around. This he comments was not cleaning. The sweepers were there to symbolize their status as sweepers in the country. Western notions like efficiency are swamped by the dominance of tradition.

In *Magic Seeds,* Willie arriving in India sees a sweeper operating in the same manner, "giving the floor a suggestion of thinly spread grime" and the sight prompts the reflection, "Twenty years ago I wouldn't have seen what 1 am seeing now. I have come from a world of waste and appearances. I saw quite clearly sometime ago that it was a simple world, where people had been simplified; I must not go back on that vision. I must understand that now I am among people of more complicated beliefs and social ideas, and at the same time in a world stripped of all style and artifice. This is an airport, it works; it is full of technically accomplished people. That is what I must see".

The movement between these two different ways of seeing might have been interesting, but while Willie continues to criticize his former self, his conclusions don't actually represent any important shift in the opinion. It is as if the author, reading his more hostile critics, has set out to prove that he is capable of responding to the contemporary world. The difficulty is he isn't.

Naipaul's great subject is humiliation. His books are about myriad means by which people lay each other down-sexually, violently, caste and class privilege, and related to all these is the profound historical humiliation of the Third World. To have been put in contact with the forces of history, but to be unable to understand their sources, to live in a place where things move along like a river but you can only see a short distance into the past or the future. This is a humiliation. There is first the work of understanding of history, the beginning of vision. There is also property in *A House for Mr. Biswas;* it is the house itself, though irretrievably mortgaged that saves Mr. Biswas's honour in the few months before his death. 'That he should have been responsible for this seemed to him in these last months stupendous". There has always been in his fiction the escape from the Third World humiliation, into the solidity and the anonymity of London, counter to all these aspirations has been the lamentable urge towards violent revolution, to burn down knowledge, houses and lash out at London.

Magic Seeds though bleak is uniquely moving, uniquely universal in no small part for it deals so honestly with

Naipaul's humiliations and uncertainties. In interviews Naipaul speaks with mournful honesty of late in *life* he received the Nobel Prize of how little pleasure he will be able to have from it.

The book attempting to explain multiracial Britain seems to be located within a depressing! of archaic framework of ideas about race. While in London, Willie notices that the appearance of London has changed. "There were black people everywhere, and Japanese and people who looked like Arabs". In the concluding and most telling scene is a wedding - a successful black diplomat's grandson, white of skin, African by heritage precisely the mix his grandfather, Marcus the diplomat, had dreamt of achieving - to a girl from once eminent British family now fallen in undistinguished time. What the girl now has to offer is her name, the skin, a kind of pedigree. Cultural ideals, old and new, jostle to the overland drumming of Surinamese band, in the dilapidated garden of a ruined roofless country house - a kind of skin colour migration from black to assimilated white or such changes be only skin deep. A marriage of mixed race celebration convey to Willie not just festivity but also the true look of a world where traditional lines of division of expectation have been erased, redrawn so much as to be no longer useful. Willie accepts this. "It is wrong to have an ideal view of the world. That's where the mischief starts. That's where everything starts unraveling". In the opening lines of *A Bend in the River,* "The world is what it is men who are nothing, who allow themselves to become nothing have no place in the world". But in *Magic Seeds* there is a change of emphasis, Willie, who allowed himself to become nothing, has put himself smack in the middle of everything. He would say that the old thinking is dead, that there is a place for everyone - but is this progress, it is hard to say. For Naipaul progress has become a part of the problem, it belongs with that ideal view of things we need to outgrow once and for all, *Magic Seeds* seems to represent some sort of a struggle to reassure and defend his life's work. In the end the struggle is a failure, largely because Naipaul has nothing new or interesting to offer.

Naipaul declared that he was going to quit writing, instead read Balzac. It is some kind of life that allows a man to read all of Balzac. Willie Chandran deserves at least a measure of that dignity. Even during the time he was involved with the Movement, Willie surrenders not because of any change of ideology, but because he can't stand the idleness of life in the jungle, between skirmishes. After being sentenced to prison, the idleness of his incarceration seems less oppressive. He seems almost at peace with the "regimented protected life of the jail". Getting an early release on the strength of the stories he had published during the college days. His return to London, where he pursues a dispirited affair with a woman for whom he had a passing infatuation some twenty years before, and now who is the wife of his saviour and friend Roger. The friend too is involved in his own dispirited and dispiriting affair. At the age of 60, towards the end of the novel, Willie is still crashing at his friends. Even in the post war West, forty years is too long for that self exploratory period after college. Willie should at least be allowed to find his own apartment. In *Half a Life,* Chandran reflects "the world is full of slippery substance".

Half a Life and *Magic Seeds,* like much of Naipaul's work, constitute a consideration of what it is to find a place in the world. Even Willie's book is reviewed as that it seems "is the most unsettling way to come out of a no settled view of the world".

It is taxing to follow a protagonist who is a blank spot in his own life but Naipaul writes a pure direct prose that carries the readers along and provides a thread of continuity. *Magic Seeds* makes high art of the convulsions of a life "as tangled and unplanned as wild jungle wine".

Magic Seeds, even more than its predecessors, is a horrible novel- icy, misanthropic, pitiless. If *The Enigma of Arrival* (1987), is a sad and wonderful book, belongs to Naipaul's 'autumnal stage', this is 'bleak winter'; the cold fury before the end. Naipaul was just playing up to his reactionary reputation, as he does in various interviews, railing against multicultural (a racket) New Labour (a socialist revolution producing an aggressively plebian culture that celebrates itself) or Saudi Arabia and Iran (they probably should be destroyed actually). The great diagnostician of Societies, as V.S. Prichett described him, seems to have given up the job-he now just jabs the patient playfully in the liver or pokes him viciously in the eyes.

Magic Seeds confirms the forbidding drift of Naipaul's talent. Since *A House for Mr. Biswas* doomed to be more admired than loved, and since *A Bend in the River* more respected than reacted, as Thackeray said of Swift, Naipaul leaves his readers with conflicting desires, wanting both to damn him, "filthy in words, filthy in thought, furious, raging, obscene for as it were given up on being human, but also to acknowledge the gloomy genius. So great a man he seems to me that thinking of him is like thinking of a great empire tailing. Though after he has made himself difficult to be liked, but even more difficult to be ignored, resulting in his recognition by the Swedish Academy to be honoured with the Nobel Prize.

References

1. V.S. Naipaul: *Magig Seeds* Picador 2004.
2. Mike Philips: Growing in Pain Guardian 25 Sept. 2004.
3. Carey Harrison: Review, Sunday 9 Jan. 2004.
4. Michael Drida: *Magic Seeds* Sunday 19 Dec. 2004.
5. Richard Wakefield: *Magic Seeds* Journey in India Unearths a tangled life. Sunday: 2 Jan. 2005.

2

Arun Joshi: *The Apprentice: A Spiritual Odyssey*

The Indian novel in English began as a 'hot house plant' but now it has taken firm and deep roots. The development of the novel can be traced from the experimental stage to realistic stage to the psychological. The realistic novel in English came to be written in India for the first time in 1920 when with the surging nationalistic feeling the "scene shifted to contemporary battles and agitations" The novels written between the two World Wars were chiefly concerned with explorations and interpretations of the social milieu, as is evident from the novels of R.K. Narayan, Mulk Raj Anand and Raja Rao *Swami and His Friends, (1935), Untouchable(1935) and Kanthapura (1938)* These novels did not make any conscious efforts in dealing with the individual personal predicament. After the 1950s the novelist's interest shifted from the public to the private. "If anything is to distinguish Indian fiction.....it would be a literary attempt to portray the conflict of the contemporary Indian" (I)

Arun Joshi is one of the few novelists in Indian English who have broken new grounds. In his search for new themes he "has renounced the larger world in favour of the inner" and has engaged himself in "a search for the human living" (2) Joshi has chartered in all his five novels the inner crisis of the modern man. The most common problem that man faces today is the problem of alienation and meaninglessness of life. As Edmund Fuller remarks "in our age man suffers not only from war, persecution, famine and ruin, but also from inner problem, a conviction of isolation, randomness and meaninglessness in his way of existence." (3) The problem of meaninglessness is so pervasive that it threatens to erode every sphere of life. Man fails to perceive the purpose and relevance of his existence in a hostile world. Notwithstanding his unprecedented science and technological advancement which have added immensely to his physical pleasures and comforts yet he is doomed to find himself in a tragic mess. He is estranged not only from his fellowmen but also from his innermost nature having nothing within or without him to fall back upon in moments of crisis. The age has seen the dissolution of old certainties and dogmas. Paul Burton observes "Never before were so many people plunged in so much uncertainty so much perplexity and unsettlement" (4). Deprived of the succor of ancient wisdom, which provided the much needed basis for value and meaningfulness to life, the modern man has no substitute for faith and religion except science and information. Huxley has aptly pointed out "ours is a world in which knowledge accumulates and wisdom decays" (5).

The past and the opening year of the Century has been an age of great spiritual stress and strain making it an 'age of Alienation'. It has shrunk in spirit languishing in confusion, frustration, disintegration, disillusionment and meaninglessness. Everything is conspiring towards a philosophy of meaninglessness boredom and the absurd. The existential encounter with nothingness and the tenuousness of human existence are prototypal of modern existence. The hiatus between what the individual aspires for and the hard reality of what he achieves between what he professes and what he practices and between what he really is and what he would like to appear, has crippled his life leaving an insidiousness in his inner life. The injuries inflicted and the scars left on his psyche generate a cynical attitude towards the established social norms and values and makes him grope for life's relevance.

Man is shocked to find that he is no longer the master of his destiny. There are forces which threaten to wither his life and all its joys and hopes. He "comes to feel helpless in the fundamental sense that he cannot control what he is able to foresee" (6). He suffers from a deep sense of powerlessness and meaninglessness and is in deep terror of the world augmented by its randomness. Life has grown indefinitely vast and without any proper shelter or linkage to hold from falling apart. "In the 19th century the problem is that man is dead. The danger of the past was that men became slaves. The danger of the future is man may become robots "who will destroy the world and themselves because they cannot stand....a meaningless life" (7). The absence of meaningful relations is the greatest curse of the age. We suffer from a gnawing sense of meaninglessness which may be manifested in "alienation from oneself, from one's, from one's fellowmen and from nature, the awareness that life runs out of one's hand like sand, and that one will die without having lived ,that one lives in the midst of plenty and is joyless(8).

The existential state of disappointment, isolation and meaninglessness have received attention in the West, novelists in India too have made serious efforts to delineate the predicament of the modern man. The works of Joshi particularly read like the spiritual odyssey of the modern man who has lost his spiritual mooring and is in quest of harmony and peace.

Arun Joshi emerged on the Indian English literary scene with his *Foreigner* (1968) which at once established him as a mature and outstanding novelist, and the novel itself as one of the most compelling works of fiction. The story revolves around Surrinder, Sindhi, his anguish following his loneliness and so called rootlessness. Sindhi finds himself lost in the maze of worldly existence and is deprived of any familial, social and cultural ties, and his soul cries for a way out of these confused ways of life. Sindhi Oberoi is born a 'foreigner' a man alienated from all humanity. The only son of an Indian father and British mother, born in Kenya, orphaned at an early age, grows without family ties, and without a country under the care of his uncle, Educated in England and U.S.A he is fed up of his life at "twenty five years largely wasted in search of wrong things in wrong places" To find a solution to the problem of his restlessness and foreignness, Sindhi tries to detach himself from, the world. He develops a philosophy of detachment which is a mask for his fear of getting too deeply with others. His philosophy of detachment, causes a tragic end to his American friend June Blyth and his Indian friend Babu. This later brings him to the realization that detachment means getting involved with the world. He follows the Karmic principle of the *Upanishad, Gita* and Gandhi and changes his name from Surrender Oberoi to Surrender Oberoi. The novel shows the protagonist's journey from inaction to action, from detachment to attachment and from illusion to reality. It shows the struggle of the individual to seek a way out of the intricate labyrinth of life which one passes through.

It examines the problem of alienation, isolation and involvement and man's despair at being unable to find a meaning to his existence and attempts to explore its genesis its course and cure. He is an existential character rootless, restless and luckless in a mad, bad, absurd world. He belongs to no country, no people and regards himself as ".... An uprooted young man living in the latter half of the century who had been detached from everything except himself (9).

The Strange Case of Billy Biswas (1971) was Joshi's second novel. It presents a hero alienated from higher middle class society in which he is born and brought up and which he is compelled to live though he feels an overpowering urge to march to a different dawn altogether. Right from his adolescence Billy had been conscious of an urkraft-great force-a primitive force within himself. In reference to it and in quest for peace and harmony he vanishes into the forest of Maikula Hills. The novel appears to be a sequel to *The Foreigner* in regard to the spiritual quest of Sindi, the hero and his itching to identify in the modernized superficial world. Sindi measures a day all through from Boston to New Delhi with the purpose of knowing the meaning of his existence and finding a place which he may call as his own. In *The Strange Case*[1] *of Billy,* Billy continues the Odyssey and leaves Delhi to Maikula Hills in search of inner peace and his spiritual roots. According to Arun Joshi *Billy Biswas* is about a mystical urge, a compulsion which makes Billy go away ".... in a number of Indian legends and religious texts people go away to forests to heal themselves spiritually. Possibly that's what he is suggesting though not consciously" (10). It presents the theme of man's restlessness in modem materialistic life and his futile attempt to escape it. For the theme he goes to Mathew Arnold's Thyrsis "It irked him to be here, he could not rest". The novel deals with the chaotic state of the human mind in the modernized world. He presents the conflict between the norms of the civilized and the primitive life and the spiritual quest through primitive passion.

"*The Strange Case of Billy Biswas* is a study in the total alienation of the protagonist Billy Biswas from the modern bourgeois society of India .... An apocalyptic light spreads over the novel, the promised land gets lost in the promised End"

Arun Joshi's vision of life as presented in *The Strange Case of Billy Biswas* shows that in the conflict between the civilized and primitive way of living, it is the latter that prevails. Real peace, pleasure and perfection can be found in the natural and primitive atmosphere rather than in the din and dust of big cities like Delhi.

Joshi's third novel *The Apprentice* is the tale of conscience torn man with a curious mixture of idealism and docility a vague sense of value, a helpless self deceptive effort to flout them for the sake of a career-in short with a deep awareness of the conflict between life and living. If in *The Foreigner* Sindi Oberoi in search of his identity and roots withdraws himself from humanity, but later realizes that sometimes detachment lies in actually getting involved, In

The Strange Case of Billy Biswas Billy withdraws from the materialistic and emotionally dehydrated 'upper-upper crust of Indian Society' which he belongs to .He identifies with the primitive world of the unsophisticated tribes. In *Apprentice,* Ratan Rathor, alienated from his pure self is a victim of the money minded corrupt society. Finally, he tries his atonement through humility and penance by wiping the shoes of the temple visitors everyday. *Apprentice* presents the most acute kind of alienation of Ratan Rathor, a government official who after alienated from society adopts the ways of the world to achieve power, status and material prosperity. He moves ahead in the race with a devil may care spirit, indifferent and insensitive towards people around him, in which he becomes the cause of the death of his Brigadier friend who had to leave the battlefield because of the supply of defective war material. Ratan later realizes his fault and holds himself responsible for the Brigadier's death. His morality is completely eroded and he realizes the hollowness of life. He suffers from acute alienation and loneliness within and without and out of mental agony he begs forgiveness from all those whom he had wronged and as a penance for his guilt he wipes the shoes of the congregation before the temple gate daily on his way to office. Written in the form of a dramatic monologue Arun Joshi makes the hero bare his soul before a silent listener. Ratan's penance is not physical but spiritual. He is willing to pay the price by suffering humiliation.

Joshi's fourth novel *Last Labyrinth* (1981) probes into the turbulent inner world of Som Bhaskar an industrialist, who becomes a millionaire at the age of thirty. He marries a woman of his choice and has two children. Yet he is driven relentlessly by undefined hunger. He suffers from loneliness in spite of all material possession and a happy life. The novel raises some pertinent questions about life and its meaning and tries to unravel the mysteries of God and Death.

In all the four novels Joshi focuses on the inner turmoil while in *The City and the River* he works on a vaster canvas depicting the predicament of the whole race. It is in fact an account of human predicament and divine salvation of mankind Using a mixture of fantasy, prophesy and a startling new vision of everyday politics he makes it truly a parable of the time. Joshi has turned to a "full-fledged allegory both existential and political" (11)

It appears to be "a scathing indictment of the notorious Emergency proclaimed by Indira Gandhi in 1975 mainly to be in power at all cost"(12)However it will be an injustice to Joshi if it is taken only as a political novel. The political body of the novel has been adopted by the novelist to present a spiritual vision of life. As Tapan Kumar Ghosh observes"......despite the satire in the novel of the present day political situation, it transcends the realm of political and explores fundamental truths about human life with it's spiritual destiny and that it's ultimate world view is not political but mystical or metaphysical(13)

Divinity dominates the whole world. Joshi makes a successful attempt to show the significance of an inseparable relation between religion and politics. Like Gandhi he seems to say that politics in the absence of religion and truth will only lead to death and destruction. *The City and the River* exhibits that it is ego, over-powering desire and self centered attitude that causes the predicament of mankind and it is only through purification, suffering and self sacrifice that divinity can be attained which in turn leads to the salvation of mankind.

APPRENTICE

In his third novel *Apprentice* (1974)Joshi adopted the technique of dramatic monologue like Robert Browning Joshi makes his protagonist Rathan Rathore lay bare his soul before a silent listener. Jean Baptiste Clamence in Camus's *The Fall* narrates his life tale to a French man in the bar, and as *The Ancient Mariner* in Coleridge to a wedding guest, in the same way Rathan Rathor pours out the details of his life to a nameless young student- a National Cadet who came to Delhi to participate in the Republic Day parade. Ratan tells him over a period of three months his life story-one of hypocrisy, cowardice, corruption and debauchery to this silent listener.

The novel opens with Ratan Rathore, the protagonist narrator, government officer in the Defence Ministry, busy in the humble work of shining the shoes of the congregation on the stairway of a Delhi Temple. A National Cadet Corps cadet approaches him seeking direction to the Republic Day parade ground. Rathore offers to give the boy a lift in his expensive limousine. To satisfy the curiosity of the young cadet why he does such a menial job Ratan relates him his story from his childhood to the present with sporadic flashbacks interspersing it.

Ratan comes from an impoverished middle class family he is a child of double inheritance, the patriotic courageous world of his father and the worldly wisdom of his mother who often reminded him "... It was not patriotism but money.... that brought respect and brought security. Money made friends. Money succeeded where all else failed. There are many laws.... but money was law unto itself. (14)

In R.K. Narayan's *Financial Expert,* Margayya comes to the same realization "Money alone is important in the world. Everything will come to us naturally if we have money in our purse."

Ratan is torn by these two conflicting philosophies of life, finds it extremely difficult from the beginning to live smoothly in the 'petrified and frozen world of civilization' His parents were a study in contrast. His father he recollects was a strange man, strange even to look-more than six feet tall. On the contrary his mother was "short and dark and tubercular". His father was a lawyer, a successful one, money then was no problem. But, under the influence of Gandhiji, his father "had abandoned his practice, given away most of his wealth, in short (they) had no means of living" (p. 18) and finally was shot dead for defying the sergeant's order to stay back, while leading a political procession. This heart rending moment of heroism, "is frozen as a moment of great silence" (p.23) in Ratan's mind. Within a period of one year his father had been forgotten by those "for whom he had squandered a lifetime" (p. 10). These events were a turning point in his life.

A very tough time was waiting ahead after the death of his father" He, his mother and and her disease, were left to face the adverse situation. He remembered a day of poverty when his mother" was sick.....was coughing and spitting blood, there was no money and every night my mother spat blood. Every night, night after night (p.48)

His friend had become a brigadier with the help of his father. He could not complete his studies. He recalls how he was the fastest sprinter in the college and had also won a prize for poetry. It was not the present but the future" It was the future that loomed before me, like a mountain range, a sense of question mark...... wanted to join the Medical but money was a problem" (p.30)

Like his father he also wanted "to be good, respected. To be of use....things as basic to life as air and water. And so difficult to get (p,32)He cherishes the ideals of his lather and even decides to join the clandestine army of Subash Chandra Bose. He tries to eliminate the panic of his life by following the heroics and sacrifice of his father. His mother strongly dissuades him .She tells him "......it was not patriotism but money......that brought respect and bought security. Money made friends. Money succeeded where all others failed. There were many laws ....but money was law unto itself......if he underrated the power of money .....he would be sorry one day (p.34)

Not paying any heed to it he sets out on his cycle towards the town to join Subash Chandra Bose's army Rathor had a feeling as if he had been on his way to a pilgrimage" I am very excited. I am on my way to greatness....about to lay the foundation of a glorious future. I have at last found the courage to do what J had always wanted to, (p.35) But unfortunately he lacked his lather's courage lo ignore his mother's advice to move with the flow of the world All of a sudden the momentary heroism and temporary feeling of patriotism and sacrifice collapsed. The countdown of his courage started with each succeeding mile. Finally "sweating and exhausted, in sight of his destination, he sat in a mango grove and wept, (p.39) Despite his desperate struggle to forget that shameful evening at unexpected moment it overpowered him.

Ratan leaves home comes to Delhi for "it was a city of opportunities. To fail in Delhi would have been the sign of the greatest incompetence (p.29) Ratan fails to get help from his friend's father. Alone, disheartened, deflated the world appears to him "a bundle of mirrors, tempting and somehow held together, but on the brink of always falling apart (p. 17) Getting a job is by no means an easy task for".....it was expected that the jobs would be filled by people who had, in some manner been pre-selected(p.29)

What hurt him most was when he" was looked at-examined, interviewed, interrogated and rejected (p.29) Ratan's humiliating experience of job hunting makes him realize the cruelty of the human lot. The reservoir of his hope had been steadily dwindling drop by drop.

He does get a temporary job as a clerk in a government office for war purchase with the help of his room mate at the inn where he was staying. He was sure with his qualification, intelligence, culture he was sure to rise. Hence forth his only aim in life was to make his career and gain material prosperity

He had become at the age of 21 a hypocrite and a liar, in short a sham.

> .... I had added a new dimension to my life. I had become at the age of 21, a hypocrite and a liar, in short a sham.... I had become a master faker (p.27).

When Ratan reached Delhi, he was full of enthusiasm and dreamt of making a mark in the world. He whole heartedly devoted himself to the advancement of his career, "the magic word" which his father used to scoff at. In the rat race he often remembered his father's comment in making a career, which he called 'bourgeois filth', But, the polluted atmosphere of the post independence society gave him a severe blow.

> "I embarked upon the solemn and relentless pursuit of a career. Bourgeois fifth. There have been moments in my life when I saw nothing but filth around me. At such times my head would explode with violent rebellious thoughts" (p.39).

He got hardened and thought himself to be a thick skin and a washout. He condemned himself "what was to be done? One had to live. And, to live one had to make a living. And how was a living to be made except through careers. Then the turbulence always died until it ceased to erupt altogether" (p.58).

Initially, when he refused to take a bribe of ten thousand he felt proud and self righteous. He approached his boss to help him, but his answer puzzled him. "There was no point in looking for truth aside from the truth of God. Money in the world always changed hands. God was only concerned with what one did with the money..."

It added to his confusion and made him feel ".... What about the consequences, consequences for what was termed as the character of the giver and taker or was character just a myth that I had somehow picked up" (p.42-48).

Ratan's one and only intention was progress for which he had to ignore-his ideals, values which he once upon prized and his father cared for. He worked hard and impressed his boss by his quick pick-up and his docility that verged on sycophancy he remarks. Some survive through defiance, others through ability; still others through obedience by becoming servants to the powers of the world. They are like these heavenly bodies that in themselves are nothing but reflect only the superior and more powerful lights. (P.33)

Ratan lay in the second category. The single motivating force in life was (to rise high) to please his superiors. His docility was not a put on affair; it was spontaneous. His colleagues sneered at him for 'shamelessly sucking up to the bosses'. This docility was accompanied by his skills that were not to be found among others. He was very hard working and could not rest until a job assigned to him was completed.

Ratan's life was one of compromises with the deceitful compelling society of post independent India. He was afraid of losing his job after the war. But, his boss promised not only confirmation but promotion too if he agreed to marry his niece. He agrees, though he feels humiliated for making such a bargain, and his colleagues started calling him a whore. He never forgot the bargain lying at its foundation. He mocks at himself. "The nation for which my father had given his life was moving and so I thought was I nothing....Nothing is more deceptive than a man's ideas about getting ahead" (p.50).

By now he comes to understand that the world runs on the basis of deals. "If men forgot how to make deals the world would come to a stop .... It is not the atom or the sun or God or sex that lies at the heart of the universe: it is deals" (p.48).

Though Ratan progresses, he also progresses in being fraudulent and unscrupulous. "The more money I accumulated, the more dissatisfied I-was, and the more I was determined to 'enjoy life" (p.85). He confesses he had become a 'master faker'. He had added a new dimension to his life. Right from the age of 21 he was growing into a hypocrite, a liar, a docile, obedient, corrupt, readily accepting bribes.

Though he had become a member of the money hunting society he had still not lost his patriotic self. During the Indo-China war he donated money, blood and offered his service to the Red Cross. He felt strongly for his country which "had come to such a sorry pass (p.54). The Indo-China war was a great debacle. He contemplated who should be blamed for it, the ill equipped military, the incompetence of the politicians or the bad weather; no, it was the 'Indian Character'. In his essay on "Crisis in Character' he hits at the corruption in society and describes the Indian people as 'glorious monument in ruin' (p.57).

He tried to get the essay published but when failed to get it done he cyclostyled and distributed only to be mocked at and nicknamed as Mr. Crisis of Character. Ironically there is a crisis in Ratan's while struggling through the political question involved when making war purchases, he accepts a big bribe from Himmat Singh, popularly known as Sheikh. He passes a contract for defective and rejected war material. The deal was done so fool proof that no evidence could be traced.

Ratan justifies his guilt-attributing it to the general degenerate atmosphere. He thinks how can he be his own master when a system is his master He tries to seek solace from the living example of corruption prevalent in society.

".......if I have taken bribe I belong rather to the rule than the exception. Peon....government officials....traffic police.... railway conductors. A bribe could get you a bed in a hospital, a place to burn your dead. Doctors had a fee to give false certificate, magistrate for false judgment. For larger sum they declared wars. Bribery was accepted by factory inspectors, bank agents, college professors, by nurses, priests... by all those who acted in the public interest....All this I knew and had known ,for twenty years (p. 108-9). Even a M.P, a trustee of the Republic feels unconcerned about the war....who cared for wilderness that we were quarrelling over (p.82).

Sheikh understood the Indian reality more than anybody else "this country has two kinds of people....The rulers and the ruled. The rulers were a fraud....phony people who knew only to make speeches, be cruel, and feather their nests. The ruled were brainless" (p.80) and he holds that the laws were not written by God but by a silly society that could do anything for money.

There is further downfall. He is now a lover of wine and woman. 'I felt bold, unfettered, I stared at them, the women, openly willfully' (p.74). He visits prostitutes. He is now at the "top of the dung heap and had been climbing all my life', (p.82)

Ratan was chasing his career so blindly that he cared for nobody. When he transferred a sincere officer he told Ratan "If I had asked for a transfer not because you have defeated me but because I consider a waste of time to work with men like you it is a pity because my first impression of you was that you were a bit like me. But I was obviously mistaken" (p.68). This shook his inner self, He felt he belonged to a society which had no principles, direction or purpose. After clearing the rejected defective war material, he found his soul turned to ashes.

The result of the war shook him further especially when he learnt that the Brigadier who had deserted was on the verge of insanity hundreds had lost their lives. Directly or indirectly he felt responsible for all this. He was summoned by the Police for interrogation in the matter of supplying sub graded war material. But, as the deal was fool proof, they could not hold him guilty. But the Superintendent of Police spat at him and said "You are lying Mr. Rathor". He called him a crooked liar; he had come to know through reliable sources that he had cleared the defective war material for a big bribe. He was put behind the bars but could get out with the help of Sheikh. Up till now he felt no regret. He only justified his action by seeking consolation from the annals of corruption. While he was coming out of the jail the S.P. said his friend could be saved from being court-martialed if he would make his confession. Though, he wanted, at the last moment lost his courage. This lack of courage in him resulted in the ultimate tragedy. The Brigadier shot himself to death. The Brigadier was his friend and whose father had helped him to graduate and often helped them after his father's death.

The death of the Brigadier terribly shook the inner self of Ratan. When he went to the morgue to see his friend's dead body, he was deeply struck "What I had seen that morning at the morgue was not so much a shattered skull as the vision of the vast pit at the bottom of which my life crawled. Like a worm", (p.R6). According to Tapan Kumar Ghosh "The Brigadier's death served as a catalyst that shocked Ratan out of his moral inertia and initiated the process of inner transformation in him. He was jerked out of his self complacency, pseudo-security and illusion and was confronted with the responsibility of his gruesome crime" (15).

Joshi presents death as an instrument of self realization. In *The Foreigner* Sindi's self realization started after the death of Babu and June.

The Brigadier's death hurt him and a feeling of loneliness came over him. He became tongue tied like a stone "no occurrence, no conversation, no visit of either friend or foe, no sleep...no relief, no respite from the hands that pulled me steadily down towards these caverns where I felt certain the Brigadier had gone" (125). The death had left him totally frustrated and shattered.

Ratan on a frenzy decides to kill the Sheikh who had persuaded him to take the bribe, but when he reaches he finds the Sheikh was already dying and came to know that he had only been used as a scapegoat, the master mind behind were the Minister and the Secretary. He was made the scapegoat for he was a 'spineless flunky'. He tells "You are bogus Ratan Rathor....From top to bottom ....your work, your religion, your friendship, your honour, nothing but a pile of dung. Nothing.....but poses a bundle of sham" (131) The Sheikh makes him aware of himself. When he recalls his past he is pained to see that it has been a waste "Twenty years earlier I had come to this city .....to learn to work, and in the process to make my mark I had come full of hope, ambition goodwill and all that was felt was a pile of dung.... And nothing gained. Pushing files? Maneuvering .At forty five all that I knew was to maneuver. A trickster that was what I had life make me"(133)

Sheikh advises Ratan to be like his father" Try to get yourself to use......it might be too laic, you have been too long a slave.... But give it a try" "My soul was killed you put yours to pawn. But souls that are pawned can be retrieved" He realizes the meaninglessness and purposelessness of the sort of life he has so far led. He visits temples in quest of peace harmony and purpose. Even there he finds priest ready to bribe him to save his son, a contractor who had used substandard material in construction resulting in the collapse of the roof killing a number of people. Ratan is shocked to see bribe in religious places too. He realizes the futility and hollowness of his whole life. Having lived for two decades as he says" in smog, confused, exploited, exploiting. deceiving"(133) he is tired of body and spirit. Penitent after he learns that even the temple priest is corrupt he takes to cleaning the shoes at the temple congregation. Each morning before going to office, he goes to the temple to wipe the shoes of the people and seeks forgiveness from "my father, my mother and the Brigadier and all those he had harassed with deliberation and with cunning" (143) He thinks that this act of his will bring forgiveness and humility of all those who had been the victim of his cleverness, those whom he could have helped and did not.

For the purgation of his filthy self he does not renounce the society but remains there and atones through humility and penance. He says "I am learning to be of use, I know it is too late in the day But must try and not lose heart, not yield at any cost to despair"(143"The ending of the novel at dawn signifies the ray of knowledge that Ratan comes to gain. The fall of Ratan is an act of purification, he falls only to rise from corruption to purity and innocence. "*Apprentice* is the tale of a conscience stricken man with a curios mixture of idealism and docility, a vague sense of values, a helpless self effort to flout them for the sake of a career- in short with a deep awareness of the conflict between life and living"(16) To Ratan though the future appears gloomy he still has faith in the younger generation who "might yet hold back the tide"(144)The novelist pins his hope in the new generation and ends the novel on a positive note" There is hope as long as young men are willing to learn from the follies of elders. Willing to learn and ready to sacrifice, willing to pay the price" (144)

Apprentice is a confessional novel which" in the process of confession, he tells his story of degeneration, and the darkest and filthiest part of his life, for he is willing to pay the price by facing humiliation. He believes in what Gandhiji said "A clean confession combined with a promise never to commit the sin again, when offered before one who has the right to receive it, it is a purest type of repentance" (17)

In spite of the Western influence on him he was deeply rooted in Indian culture and philosophy. Joshi went to Indian philosophy for the solution of the crisis of existence in the universe. Hinduism Joshi believes is highly existentialist oriented philosophy since it attaches so much value to the right way to live-to exist-In *The Foreigner* Sindhi Oberoi, a rootless hero who seeks detachment from the world comes to realise the actual meaning from the Gita "sometimes detachment lies in actually getting involved" In *The Strange Case of Billy Biswas* , Billy goes to the hills like the great seers in Indian legends in search of spiritual height and inner peace. In The *Apprentice* Ratan tries his redemption through humility and penance. In the *Last Labryrinth* Joshi presents the mysteries of love, God and Death In *City and the River* the cultural and spiritual ethos. Under the influence of Gandhi all the protagonists make confession and suffer all through their lives to self realization. His experience have been a perennial source of his novels A committed writer he states "My novels arc essentially an attempt towards a better understanding of the world and of my self..... if I did not write I imagine I would use some other method to carry on my exploration(18) The novel is a study of the loss and retrieval of one's soul. It commands the value of humility and self purification. The cause of attenuation and inner emptiness of Ratan is neither the rootlessness of Sindhi nor the unusual urge of Billy but the compelling forces of civilized society which has turned cynical and hypocritical *Apprentice* is a also a study of a crisis in character .A crucial decision may plunge the self, family and society to acquire a new meaning. The new meaning emerges as a sort of cleansing of the soul, The self becomes an apprentice to it self so that it may explore the labryrinth which is itself. Ratan becomes an apprentice in order to retrieve his soul.

Ratan realizes that one cannot live for oneself because no human act is performed in isolation without consequences. He remembers what his father often used to say" whatever you do touches someone somewhere "hence each should be performed with a sense of responsibility. Unlike Billy Biswas who opts out the modern world in a bid to seek his communion with the primitive world. Ratan lives in a modern world to sock mental peace and fulfillment in serving others in the humblest form in the symbolic act of shoe shining. With deep remorse, he realizes the futility of his life and decides to be of use to others. The theme of alienation in Arun Joshi's novels is right from his very first In *Apprentice* it moves from alienation to community. Horn alienation he moves to humanism and religion which alone can be the saving grace of mankind steeped in corruption.

References

1. The Reporter: *Fiction in India,* February 14, 1965, p. 59.
2. C. Paul Verghese: *Problem of Indian Creative Writers in English,* Bombay, Somaiya, 1971, p. 124-25.
3. Edmund Fuller: *Man in Modern Fiction,* New York, Random House 1958, p. 7.
4. Paul Burton: *The Spiritual Crisis of Man*. London, Rider 1952, p. 7.
5. Adlus Huxley: *Adonis and the Alphabet,* London, Chatto and Windus 1956, p. 124.
6. C. Wright Mill: *White Collar,* New York OUP 1981, p. 157.
7. Eric Fromn: *The Same Society,* New York Holt, Rinehart, 1955, p. 120, 130.
8. Eric Fromn (ed.): *Zen Buddhism and Psychoanalysis,* New York Harper and Row 1970, p. 86.
9. Arun Joshi: *The Foreigner,* 1970. p. 28.
10. Purabhi Banerjee: "*A Winters Secret*" Interview 'The Sunday Times', February 27, 1983.
11. Arun Joshi: *City and The River,* Orient Paper Back 1994, p. 1.
12. M.K. Naik and Shyamala Narayan: *Indian English Literature 1980-2000, A Critical Survey,* Pencraft International 2001, Pencraft, p. 28.
13. Tapan Kumar Ghosh: *Arun Joshi's Fiction, The Labyrinth of Life,* Prestige Books, New Delhi, 1996, p. 152.

14. Arun Joshi; *The Apprentice,* Orient Paper Back, Vision Books, Pvt. Ltd. Delhi 1993, Further quotes pertain to this edition.
15. Tapan Kumar Ghosh: *Arun Joshi's Fiction The Labyrinth of Life,* p. 112.
16. C.N. Srinath: *The Fiction of Arun Joshi: The Novel of Interior Landscape,* The Literary Criterion Vol. XII, No. 2-3,1976, p. 219.
17. M.K. Gandhi: *The Story of My Experiments with Truth,* Navajivan Mudralaya, Ahmedabad, 1927, reprint 1992, p. 31.
18. Arun Joshi: Interview, Reply to M.K. Dua, LIT, September 3, 1971.

3

Indira Goswami: Living But to Die

Widows ekeing out a miserable, existence in innumerable homes across the country. discriminated, subjected to violence, humiliation, deception- a casteless outcast-are a continuing presence in society, a reminder of the degradation women experience. However, much one may try to erase the figure of the widow, she is very much there especially in the individual memory as well as the social. Most of the house-holds have an aunt, sister, mother, grandmother or a distant relative who came to live with the family and remained to become a servant-an unpaid one. She is expected to do all the work right from the kitchen and as time demands to be a baby sitter, nurse, escort, doing errands-at the beck and call of everyone- at the same time be an unseen presence. If the family does not find her presence useful or reluctant to maintain her, can lead to her abandonment, preferably to a place tike Kashi, Mathura- Brindhavan so that the act of abandonment can be masked under religious preventions. As one walks down the lane their helpless eyes leave their imprint on one's mind. If not the pilgrim tracks there is the odd documentary film or article which keeps the widow alive in public consciousness, however hard one may try to ignore them.

Man's dependence on women for the continuation of the family/ lineage providing 'sons, serving and nurturing the family was duly recognized. She was given the place of important, seen as a 'Laxmi' a 'Sumagali'. But once she lost her husband, her practical utility was over she was now an 'anmngali' a sight to-be, detested. She had to hide her face as if she had committed a heinous crime, and forced to spend the rest of her life in a dark corner, Unloved by God, despised by men, a social pariah, a domestic drudge, she cannot-move "about freely as she is treated as an untouchable. As a widow she is an -unclaimed property-an unwelcome sight, a bad omen, Starvation and death stare' her no ray of hope penetrates her densely darkened life even a housemaid can concort lies and admonish her. A child widow a childless widow does not know what is compassion, kindness or sympathy which makes them sadly say " we just go on living, since we do not die that easily. We have to live".

A feminist-reading shows that there is a relationship between material structures und ideological and cultural practice and to the specific dimension of widowhood according to caste, community, religion and region. Religious minority groups such as Christians, Buddhists, Sikhs'. Muslims do not prohibit widow remarriage. The levirate system was also followed by them as well as the lower caste 'Hindus. But the formative structures of Brahmincal patriarchy, put a ban on widow remarriage. A sacred indissoluble marriage was regarded as a sign of superior culture and the Brahmins as the highest caste were supposed to be the custodians of the sacred rituals. The ideology of 'pativratya' or 'Satitva'-Chastity and devotion to the husband was made to control her sexuality-and avoid transgressing patriarchal norms. Pativratya" entails a complete withdrawal from social life of the community and the imposition of the severe discipline which made her existence a virtual social non-entity. She was to all intent and purpose an ascetic and any breach of her austere discipline not only made her viable to a very unhappy rebirth but also endangered the welfare of the soul of her departed husband who might suffer from the short coming of his other half on the earth. For a upper caste widow therefore, there were only three choices left-immediate death through Sati, life long condemnation to segregation and drudgery and subjection to clandestine sexual exploitation by the male of the family or locality. Code of bodily mortification, food restriction, symbolic relationship with colors, dress, non access to ceremonies were elements that reinforced pattern of belief wherein the upper caste widow was regarded as entering a social death with her husband's death.

Considered ritually impure, inauspicious, dangerous someone to be shunned and treated with suspicion, they were subjected to severe restriction on their diet, attire and movement, their heads tonsured in an attempt to de-feminize and de-sexualize them. The right to inherit property under the dominant legal systems of *Dayabhaga* or *Mitakshara* as daughters or widows were hemmed by the institution of the joint family system, legally expressed as co-parcenary in which three generation of men residing in the joint family system alone could be members, women were automatically excluded from inheriting immovable property, as they were not accepted as co-parceners. This made a widow vulnerable and dependent on her family. However, around the 12th century, the legal practice settled around the widow's right to maintenance unless her husband had already claimed as co-parcener before his death, in which case a widow could have a life estate, in case she was without a son, the property would revert to her husband's nearest relative-a male, after her death. In either case all this depended upon her leading a chaste life.

The various legal changes and judicial interpretation in recent times have on papers freed women from her bonded status to one where she has greater choice in matters of remarriage and control over property, but little has changed by way of actual experience in the lives of widows especially in rural areas. Contemporary studies show that prejudices and taboos continue, many widows still suffer from various forms of social ostracism, deception, violence at the hands of relatives. Traditional biases still continue. Denied of personhood widows are subjected to what has been evocatively described as "linguistic oppression", abusive and suggestive terms are used to refer to them as if they were piece of stone or inanimate object that has no feeling referring to her/ them as "that" and "it"

Despite rhetorical concern for the widow for almost two centuries widows are among the most vulnerable section, social oppression and ostracism exists along with economic exploitation. Especially in remote rural areas where most of them being illiterate and ignorant they are either unaware of their rights or cheated of their right to property. With restrictions on their movement, they get employed only under terms set by their in-laws. Despite being economically and physically vulnerable they have rarely figured in public policy. As Chen points out widows are rarely mentioned in the literature of poverty, in public debate or social policy or women's movement. All that the widow wants is wholeness, dignity for a positive social image and for being accepted as useful members of society.

The widows were not only socially marginalised even early literature seems to have given them only a marginalised place, widows are mentioned only in the context of the death of their husband and dismissed after a conventional description of their tragic state and not as a problem. In *Ramayana* and *Mahabharata* widows are shown enjoying greater freedom. They had the choice of Sati, remarriage, take a levir to perpetuate the princely lineage. Young widowed mothers dedicated themselves to the task of raising their children, those with grown up sons held prestigious position in the family though the ideology of "pativrathva" was still valued as the most sublime and most perfect,

Puranic literature, eighteen in number, contain many stories about virtuous women who with the power of 'Satitva' protect their husbands from disaster and death. The stories illustrate the super human power of "Pativratha' but ignore the problem of widows. Buddhism and Jainism which rose in protest against the oppressive caste system and hegemony of Brahmins, adopted a more liberal attitude. The widows were considered as living human being-rational and sensitive. They were granted freedom to chart their own lives. They were permitted to join the Sangha, go on pilgrimages, seek spiritual fulfillment outside the domestic sphere.

Sanskrit poetic literature 'Kavya' which was written in courtly tradition sang 'the heroics and amorous exploit of Gods and kings, celebrated the beauty and the varying shades of young women or Nayakas as beloved, mistress and wives, widows had no place in courtly romance. The concept of man and women made a complete whole. Women as a widow was a word without a meaning, bereft of life and significance even Kalidasa had nothing to say about the widows, the only notable exception being Pandita Kausiki in *Malavikagnimitram.* Classical Sanskrit literature aimed at "rasa" hence the grief of a widow was used only for evoking 'karuna rasa'. The hero's death was an anathema, an Indian classical literature did not conceive a tragic ending, but the death of an adversary killed in the battle was moaned by his widow, in Sanskrit literature the widow functioned as a motif for depicting sorrow.

The Bhakti movement opened up the cult of devotion to God. The chief mood of Bhakti is 'Sringara' seen almost from the point of view of women whether on the phase of union or separation with the loved one. The new cult inspired women in another direction-spiritually. Now they could transcend their familial and social role direct their sexual and emotional energy to God and find peace as Andal, Mahadevi. Avvai, Meerabhai who rejected marriage, family and widowhood Vaisnaism which is an offshoot of Bhakti movement promised liberation through devotion to Krishna, whom the devotee could worship as master, friend, child, or lover. Vaisnavism took a liberal view of caste, assigned sublime value to human love and promised liberation to the followers through devotion. The widows found refuge in Vaisnavism, lived away from the families at Kashi, Brivandavan and Mathura. But this relief too could not be tolerated since the orthodox Hindus and social reformers saw it as an order of debauchery, under the cover of religion and looked at it askance. The widows bound by man made codes and restrictions remained mute and her Voice was rarely heard.

From time to time there were efforts to liberalise attitude towards widows to abolish 'Sati and give them more freedom. The new literature which emerged in Indian languages in the middle of the 19th century marked the appearance of the novel. This new genre represents a shift in the presentation of reality and focussed on themes not addressed before Once the literature of social realism found its arena of expression in the novel, it became the preferred genre for creative writing the theme of oppressed widow was bound to dominate, For a variety of reasons, including the nature of class formation in the 19th century, over determined by the upper caste, the widows were the first category to be perceived as oppressed long before the exploited peasants or the dalits appeared as the focus of the novels of social realism.

It was in Maharastra that the oppressed suffering widows first attracted the creative imagination of the writers A year after the passing of the Widow Remarriage Act (1856) appeared *Yamuna Paryatan* (1857) portraying the travails of a young women, which culminated in her widowhood, was written by Babu Padmanji, a reformer converted to Christianity. The novel deals with the oppression of widows, it's aim was to propagate widow remarriage. The same was translated into Kannanda and the first original novel in Kannada *Indra Bhai* (1899) realised the full potential of the novels of social realism. The first Assamese *Ram Navami* too centered on widow remarriage.

The most ambitious handling of the widow question within the larger frame work of social reform was Goverdhanram Tripati's *Saraswati Chandra* (1901), written over a period of fourteen years, it was recognized as the epic of the lime, The book is a classic example of the ambivalence of its time about the desirability of widow remarriage. Social stability wins over reformist and humanistic impulses. The renunciate model of widowhood remained the preferred ideal. More than any other novel on widow remarriage *Saraswati*

Chandra exercised a spell over readers, not because it offered solution but because it raised questions which the then contemporary society regarded as insoluble and it struck the chord. The theme of widowhood excited the imagination of Bengali writers for nearly seventy years. Writers like Bankimchandra, Rabindranath and Saratchandra handled it with great power, their works were translated into many languages The theme of the young widow was developed along a different line in Bengal-of widows in love, transgressing widows and the fallen widows. In *Vishavriksha,* Kunda an innocent widow in love commits a moral offence when she accepts Nagendra's proposal of a second marriage Binodini in *Choker Bali* is wayward and rebellious who seduces Mahendra a married man, is however transformed by her love for Bihari A fallen widow is depicted as one who has committed an indiscrete act in the past and has lost her place of respectability. She may love but never marry, she is torn between desire and guilt. The theme has enabled a play between the inherent will to enjoy and circumstantial will against enjoyment, between the desirable and unspeakable. The theme is best represented in Saratchandra's *Charitraheen* and *Srikant.*

The sexuality of the young widow which had figured in much of the creative writing on widow remarriage in the later part of 19' century and early part of the 20th century was explored as an independent theme in regional languages. Lakshmidhar Sharma's *The Rebel Woman* (1930) in Assamese, U. Ananthamurthy's *Ghatashradha* (1934) Pudumaipithan's story "*Sarasu*" in Tamil marks a shift in the handling of the celebite widow, as it is sharply critical of the one point agenda of male reformers-widow remarriage. All these stories provide a critique of enforced code of widowhood and Brahminical patriarchy, but engage with the widows sexuality in very distinctive ways.

Phaniyamma in Kannada by M.K. Indra, is a milestone in Kannada literature. Located within the insular and orthodox Brahmic community of Malnad in Karnataka, with its joint family system and strict adherence to the ideology of "madi" or caste purity, it recounts the life of an upper caste widow. The main burden of observing "madi", fal ls on the widows. They have to renounce their sexuality along with their hair, ornaments and colourful attire-wearing only white/off white or a dark maroon (in Karnataka) with no border, keep themselves confined to kitchen, puja room, infirmary and ensure that they do not fall within the view of anyone - for the widow is the symbol of ill omen.

Born and brought up in this environment Phaniyamma goes about her work silently (married at seven widowed at eleven) observing all the present rituals and conventions. However, her discerning mind sees through the hypocrisy of the Brahmins and questions the arbitrariness of the convention of purity and pollution and the double standard. The novel ridicules the elitists notion of the Brahmins as pure upper caste and also challenges the wisdom and authority of men who oppress and enslave women. The corrupt religious establishment with its double standard which sits in judgement on the sexual conduct of women-which has been so seriously attacked by U. Annathamurty's in *Samskara.* Towards the end of her life she narrates her story to her neice Banashankari to be passed on future generation. The novel is a radical feminist text, striking at the very foundation of Brahmincical patriarch), Some of the novels that shift the focus away from the upper caste widow oppressed by the Brahminical code of ascetic widowhood is Rajendra Singh Bedi's *Ek Chader Maili Se* (1962), Premchánd's *Beton Wali Vidhwa,* which takes the middle class upper caste widow who loses control over the family after the death of her husband not only in financial matters but even in the kitchen. In Mahasweta Devi's *Rudali* grief is used as an asset, especially for those who throughout their life have only exploited and oppressed and in the end have nobody even to mourn for them.

"Al-haj Subaka, as referred by 'Puratchi' a Tamil journal identified with women's self respect movement gives an account of oppression suffered by Muslim widows. Despite the tall claims the condition of Muslim widows is far from

human and normal, She openly proclaim "Muslims women are slaves, the situation of Muslim widows is far from wonderful This is a challenge to those Muslims who claim profoundly, 'Islam has granted all possible rights. This in spite of Mohammad the Prophets efforts to uplift the widows, by himself marrying a widow older than him, and later several more to give them a dignified status.

The Muslim of today are a far cry from the example set by Muhammad. They oppress the young widows and do not permit them to remarry. They are highly critical of those handful of progressive Muslims who choose to remarry. They are a virtual prisoners remarriage is against the family honour. She states that at least Hindus are willing to admit to their repressive practices and are prepared to reform, but the Muslims are hypocrites when they call themselves progressive. A significant poem describing the abject condition of the widows (Muslim) is *Munajat-e-Bewa* (1884) (The widow Prayer) by Altaf Hussain Hali (I87-1914). Though the Muslims give freedom of remarriage, but this is denied to the upper caste Muslim as is described in this poem.

Hali vividly portrays the lonely and dreary life of a widow who has to face the indifference and contempt of others and struggles with her own suppressed desires She grieves not only for her wasted life but also for these unhappy child widows who do not even understand the meaning of marriage and who can look forward to no joy or comfort in life.. The poem ends with an anguished plea to end such cruelties of conventions and customs, wreck many innocent lives and turn it in to a weary struggle Kashi Prasad Ghose brings out the pathos of a young widow in his poem 'To *A young Widow*".

Ah, fair one, lone as a desert flower.
Whose bloom and beauty is in vain.
How dark was that fatal hour
Which brought thee lasting grief of pain
From every joy rudely torn
How drear and comfortless thy fate

Doomed to remain for ever more
As if in this world were not
And is there none, O, can it be
None warm or friendly in thy cause
Has pitiless humanity
Forgot its sacred ties
The rigour of a life austere
Followed by every fear and stare
What is thy being but a name
Thou may'st and dar'st not must not hope
A joy upon the world beneath
And thou must, even with sorrow cope
Sorrow which only ends in death

Rabindranath Tagore in '*Saved*' exposes the hypocrisy and double standard. Manjuli is forced to marry an old man for he was a Kulin Brahmin, who leaves her widow within a couple of months after his wife's pleading to get her married to a young doctor, who loved Manjuli, But the father is dead against it, but he is ready to contract a second marriage soon after the death of his wife, taking recourse to Hindu sastra. His hypocrisy stands exposed.

The intensity of concern with the repressed widow and her sexuality and the possibility of remarriage form the central thematic concern of Indira Goswami novels especially in *Neel Kanthi Braj* (1976) and *The Moth Eaten Howda* (1988)] Most of her novels center around the tragic protests of women as -well as their search for sexual fulfilment and self realization in a repressive world full of socio-religious conventions and predatory men The novel *Neel Kanthi Braj* (1976) *The Blue Throated Braj* is a fictionalized account of the authors stay in the temple town of Brindavan while she was researching the origin of *Ramayana.* She vividly recreates the atmosphere of the Braja region- held sacred by the devotees of Radha Krishna with all its glorious tradition of Hindu philosophy, art, architecture music dance devotion as well as the squalor misery and corruption rampant in Brindavan. She describes the turbulent history of the town, the abundance of Hindu relics, descrated by Muslim invaders, the maze of narrow lanes and alleys, the profusion of large and small temples, the ghats, the cremation ground on the banks of the flowing Jamuna. The town thronged by pilgrims, pandas, beggars and destitute widows called Radhasyamis. Abandoned by their families living in pitiable and pathetic condition, having no financial social or emotional support They live on the edge of survival begging near the temple, singing devotional songs for a pittance. The Radhasyamis are dehumanized by extreme poverty, incurable diseases, sub-human living conditions and subjected to every form of indignities. Many of them are depicted as merely waiting for their death with their meagre savings tied in their waistband hoping to be given a decent funeral by their mates.

Neel Kanthi Braj structures itself on the three women brought together by different circumstances to the holy shrine of Mathura. The main story centers around Saudamini- her story of agony. Widowed after a year of happy marriage and now stranded in her emotional life, because of her forbidden love for a Christian youth. In fact the family had shifted to Mathura to snap their emotional link. Saudamini's father is a doctor and he expects his daughter to transfer her love and warmth to the service of the sick, and gradually cure her of her infatuation for the youth. In Mathura women came to transfer their love to God and die in peace. But the reality of Mathura is it is a living hell, Indira Goswami shows considerable courage in depicting the different forms of perversion that are rampant in this holy land, the land of idyllic love has in fact swallowed poison and has not digested it. One sees unrelieved ugliness and pain against the resplendent architecture of the temple of Ranganathan. Saudamini found no consolation and her rebellious spirit grew. Her mother was apprehensive that the Christian youth might return and claim her. Saudamini confesses to the old artist. Chandrabanu, who loved her like a father. She was made of clay and was not ashamed of it. "You are an artist, you have feelings, You understand physical desire, love, And I tell you I have not overcome it."

Seven years were not long enough to wean her away from the desire for physical contact with her lover. She felt like asking all the thousands of the widows, whether they had overcome physical desire, were they ever freed from that terrible loneliness. One widow, with tears in her eyes confesses that she did long for a new love. Even while counting the prayer beads, in the holy sack, she was silently imagining the touch of something soft like the Jasmine. Saudamini hated her mother but loved her father, was close to him. It was he, who when he finds that his wife Anupama's condition was on the decline, depressed and all his saving exhausted tells Saudamini "Have you kept count of these who have disappeared from the scene within a short time. Thakur Sahib breathed his last the other day. Who knows, for us too the final hour is not far off.... Look at this hand of mine. For some times now I feel as if it has become benumbed and insensitive. Very soon I am afraid, I, too shall have to live a helpless life like a cow that's unable to move and feed itself (135-36) therefore he resumed." I have written a letter to that friend of yours. It is very necessary for him to come here at this particular time and later comes to her with a lantern "your friend has arrived. He is at the moment waiting for you at the Vaishnavachatlri near the ghat. Its an odd hour. But there's no help. Anupama is asleep. She will wake up in the morning. Now get ready protect yourself well with a scarf, for outside is pretty cold he lighted and escorted her to the waiting boat. At last she met the man she wanted. They enacted a passionate love against a cyclonic wind. She was turned into a demoness of desire for that warmth of love... I'm hungry like a wolf. I'm ever after that warmth- the warmth of the body and mind, the mysterious warmth of a Christian, and a Hindu in wild ecstatic embrace. The warmth in which I find all the meaning of my life and existence. How I wish others too could hear the rhythmic beats of our warm hearts. There who call you an outcast because of your religion are no better than butchers, I would call them butchers....(142)

But for all her longing, she cannot go with him, she can

only tell her love. "Forgive me, retreat, Forgive me" (143). She wanted to die before her mother. She could not allow her to triumph over her. What remained, finally was only a scandal, another tragic end of desire on the river bank. The conventional ending of the novel does not take away the stark realism. The frank description of the plight of the Hindu widows cast away to die in the so called holy town and the blighting of young lives by convention which does not permit a natural expression of sexual desire, is powerful indeed.

The other widow in the novel is Shashiprabha, a young widow in the service of Alamgadhi, an elderly impotent priest, Shashi is hopelessly in love with a young swami, whom she can gaze only at from a distance. However when the temple is sold off, which was the property of Thakur Sahib, Shashi is left alone to fend for herself She takes shelter in a ghetto but the Radhe Shyamis living there threaten to throw her out, she becomes a target of drunken louts. Her situation worsens alter the death of Alamgadhi. She is thrown out of the hovei and running for life she finally reaches Mrinalini's who offers her shelter.

In *The Moth Eaten Howdah of a Tusker* (*Datal Hatir Une Khowa Howdah)* (1988) the focus of the novel centers around the family of a spiritual head of a Sattra, a Vaishnavaite monastic institution, which endowed a family of high born Brahmins with hereditary rights over vast areas of land gifted usually by the king for the spiritual responsibility vested on them for carrying out the religious duties of the people owing allegiance lo the sect. These spiritual homesteads were powerful centers of culture in early times but eventually lapsed into feudal holdings commanding allegiance in the name of sect. With the decline of religion in modern times the power of institutions declined and with the coming of the ceiling act the large holdings became insecure. The novel presents the family in the last stage of decline centering on the emotional deprivations of the main characters because they are prisoners of that system which alienates them from others. Men's lives are governed by rituals and dissipated in frivolous activities, women are victims of the tyranny of orthodoxy. Girls had to be married off before the onset of puberty- as Giribala in the novel - to a groom of high caste irrespective of his age, and character. If widowed they had to observe restriction in food, attire movement social intercourse all of which made them virtual prisoners. Invariably they face torture, harassment by their in-laws, who are eager to get rid of them and possess their property. The novel is based on Indira Goswami's own childhood memories and her deep research in a feudal Vaisnavaite Sattra in the South Kamrup district in Assam in the post Independent period. The novel is a protest against the Assamese feudal and religious tradition.

The main focus of the novel is on the three widows of the family, the other character only creates a scaffolding for them. The patriarch, the spiritual head of the 'sattra' is hardly shown, he is only referred to, his son Indranath holds the thread of the narrative but not the one who shapes the events. Indira Goswami finds the subjective co- relative in Giribala the young widowed daughter of the family and the other two are aunts of Giribala. As in many of her novels this novel too concerns with desire and fulfilment which accounts to search for freedom by the female protagonists.

Durga, the elderly widowed sister of the adhikar is an unhappy women harassed and rejected by her husband's family as an inauspious woman. She lived with her brother where she is treated as a servant. Her life is bereft of happiness, which leaves her brooding over her unfortunate life. Her hope that she would get a share of property or called back by her in-laws is frustrated. Abandoned by her husband's family neglected in her brother's household, Durga is the traditional image of a Brahmin widow neurotic and unconsciously perverse because of her crushed sexuality, she is an abject image of pity. She wants to get away from here, and live her life going on pilgrimage. Since nobody is ready to finance her, she decides to sell her ornaments which she had kept in the safe custody of Saru Gosainee, only to find to her utter shock, that it is missing, perhaps stolen by Saru's trusted agent Mahidhar, and trying to involve Saru in the theft. Frustrated at all quarters, she is condemned to live here, her health deteriorates, she waits for death which alone could give her the much desired freedom. She requests Indranath, her nephew to send her to Chikarhati. to her in-laws so that she may die in her husbands home and keep the dignity as a high caste Bhrahmin widow. Durga who led a religious life dies unhappy. Leading a religious life is meaningless, she dies cursing her tormentors. Durga's last words of agony before she died were "God above are my witnesses: I am a widow of Chikarhatis Gosain.... Who will die now from the sorrow of not offering her husband's funeral bones to the holy river.... Let my curse fall upon those who have done this harm to a tortured soul" She was hounded by the human vultures who snatched away her possessions.

Saru Gossaine is a young, thirty years old widow of Indranath uncle, who was banished from the Sattra by his father for daring to object to his dissolute ways. Coming from a rich family, she was the Gossainee of three Sattras. Her disciples were scattered in places like Pat Haldhia, Chakrod, Dakhala, she regularly visited her disciples like the male Gossains of Kamprup. She is dignified, independent lives all alone. After the death of her husband, for sometime the adhiars (tenant farmers) paid their revenue of half paddy, but gradually they started cheating on their contract taking advantage of her helpless condition as a lonely widow. Added to that was the problem of the naxalites, she was no longer rich but carried on bravely with the support from Mahidhar Bapu a Brahmin, Saru who led a strictly regulated life, almost like a sanyasini maintained a distance from him. Yet he gradually becomes part of her dreams and fantasies, she cooks for him, waits for his returns. Her dream of love and desire are woven around this man. She is deeply concerned about him. Once after a stressful day she walks to his house at night, sees him sleeping wants to touch him but holds back her desire. Her story of desire and frustration is woven very intricately. Her inner life could be only described in terms of silent monologues and dreams, she dreams of

Mahidhar escorting her across the river Torcha to see the icon the four armed Vishnu. Mahidhar saves her from the elephant, stretches his hands and shouts, "come madam take my hand. I can subdue elephants on the musth..... Madam how long can you carry a dead body on your shoulder ....." Her love for him makes her blind to his evil designs.

There is an episode when she is waiting in the rain, almost risking her life and exposure to scandal. She returns home drenched and exhausted to lie awake in bed, dreaming of Mahidhar. A noise and knocking awakens her- to find a group of men with torches in their hand bringing a man caught in a fishing net with hands and feet tied. It was Mahidhar killed in an encounter, caught while trying to sell Saru"s land with a forged letter of authority. A shattering end to her dreams, bringing together a revelation of character, action and ideas. With him dies her love, her dream and her hope for future happiness

Among the three widows in the novel Giribala appears as the heroine. An exceptionally beautiful girl, lilthe, long haired daughter of the Gossain who is widowed at the age of sixteen. In keeping with the tradition of a Brahmin family, she is married off in a hurry at a tender age, to a sickly and dissolute man who neglects and humiliate her spends his time with a theatre group and low caste women. She could not tolerate the cruel and torturous rituals at Bangaru Sattra, her in-laws house. She unsuccessfully protests against the social convention which oppress and ossify her life. Even the child, which she conceives before the death of her husband, dies in her womb as a result of inhuman ritual she was forced to obey. Giribala revolts and her widowed existence is a progress from crisis. The greatest problem is the suppressed sexuality, she could not live like aunt Durga.

Following the death of her husband, she is brought back to her parents, who could not bear the agony of their daughter. Indranath wanted to save his sister Giribala from the fate of Durga, and helps in directing her energy towards a more purposeful activity. She is introduced to the European missionary, to help him with his research on religion. An out house of the Sattra was provided for his stay and Giribala was allowed to assist him in reading the manuscript. It was a very daring thing on the part of the family to allow her to attend him. But gradually, besides sympathy and friendship based on shared interest she is attracted to him. Mark has a great respect for the family tradition, and the reputation of his hosts. Moreover he is committed to a life of celibacy and poverty, and shows full restraint in his relation with Giribala.

Total lack of love on her husband's part, left her with no sweet memories to fall back upon. Giribala rebels and wants to disappear in the golden sunshine of love. She demands love from Mark, not his sympathy. Morals have no relevance She tries to assimilate Mark to her world through her love. Such resolution is bound to fail. The bitter moments of her husband's illicit relationship and his proud and bold confession leave harsh memories, which makes her violate the norm by eating meat at the Shraddha ceremony-which was a taboo foe the widows. This causes a big scandal in the village and was forced to do hard penance for violating one of the sacred injunctions of widowhood, but she never felt any remorse There are several scenes in the novel which show Giribala's open admission of her growing attraction to Mark, and her desire for freedom. Once on an excursion she tells him she had no sense of sin. She could not live the life of aunt Durga-the traditional life of a widow. Her frankness embarrassed Mark. On one such excursion to the ruins it was raining, the cart was broken down by the elephant. The rampant elephant in its 'musth' state created a terror and she threw her self in the arm of Mark. In that, moment she thought even if she were to die now, killed by the elephant she would have found fulfilment. To die in the arm of an infidel would soothe her conscience. But the elephant was driven away by the villages, but they had not failed to notice the intimacy between Giribala and Mark, which spread like wildfire in the village, it reached the in-laws too who to save the reputation of the family acted swiftly. A daughter in-law of a reputed family could not be allowed to hobnob with an infidel foreigner. Messengers were sent to bring her to her in-laws. And the instruction was if she resisted, to drag her by her hair and bring her. Giribala escapes from her house, comes to Mark's cottage all drenched, clothes sticking to her so close that she looked almost transparent Giribala's appearance shocks Mark, she asks him to close the door, he does but requests her to go back. But Giribala was determined, she looked at Mark and said, "My father-in-laws people are sending men to take me to their home. To go with them would be living death to me, and I shan't go." "Mark felt deeply, wanted to console her. but never came close, there were tears in his eyes, The night passed.

Next day a group of men appeared led by the family priest, Marks' door was kicked open. Mark seduced a pious Brahmin widow and defiled her religion. They tied up Mark with a rope and dragged Giribala out, she had become impure as an outcast. The priest wanted to purify Giribala before she could enter the precincts of the Goswami household. She was to be brought to the back of the homestead where elephants were tied Giribala sat under the jackfruit tree indifferent to what was happening, took the whole thing playfully. She called the boys to play at burning the goat, and set fire to the hut and she would run out like a goat. The priests too agreed for it would serve the purpose. But when the fire is lit, she does not run out but prefer to die. Stunned all looked at the awful sight. She choose death instead of a life of bondage and humiliation and dying everyday. Her suicide is a final act of defiance against a system which annihilates her for being a widow.

Indra Goswami in novel after novel, shows that love is the only value which gives meaning to life. Saru Gossainee, the only woman who fights the male dominated Satha system and survives, she is independent and courageous but hungry for love. What distinguishes her from Giribala is the loving memory of her husband, which is still fresh in her memory, which implies her to an attitude of trust. Love is based on trust and being of a loving nature, trusts others including

Mohidhar, but is sadly betrayed. Like Indranath she tries to bring a human touch to her activities. Giribala is forced to commit suicide, because the young passionate widow can find no way to break the shackles of the ruthless feudal Brahmincal system. Mark, sympathises but lacks the courage to take her out of the oppressive system, though he wants he cannot, for she is a part of the system to which he is only a foreigner. Indranath's beloved Elliman, the daughter of the priest, love too falters because Indranath lacks the courage to stand up to her love.

Love can give meaning to life only if it is reciprocated, but such love is difficult to find. Betrayal, cowardice, rigid traditional morality all go to stiff love. One is left with an arid landscape of dryness and drabness denoting death in life. No one finds fulfilment, love makes one more lonely. On the whole the world is gloomy, one sees the despair and death of love, rather than fulfilment. This is what makes the novel significant to modern reader. Though yearning for love, love is unattainable. The novel tries to show that tradition are a dead weight on men and women. Tradition have become meaningless, but a modern way of life has not emerged neither is there any hope that the modern faith in love is a panacea.

The Indian novels of social realism has followed two different courses- the documentary novels which present the social problem and suggest possible solutions and the romantic novel which explore the complexities of human relationship and the moral conflict within an individual and society. While the documentary novels record social reality, the romantic novels raises moral issues. The power of a great novelists like Indira Goswami lies in combining realism with comprehensive philosophical and moral vision, which has added new dimension to Assamese novels.

References

1. Rojal Sugan: *The Hindu Widow in Indian Literature,* OUP Delhi 2002.

2. Uma Chakravarti and Preeti Gill: *Shadow Lives: Writings in Widowhood,* Kali for Women Pub. Delhi 2007.

3. Indira Goswami: *Selected Works of Indira Goswami,* New World Series-12 B.R. Pub. Delhi-88.

4. Indira Goswami: *Shadow of the Dark* (translated Prafulla Kotoky, Gaurav Pub. House Delhi 86.

5. Malaya Khaund (ed) Indira Goswami Critical Studies New World Literature Series-74. B.R. Pub. 1994.

4

Bharati Mukherjee: *Jasmine;* Alienation to Assimilation

Canada, like United Slates, was peopled by waves of immigrants coming from various parts of the world. As John Marlyn said, "It is meaningless to call anyone a foreigner in this country, we are all foreigners" (1). But, Canada like U.S., did not believe in the 'melting pot theory'; which, in the words of Handlin, "all individuals of all nations have melted into a new race of men where labour. will one day cause changes in the world". Even those who did not support this theory believed that American society constituted a federation of culture that the American culture had much to gain by permitting each of them to develop their own particular tendencies and believed that by encouraging differentiation through mental and psychic cross fertilization reach a higher level of humanity and to afford all an unfettered start and a fair chance in the race of life. (2) Canadians too. like many Americans, who did not support the 'melting pot theory' believed that each distinct group could maintain its identity and, hence, Canada would have a mosaic culture, with each contributing to the fabric of the country. But, in actual practice, Canada rigidly believed in racial purity as is evident in *"Saturday Night"* in which the dominant theme was racial purity. Canada, according to the magazine, was a White man's country. Stephen Leacock, one of Canada's heroes, wrote in 1911 in "*Saturday Night*," that the new Anglo Saxons immigrants were fit objects for pity but indifferent material from which to builda Commonwealth of the future.

Bharati Mukherjee entered the Writer's Workshop at the University of lowa in 1961 where she met Clark Blaise, a fellow Canadian student and married him. Her first two novels, *The Tiger's Daughter* (1972) and *Wife* (1975), were well received. But, ten years passed before she brought her third novel. Her decision not to write fiction was not made by choice but because by 1970 Canada had become a place of 'rapid racial discrimination', As a result of the influx of South African immigrants into Canada, frightening outbursts of 'Pakibashing; and 'dot busting' towards Asians by White Canadians had started taking place. She told Alison Carb

"The 1970's were horrendous years for Indians in Canada. There was a lot of bigotry against Canadian citizens of Indian origins, especially in Toronto, and it upset me terribly when 1 encountered this or saw other people experiencing it."(3)

She noticed several ways of discrimination. She was refused service in stores. Though first in the queue, she would have to board the bus in the last. She would be followed by detectives in the departmental stores for she was considered to be a shop-lifter or treated like a prostitute in hotels, and was physically roughed up in aToronto subway station. The Canadians did not feel shy in rhetoric while talking about immigrants. In polite company she was an 'East Indian' and in impolite company a 'Paki', a British slur unknown to Americans. Most Indians faced violence, physical assault, spitting, name calling, bricks through the windows, pushing and shoving in the sub-way. The government gave implied consent to racism.

Her coming to Canada was with a desire to be accepted as a Canadian writer. There were political reasons for choosing Canada-Clark Blaise, her husband had roots in Montreal and she herself got an offer lo teach at MacGill university. But, even after having published two novels, *Tiger's Daughter* and

Wife, she still felt to be an outsider in Canadian literary circle. She was insulted by the Canadian Council letters addressed as Mr. Bharati Blaise. The conclusion she drew was

"If you don't have a family compact nature, forget about joining us; if you don't have Canadian content, forget about publishing here. ACBC interviewer was rude point-blank. How can you call yourself a Canadian writer if you didn't play in the snow as a child? How do you justify taking grams and then not writing about Canada?" (4)

Like other immigrants, Bharati Mukherjee and Blaise, saw scope and promise in Canada. Hence, they chose to live there, which only ended in deep regret.

"We were slow to .acknowledge the gathering clouds. Some of us have reacted positively working with the local or provincial government.... Others have taken hockey sticks or vigilante patrols to protect their people. Many, including myself, have left unable to keep our two selves together." (ibid: SO)

She was under such distress that she could only think of becoming 'a human activist' instead of a writer. By then, having concluded that the situation in Canada had become unbearable, Mukherjee left with her family, though she felt guilty about having uprooted her husband and children. Because "of my refusal to deal anymore with what I felt was very racially hostile situation in Toronto" she confided to Hancock "Moving out of Canada gave me back my voice." The last seven years or so in "Canada I felt was constantly being forced to sec myself as part of an 'unwanted visible minority"." (5)

Her immigration to the U.S. was to her "a movement away from the aloofness of expatriation to the exuberance of immigration." (6) Her Canadian experience as an expatriate, who felt constantly crippled in self-defense in a hostile environment made her welcome the freedom of the anonymous in the U.S. Unlike Kamala Markandaya and Anita Desai who treated the immigrants situation as one of conflict and adjustment with little understanding and love, Bharati

Mukherjee gives a new challenging perspective enabling the immigrants to emerge out of the cocoons of defense into the openness of assertion and say that they do belong. She was determined that the cold unfriendliness of a foreign land is not going to drive the immigrants away. They are determined to endure hardships until they are accepted, until in fact Canada is no longer a White country.

Acculturalism or adaptation of change in external behavior begins early enough but 'assimilation' or the ability to react instinctively and emotionally to a culture is a far slower process. Breaking away from one's ethnicity and absorbing the new culture is the only way of survival. The tremendous difference between two ways of life, leads a person to a feeling of depression and frustration which could be termed as cultural shock. The expatriated immigrant faces the dilemma of being unable to return home and not being able to find a home in the adopted land. One nurtures the hope that one will be able to merge into the new culture. Bharati Mukherjee firmly believes that the multi-cultural U.S. welcomes all immigrants irrespective of color and race. Canada and the U.S. have different ways of treating newcomers. Mukherjee told Sybil Steinberg '"here diversity is accepted. The melting pot helps the newcomers to feel more welcome." (7) In sharp contrast to Canada, U.S. stimulated a different feeling.

"The U.S. was 'violent' 'mindlessly macho' 'conformist' 'lawless'. If I am not exempt from victimization here, neither are Clark or my sons and neither am I exempt from redress, I am less shocked, less outraged and shaken to the core by a purse snatching in New York in which I lost all my dowry gold than by a simple question asked of me, in the summer of 1978, by three high school boys in Toronto 'why don't you go back to Africa?' It hurt because of its calculations, its calm ignorant satisfaction, its bland assumption of the right to break into my privacy. In New York I was violated because of my suspected affluence and my obviously foreign, needless, non defensiveness." (8)

In U.S., she was not considered a grubby, dishonest,

smelly, ignorant, job snatcher, baby breeding, an unassimilitable malcontent. Diasporal dream figures prominently in all her fictions. But, its treatment after her settlement in America seems to be more assured and more comprehensive in its coverage of the many moods of expatriation- nostalgia, frustration and hope than in the Canadian phase of her life where uncertainty and despondency prevailed. Bharati Mukherjee pays glowing tribute to America as a country where "there is a kind of curiosity and exuberance" thus offering a sharp contrast to her pained outburst "In Canada I was frequently taken for a shop-lifter.... assumed to be a domestic and praised by my astonished auditors that 1 did not have a sing song voice." (9) She rightly sees an echo of this dejected state in the 'pathetic put upon' appearance of the heroines of *Tiger's Daughter* and *Wife.* The shift to America wrought a sea-change in her personality and gave a new fillip to her literary aspiration. Her own acknowledgement of this "For me it is a movement away from the aloofness of expatriation to the exuberance of immigration." (10) To Bharati Mukherjee, "immigration is a two way process both the Whites and the immigrants were growing into a third thing by this interchange and experience". (11) While Tara and Dimple in *Tiger's Daughter* and *Wife* become isolated rootless aliens because of their ambivalent attitude to their native tradition as well as the culture of the new world, Jasmine enjoys the assimilated status of immigration by a sheer will to bind herself to the adopted land.

Written in this frame of mind, Jasmine's story, the heroine of her third novel of the same name is really the making of an American mind. She seems vibrant with Bharati Mukherjee eager savouring of the bracing typical American reference for the autonomy of the individual. Informed by Bharati Mukherjee's special insight into American life that of observer participant' as Clark Blaises wife. The novel has about it the authentic ring of an experience tested against the pulse of the author's existence. But this does not in any way mean that the novel is autobiographical. As Bharati

Mukherjee herself admits, "*Jasmine* becomes the summary of my own emotion without any of the events or characters being in any way autobiographical. My fiction comes out of my own personal obsession. I listen to the voice in my head. I find metaphors, the appropriate metaphors for getting across for embodying an obsession". (12) Bharati Mukherjee's own background in real life - top family, top school, top caste, top city and society, is a world apart from that of her poverty stricken heroine Jasmine, living in a shabby dwelling, devoid of minimum amenities like water and electricity. The similarity to quote Bharati Mukherjee is 'shape of her life' and her 'desires'.

Jyoti was born in a small village in Punjab, in a family driven from an affluent house in Lahore to a life of ignonimus poverty in a remote village in Punjab-Hasnapur-during the partition riots. Jyoti had early acquaintance with the heart-wrenching agony of people uprooted from their homesteads. Resigned to her supposedly inferior status in society for the sin of having born a girl, constantly made aware of her misfortune as a daughter who would be a big problem even in getting married for there was nothing to pay as dowry, Jyoti had an uneventful childhood. Two incidents were fixed in her memory. One was her having killed a mad dog rushing to attack her and the other the star like scar on her forehead, while she slipped and fell while running away from an irrate astrologer who had predicted her early widowhood and exile. The scar, she called her third eye, but which continued to influence her of the astrologer's words even after breaking away from Indian roots and settling in U.S.

Marriage to Prakash brings about a total change in her mindset, the city and her name Prakash the young man who always thrashed tradition. Pygmalion like he had given her a new identity and a new name. Jasmine, for she was small, sweet and could enliven the world with her presence. Enthused by Prakash's plan of eventually settling down to a much better life-style in America with his business, she assists him in the repair of electric goods, but his untimely death-killed by the terrorists - leaves her shattered. But.

Jasmine does not regress into being Jyoti again. She does not shuttle between identities. Instead, she decides to go to America and fulfil Prakash's mission and become a 'Sati' on the very ground of the university where he had got admission. Rebelling against the idea of spending the rest of her life as a destitute widow of Hasnapur, she prevails on her brothers to arrange for her transport to America, and she leaves on a forged passport.

Oncè in America, her old self strongly conditioned by the society in which she was born gives birth to a new exuberant self that denies death and welcomes the prospect of a new life. Raging against fate and norm of society which tried to condition her existence, Jasmine asserts that she is not just nothing. Her drive is seen early in life where she kills a mad dog though poor and cannot afford dowry, she still refuses to marry anyone who does not know English and is finally married to Prakash, an engineer, who too seems to be like her "to make something more of life, than fate had intended". Jyoti begins the journey of realizing her 'self and 'potential'. She joyously shares the ambition of her husband to go to America, a land of dreams and opportunities.

The daring of the rustic young girl in undertaking the hazardous trip abroad is a measure of her innate affinity to American ideal of free enterprises. Jasmine's image seems to be a personification of Bharati Mukherjee's concept of American-ness as an outlook of life. As experienced by David Davidar, "some people were meant to be American even if they never leave their village in Punjab. At heart they are Americans. It is a desire for more, more, more". (13)

The desire to hold her own against the blind forces of destiny urges her to leave India. But her American experience begins on a jarring note. She is raped by a deformed captain, whom she kills like a veritable 'Kali'.

Prakash's struggle to make something more of his life than fate intended "If we could get away from India then all fates would be cancelled. We would start with new fates and new stars. We could say or be anything we wanted.

We'll be on the other side of the earth, out of God's sight" is too deeply etched in Jasmine's mind to allow her to agree to getting engulfed by insularity and the decision to leave Professorji's house with its 'diligently guarded ethnicitism in the household which included the austerities of widowhood she is expected to observe, shė decides to leave the house and live her own life. This move is in itself an indication of self actualization which is further made possible by acculturalism to the American way of life, thinking and dressing.

Given a new insight into life by Lillian Gordon's most practical and humanist approach that made life possible for anyone, Jasmine goes to New York. But, to her horror, finds New York to be an archipelago of ghettos seething with aliens. Unlike the Vaderas, who had retired behind the ghetto walls and the 'fortress of Punjabiness', Jasmine lays to explore the new land, which intrigues her.

To Jasmine, the U.S. is her dreamland and her strange mission is soon forgotten, She sheds her Indian name and dress and adapts herself easily to every circumstance of life. In spite of occasional memories of life in India, she was never tormented by the clash of traditional values and the American world she faces. Chameleon like, she transforms herself. She exemplifies Mukherjee's 'Maximalist creed', which is essential, according to her, for every expatriate. According to her 'They are neither nostalgic for their personal past, nor afraid of their unfamiliar present. Jasmine is confident '1 had landed and getting rooted'. Her journey through life from Jyoti to Jasmine to Jane through geographical locales like Punjab, Florida, New York, Iowa and finally California At every stage, Jasmine revolted against her fate and the path drawn for her. The narrative shifts between the past and the present, between India of her earlier life and America of the present.

The present was her life as Jane in Iowa, where she was a live-in companion to Bud Ripplemeyer. a small town banker. Bud was fascinated by her foreignness, he never asked her about India. It scarred him. He courted her because she was an alien. She was darkness, mystery, inscrutability 'The past plays me into instant vitality and wisdom. I rejenuvate him simply by being who I am".

The American experience shocked Jane and disgusted her many a time.

"The country has so many ways of humiliating, of disappointing....There are no harmless, compassionate ways to remake one self. We murder who we were so we can rebirth ourselves in the images of dream".

In her process of transformation, Jane is seized by a longing to belong. She closely identifies herself with Bud's adopted son 'Du', a Vietnamese, because he was an immigrant like herself. Both had seen death closely "They had both hurtled through time tunnels, seen the worst and survived. Like creatures in Fairy tales we've shrunk, we've swollen and we've swallowed the cosmos whole". Both Du and Jasmine were in a hurry to become Americans. They tried to forget the nightmare of their early lives. Assimilation in America was easy. They had just to start letting go "Let go one thing, like not wearing our normal clothes, or a turban, or not wearing the tikka on the forehead-the rest goes on its own down the sink holes."

The next identity of Jyoti was Jase, which was thrust on her by the Hayses family where she worked as a 'care giver'. The transformation of Jyoti had come full circle. Jyoti was now a sati-a goddess, Jasmine lived for the future, and Jase lived for today. For every Jasmine the reliable care giver there is a Jase- the adventurer.

The final crisis of the book comes when Jane is confronted with the souring of the American dream through the suicide of Darrel. Du's departure in search of his family de-stabilizes her. She is caught in duty towards the crippled Bud and her love for Taylor and his marriage proposal. She makes her final choice and is not guilty but relieved. She has stopped thinking of herself as Jane/Jase. She feels potent enough once again to re-position her stars. Time would draw its own conclusion about her true identity "Adventure, risk transformations -the frontier is pushing indoor. She cries through all the lives she has lived and for all her dead......I am out of the door ... greedy with wants and reckless in hope".

As an Indian girl, she would not have dreamt of deserting Bud, denying him even his child. Having seen death and the worst of life closely many a time, having suffered and survived several times, she seems to regard her relationship with Bud as just another phase in the journey of self. It is America which has taught her that nothing lasts in that country. 'Nothing is for ever, nothing is so terrible, or so wonderful that it won't disintegrate'.

Through her innovative technique alternately highlighting one or the other of the mutations in her heroines identity- Jyoti, Jasmine, Jase, Jane - Mukherjee fills in details about different segments of Jyoti/Jasmine's life in its meandering 'course through the terrains of Hasnapur, Jullunder, Florida, Columbia, Baden and thence to the road to California. Jasmine compared to the other selves stands in total isolation as a strange pilgrim in an outlandish shrine'.

Mukherjee admits in an interview that her characters are a breed of pioneers who have the guts to forsake a predictable life in order to throw themselves into a new one. (14) In *Jasmine* she celebrates both the undaunted spirit and enthusiasm of a village girl, who blossoms out of a bruised past into a challenging personality and a complete individual and the status of immigration in the U.S. which facilitates aliens not only to be accultured but also to be assimilated into their adopted land.

With the healing touch of people like Lillian Gorden, Kate and Taylor, who treat her as an intelligent, refined, sincere and affectionate person, Jasmine blossoms from being a diffident alien with forged documents into an adventurous Jase living only for the present.

While America taught her to live with ease and confidence, despite her fluid identities and undocumented status, Jasmine gave her care, concern, love to those who believed her and who needed her. Her immigrant status in no way obstructs the emotional rapport between Darrel, Du,

Bud, Taylor or anyone. For all that America gave her, Jasmine paid back with gratitude. She serves Bud patiently and fondly after he was crippled. With her kind composure, she makes Karius, Bud's former wife, understand that it is not her enemy but it was Bud's happiness that mattered to both. She find' herself welcome in the home and society of mother Ripplemeyer and longs to belong to that tribe which represented the best of America.

To change from Jyoti -Jasmine, Jasmine to Jane, Jase to Jane is not a easy process. She survived rape and murder, terrifying challenges and unimaginable crises. She is not sentimental about her Indian identity, nor does she suffer from nostalgic longing. Instead she uses all her strength and resolve to forge new alliances in the friendly soil of the adopted land. The fusion between the East and West pleases her and she rejoices that the journey to America has unfolded her affirming self.

Jasmine presents a character whose first instinct is survival; she realizes this through multipke identities in different places. The very concept of Jasmine lies in the concept of endless possibilities. Within the few years of the life of Jasmine a life time of experiences are stored. Towards the end by choosing Taylor and not Bud, she is symbolically asserting her right to try and move her stars, instead of passively accepting her fate .She has learnt by now that nothing lasts for ever and so she need not condemn herself to a life she does not want.

The new world holds a promise of new selfhood as well as new battles against marginalization. Jasmine narrates her story in a shuffled way-through the various mutations as sati, goddess, illicit lover, compassionate care giver and a courageous exhilarating dreamer.

Mukherjee considers her self an American writer. To quote her, "I consider myself an American writer and that has been my big battle to get to realize that my roots as a writer are no longer, if they were among Indian writers, but that I'm writing about the territory, about the feeling of a new kind of pioneer in America. I am the first among

Asian immigrants writing to be making the distinction between immigrants and expatriate writing. Most Indian writers prior to this, have still thought of themselves as Indian and their literary inspiration has come from India, but my roots are here, my emotions are here in North America. Ii has many pluralities. I am writing about an American immigrant group, who are undergoing many transformations within themselves. And who, by their very presence are changing the country. America is not the America, that until recently has come through in contemporary popular fiction. (15)

Mukherjee insists on being read, not as Indian or expatriate writer, but as an immigrant writer whose literary agenda is to claim that America is being enriched by the new comers. Bharati Mukherjee refuses to be marginalized as a writer of alien material, her insistence that her themes are central and not marginal to the contemporary American society bears testimony to this.

Mukherjee's novels chronicle the transition from an expatriate sensibility to an immigrant one, A novel dealing with migrancy and belonging, Jasmine is the culmination of a literary trajectory initiated in the *Tiger's Daughter. Jasmine* is an ebullient novel offering a spiced version of the classic recipe of assimilation into dominant culture, 'and where Jasmine is ready to celebrate I am of one you".

The motto of the novel is clear 'There is no harmless, compassionate ways to make oneself. We murder who we were, so we can rebirth ourselves in the image of our dream. Jasmine cuts her tongue, burns her past, sheds her cultural baggage, changes her clothes, altars her walk and her name and instead of becoming a nonentity in the violent process of mollification a husk void of self. She acquires the desired and desirable identity of Jase/Jane. It endorses what Adrienne Rich called 'two powerful pressures in present day American culture one is the imperative to assimilate, the other the idea that one can be socially twice born' (16). If as Rich says "assimilate means to give up not only your history but also your body". (17) Jasmine is ready to give up both. Jasmine

- ignorant, traditional escaping infanticide is a victim in everyway, so it follows that when she came with an intention of self immolation, she does not need to preserve her identity.

Self assertion is the key to realize the immense hidden potential, and the end of the quest should be the channeling of energy in the right direction and not passive acceptance of all situations. Jasmine creates her destiny first with love, then courage and cunning. What changes her course is not the dignity and freedom available in the new land, but infinite opportunities to strike ahead.

Discussing her fiction Mukherjee writes "I don't think fiction as being about alienation. On the contrary I mean for it to be about assimilation ... my stories are about conquests not about losses (18)

Mukherjee desires to tell the story of the marginalized Asian, in U.S. "All around me. I see the face of America changing, but where in fiction do you read about it? Who in other words speaks for us, the new Americans from non-traditional immigrant countries"? Obviously meaning who else but T have the authority to speak for others. Bharati Mukherjee, has not redefined herself as an American, rather she is part of that long procession of people who over the years have gone to redefine America itself.

By the end of the novel all the identities dissolve into one and Jasmine becomes a metaphor for that type of Indianness which has through the ages welcomed and absorbed within itself all that is fine and decent from every country, every religion and every culture.

References

1. John Marlyn, Under *The Ribs Of Death. Survival, A Thematic Guide To Canadian Literature-Margret* Atwood (Toronto: Avansi, 1972) p. 147.
2. R M. Maclver "*Our Strength And Our Weakness." Discrimination And National Welfare* (New York: Kennikat Press, 1969) p. 1.
3. Alison Carb" An Interview With Bharati Mukherjee" The Massachuseetts Review (Winter, 1988-89) p. 644-54.

4. Bharati Mukherjee" *The Invisible Woman*" Saturday Night" 1981 p. 38.
5. Ibid p. 50.
6. Joel Yanofsky, "*The Melting Pot Lady*" Books in Canada(Jan-Feb. 1990) p. 25-28.
7. Geoff Hancoff' An Interview with Bharathi Mukherjee" Canadian Fiction Magazine 1987 p. 30-34.
8. Bharati Mukherjee *Introduction To Darkness*, Penguin, 1999, p. 3.
9. Sybil Steinberg" *Bharati Mukherjee*" Publishers Weekly,(25 Aug. 1989) p. 4 has, p. 38.
10. *Introduction, Darkness* Penguin 1986, p. 2.
11. Ibid; p. 3.
12. Interview in Hindustan Times Feb. 9. 1990, p. 3.
13. Meera Ameena "*Bharati Mukherjee*" Bomb (Fall,89) p. 26-27.
14. David Davidar": *The Immigrant Native*" The Indian Express, 9 Feb, 89 p. 5.
15. Interview, Indian Express Sept. 13, 1992 p. 6.
17. Meera Ameena "*Bharati Mukherjee*" Bomb (Fall 1989) p. 26-27.
18. Andrienne Rich "*Resisting Amensia, History and Personal Life*" Blood Breed and Poets(New York: West Norton 1989,) p. 142.
19. Ibid.
20. Geoff Hancock "An Interview With Bharathi Mukhrejee Canadian Mag. 1987, p. 34-35.

5

Salman Rushdie: *Midnight's Children—A Saga of Epic Dimension*

"With the publication of *Midnight's Children* it was clear that a rare thing had happened, we had suddenly seen the emergence of a major writer. That book's extraordinary scale and fertility, its span of style from free buoyant fantasy to murderous social invective, its mixture of radical aesthetic experiment and political courage, to power of illuminating the 'English language with the metaphors, myths and sheer loquacity's of Indian writing, made it a remarkable intervention". (1)

Few novels in recent times have unleashed so much praise and criticism as *Midnight's Children* as it did when it won the 1981 Booker Award. According to New York Times, "the novel sounds like a continent finding its voice". The New York Review of Books hailed it as 'an extraordinary novel'. It was seen as something like a Copernican turning point in the history of literature and of ideas. Balanced critical judgment and evaluation has given way to exuberant rhetoric and spontaneous overflow of enthusiasm. The most striking and most universal characteristic of *Midnight's Children* is hymnal panegyrics "a continent finds its voice, although the voice is foreign tongue" the most important and most beautiful book that was first published in autumn 1983" "a colossal fresco, a collage of autobiography and history" "world in abundance like the *Arabian Nights*" "phantastic epic" "a phantastic many voiced mixtum composition of autobiography family saga and authentic history" "grotesque absurd treatise in the montage technique of film history, as endless fairy tale, a real realistic world of wonders". And Rushdie has been praised as "bard of the Indian sub continent who presents a baroque pageant a theatre Mundi" "a mythomanic with cryptic critical humour who has offered the world a book felt with Indian soul, written with a Western pen" "the opening up of a completely new phase of self confident Indo Anglican literature." Rushdie does not present a cynical image of India as Naipaul has done in *India: An Area of Darkness (64) India: A Wounded Civilization* (77). The ingredient of the European novel realism, law of causation, psychology can be traced, but they are colourfully overgrown, or as it were interwoven into the pattern of a magic carpet, by the pungent spice of Indian cuisine-throbbing, pulsating, warm blooded and colourful The result as the German reviewers observed is a novel that is at the same time a carefully constructed allegory for artistic creation 'chutr.ey fication, selection, preservation and spicing of reality and a magic talc of 1001 children. 1001 episodes, anecdotes, 1001 adventures, told by Sabeen, the protagonist, who is man, demon, demigod in one, a male Sheherzade'. (2)

The subject matter of Rushdie's novels is fairly varied; it is neither stereotyped nor predictable. "There is nothing like a consistent theme that has emerged from his works so far... There are signs however of certain key ideas shaping up of a perspective developing in his writings". (3) One such theme is Rushdie's concept of history and its interplay with the individual. He calls himself significantly enough 'a fairly political animal". (4) He told his reviewer Gordonwise that his two novels-*Midnight's Children and Shame*- are on historical themes. "It seems to me that everything in both books has had to do with politics and with the relationship of the individual and history". (5) Rushdie's study in history at Cambridge in 1965 and his experience helped him to evolve a distinct concept of historical process and their roles. Walter Alien remarks that no sensitive writer can afford lo be oblivious of the historical forces.

In the literature of an age, its conflicts, tendencies, obsessions are uncovered and made manifest to a degree which is continually astonishing, good writers are, so to speak, mediumistic to the degree of stirring of life of their time while they are still unknown to or at any rate unsuspected by the public, politicians and current received opinion.

Contemporary novels are the mirror of the age, but a very special kind of mirror that reflects not merely the external features of the age, but also its inner face, its nervous system, coursing of its blood and the prompting and conflicts which sway it. (6)

Nobody has realized this fact more fully than Rushdie. In writing *Midnight's Children,* the novelist's aim was to relate private lives, public events and to explore the limits of individuality in a country as big, as populous and culturally variegated as India. He presents realities of public history influencing and getting influenced by individual action and aspiration. Keith Wilson views that 'the image of the writer as both master and victim of public and private material, which has been formed by in the past and is himself attempting to form in the present, dominates *Midnight's Children*". (7)The central theme of *Midnight's Children* is not so much social criticism but the presentation of certain phases of history in the course of which the world and the human nature have undergone radical and irrevocable changes.

Rushdie's masterpiece. *Midnight's Children,* is a novel about Indian independence, the partition and its aftermath. The holocaust of the Partition is dealt by Kushwant Singh in *Train to Pakistan* (1956): B. Rajan, *The Dark Dancer* ('59); Manohar Mnlgaonkar in *Distant Dreams* ('66); Altai Hussain in *Sunlight in a Broken Column* and Collin Lapierre in *Freedom at Midnight* ('79). Rushdie, however, was not happy with these novels. He felt an event as mementoes as the Partition has not been given adequate attention in Indian fiction and finds the few books written on it 'anemic and dull' (8). The freedom movement was not only a political struggle but an all pervasive experience that became part of the life of all the sensitive and enlightened Indians.

Midnight's Children is Rushdie's interpretation of a period almost seventy years in Indian modern history dealing with the events leading to partition and beyond. There is in the novel virtually all of the 20th century Indian history-the Jallinwallah Bagh tragedy, Quit India Movement, Muslim League and its role, riots and bloodshed subsequent to independence Five Year Plan reorganization of Indian States and language riots, Chinese aggression, theft of the sacred relic from Hazrathbal mosque, Indo-Pak war, liberation of Bangladesh, emergency and various other historically important events

Passages of explicit political narrative occur in the novels of other novelists too in which political events dominate the human drama. In Kushwant Singh's *Train to Pakistan,* the communal hatred in Punjab is the dominant reality. This hatred is the direct consequence of Partition, but historical events are not described. They are, however, described in Mumtaz Shahnawaz's *The Heart Divided.* Here too, the descriptive passages have not been assimilated into the fictional narrative. In Rushdie, on the other hand, bits of real history are presented, but they are made to appear as integral part of the narrator's consciousness.

From the beginning, Rushdie maintains a continuous effort at synchronizing national and domestic life, so that the Odyssey of the Azizes and the Sinais became the Odyssey of the nation. The convergence of the national and the domestic is underscored repeatedly in the course of the novel.

Midnight's Children encapsulates the experience of three generations of the Sinai family, living in Srinagar, Amritsar, Agra and then in Bombay, before finally migrating to Karachi. Saleem Sinai, the narrator engaged in the actual writing of the story, works at a pickle factory by day, and records the experience at night hoping that 'one day perhaps the world may taste the pickles of history. They may be too strong for some palate, their smell may be overpowering, tears may rise in the eyes, 1 hope nevertheless that it will be possible to say of them that they possess the authentic taste of truth'. (9) Rushdie's self avowed purpose in writing the novel was to highlight "the connection between public affairs and private lives". You cannot separate the two. They interpenetrate and that is how the writer needs to examine them, the one in the context of the other. (10) Along with Saleem's personal history we have the collective experience of the people and the history of a nation.

Halfway through the novel Saleem indulges in a playfully learned explication of the scene in which his life may be said to mirror the nation.

"Your life, which will be, in a sense, the mirror of our own nation" the Prime Minister wrote (Nehru)... In what sense. How in what terms, the career of a single individual be said to impinge on the fate of a nation. I must answer in adverbs and hyphens; 1 was linked Lo history both literally and metaphorically, both actively and passively ... The union of 'passive' and 'metaphorical' encompasses all socio political trends and events, which merely by existing affected me metaphorically... Next 'passive' and "literal" when hyphenated cover all moments at which national events had a direct bearing upon the lives of myself and my family-under this heading you should file the freezing of my father's assets also ... (265-86)

The relationship between history, social realities and their fictional treatment in Rushdie's fiction has been the subject of comment since the publication of *Midnight's Children* and *Shame*. In an interview Rushdie himself commented that "the children born at midnight on August 15, 1947, the day India was liberated was a 'metaphor' and that was exactly the parallel that I wanted to make between the action of the book and what happened in history". (11) Rushdie's "achievement is to have brought to life this benighted generation who have missed out the chance of collaborating with the British -as a great majority of Indians did during the Raj-compensated by being more patriotic than their fathers". (12). While *Shame* was seen as an allegory of a recent event in Pakistan.

Saleem is constantly reminded of the fact that "historical coincidences have littered and perhaps fouled my family's existence in this world" (25) The historical forces prove so powerful against him that he feels "buffeted by too much history and begins to show signs of falling apart" (57)The identification between the public and the private strands is so complete that it is not possible to separate them. It is this feature which gives unity to the novel, Moreover the interaction of the historical and the individual forces have made the narrator what he is:

"Who am I? My answer: I am the sum total of everything that went before me of all I have been seen done, of everything done to me, I am everyone, everything whose being in the world affected was affected by mine. I am that happens after I've gone which would not have happened if had not come. I repeat for the last time: to understand me you'll have to swallow a world'". (457-58)

Rushdie thus creates in Saleem, a character who provokes much of the history he records and enshrines in his personal heritage the identity of India itself. The interplay of the personal and national history is the most significant feature of *Midnight's Children.*

Saleem is intended to be simultaneously Rushdie's fictional alter ego and an allegorical representation of India's Independence. Saleem, like Rushdie, is born at the precise hour of the end of the Raj. It takes the author's abilities sorely to sustain Saleem's creditability as a human being, while at the same time capturing within his person all euphoria the tension and the trauma of Independence. His difficulties are compounded manifold by the fact that Saleem is also the narrator protagonist of the novel. The best would baulk at the prospect of having to sustain so many simultaneous identities. Saleem and his creator come out of this ordeal bruised, with their honour, relatively unblotted.

The dominant mood of the novel seems to oscillate between the apocalyptic and the expansive.

Political forces have created a macabre world alienated from the ideal human world. In India and Europe the phenomenon of all pervading inhumanity can be imaginatively be dealt only from a grotesque and absurdist point of view. Otherwise it would be intolerable. This is admittedly a narrative technique with Saleem Sinai, who is present as an eye witness to political and private events which is at the same time a basically human experience which is global. Saleems gradual amputation is symbolic for the loss of freedom, sanity and individuality in modern man. The dried up gnome who in the end spends his days preserving chutneys and his stories on history is symbolic of India's dried up hopes. The way the world goes and the way human destinies are shaped by inhuman historical process can be only conveyed as an absurd world. *Midnight's Children* is "a symbol of man's basic human condition". (13)

Rushdie's narrative technique, however much it may resemble those of the absurdist is a liberal humanist. This is the type of humanism which goes back to the Renaissance ethno centrism and a concern for human happiness. It does not have the dogmatic faith in the ideas of individualism, freedom, equality, fraternity as the Victorians possessed. But after all the qualification and doubts, Rushdie does in the last analysis appear greatly concerned for the survival of human values and humanness of the human race. This puts him in the tradition of George Orwell, E.M. Forster, Joseph Conrad and in contemporary literature to that of Garcia Marquez, Guntur Grass and Ishaguru.

In *Midnight's Children,* Saleem Sinai in narrating the incidents takes good care to establish his position as an unprejudiced observer of the politics of India and Pakistan. He does so by being truthful and evaluating only from a humanitarian- as opposed to a partisan, nationalistic, religious or cultural - point of view.

'"Brigadier Dyer's fifty men put down their machine gun and go away. They had fired a total one thousand six hundred and fifty rounds into the unarmed crowd of those, one thousand five hundred and sixteen have found their mark, killing or wounding some persons 'Good Shooting Dyer tells his men' we have done a jolly good thing". (MC 36)

This seemingly unemotional statement of facts brings out Dyer's inhumanity and the whole phenomenon of colonial rule in general. The narrator reports it without comments but the description of the innocent people, the deliberateness of the killing and the complete lack of human feeling by the perpetrator of the killing evokes the emotions and sympathy for the victims and indignation against the British Similarly, he is concerned with the pain caused to human beings irrespective of the side they belong to be it in the 1965 or the 1971 Indo-Pak War. The wars first victim is Truth.

The 1971 War sees the ultimate degradation of man. Saleem, who suffers from amnesia and emotional numbness as a result of the death of his parents is enrolled in CUTIA (a she dog) in place of a tracker dog. The symbolic relegation of the human to the bestial is a measure of the bestiality of the 1971 war. The bare facts of the political events have been given in the novel. On the orders of the Pak army the man dog helps in getting Mujibur Rehman arrested, "It was I who sniffed him out - they provided me with one of his old shirts, its easy when you've got the smell" (335) he tells Padma, who acts as the listener or reader. The inhumanity of the army, "the roadside ditches filling up with people who were not merely asleep - bare chests were seen and the hallow pimples of bullet holes". (MC 336) The insanity of the war is reflected in the near insanity of the three soldiers in the jungle of Bengal.

When the war is over and the narrator finds himself in India, he finds the diary of unscrupulous politicians 'just as inimical for humanity as the war had been'. The State of Emergency and forcible castration for Saleem is a stupendous event. To the children born with him at midnight on 15 August, 1947, he tells:

"Politics Children at the best of time a bad dirty business

... I am coming to the conclusion that privacy, the small individual lives of men, are preferable to all this inflated macrocosmic activity. But too late can't be helped". (435)

The final assertion of the primacy of the non individual non political action is defeatist. It is the ultimate defeat of the human spirit by the cruel and dehumanizing forces of the politics of India and Pakistan.

In *Midnight's Children* the children stand for humanity. They are exposed to strong political (and other) forces which strip them of their illusion and alienate them from others and themselves for a short time, and finally exterminate them. Saleem Sinai, the symbol of human spirit retires to the privacy of a retired life. Politics never leaves him alone, because like[1] others, he surrenders to its demand. His individuality has been eliminated and the moral courage which is imperative for opposing a tyrannical government is no longer there. He is, in fact, no longer an integrated personality. He is self alienated-which means he has created a social self which goes through the motions of living. His real self (his human self) is a stranger to this self created penance and no longer motivates his behaviour. This state is symbolized by the narrator's description of himself as being cracked.

"...now that I can swear, see the cracks in the back of my hands, cracks along my hairline and between my toes, why do I not bleed? Am I already so emptied; desicrated pickled.' Am I already the mummy of myself"? (461)

This end is as bleak a vision of the future defeat of the human spirit at the hands of the social and political as any anti-utopian novel-such as Huxley's, *The Brave New World* or Orwells, *Nineteen Eighty Four-*

"Yes they will trample me under foot, the numbers marching one, two three four hundred million, five hundred six reducing me to specks of voiceless dust". (463)

In Book II, 'Love in Bombay', he shows how if Partition divided India into two, the State Reorganization Committee's report had divided into anew-not into two, but fourteen States and six centrally administered territories. But, 'the boundaries of these States were not formed by rivers or mountains or any natural features of the terrain; they were instead walls of words', (225)

Rushdie, in an informal conversation with friends, once said that he had been inspired by Qurratulain Hyder's *Aag Ka Dariya* (River of Fire) listed in the book *New Writing in India* 1974 - a title she had borrowed from Jigar's famous lines

Ik Aag ka dariya hai
Aur doob ke jaana hai

A continental history before and after independence that would embrace India, Pak and Britain in its myriad relationships at all levels has been Rushdie's inspiration and this he has tried lo bring out in his trilogy- *Midnight's Children (1981), Shame (1983) and The Satanic Verses* (1988) and in many little pieces he has written 'Any continental history would naturally embrace the interplay of religion and politics. *Midnight's Children, Shame and the Satanic Verses* which form a connected whole because the theme of religion and politics is common to them all'. Rushdie achieves a singular synthesis between the Anglo-American genre of non-fiction novel and the far older one of political allegory. Some of the finest political allegory in English was written by Spenser in *Faire Queen,* which also contained excellent religious allegory. Rushdie's religious allegory is absorbed quickly into the political because religion has always been a potent weapon in the hands of those who ruled India.

Any continental history would embrace not only the interplay of religion and politics but also the sham and reality of the interrelationships, the hypocrisy of the English ruling elites which we as ex-colonialists have so deftly picked up, have all been woven into the texture of the novel. This way the themes sound simple, even banal, but human relationships exists at many different levels, the definition of good and evil are never easy to demarcate and define and Rushdie as a creative writer, living in and outside India seems to understand. And to bring out this crisscross of relationships and attitudes, Rushdie has borrowed the technique of the Latin-American novel where memory goes back and forth "where past and future furiously chase each other in a journey of wonderful stories and astonishing flights of imagination. The past that you know lies in front of you and the future that which is unknown recedes" *(14)* as the narrative develops. There is no linear development of the novel. Everything is structurally loose and shifty and the attempts to final meaning that literary writers often do, is at best hazardous because one meaning can be valid as another.

The non-linear technique, which the Latin American and the European have specialized, is because they identify literature with life which is never linear and has been complicated by using memory, dream and fantasies that always intercede in the flow of the novel.

Rushdie in an interview, soon after the success of *Midnight's Children,* acknowledges that he was heavily indebted to Marquez for his technique, which he, like other writers, has picked up to explain the politics and religion of the sub-continent and British perfidy in strengthening obscurantism and fundamentalism. It is not easy to understand Rushdie and his works; neither are his characters simplistic, because they are torn apart by their own contradiction and the history of religion and politics of the sub-continent in the trilogy too is not simplistic because they centrally interweave.

Midnight's Children is a vast sprawling narrative of a nation's history over a period of 62 years-indeed it is proper for it is the history of three nations over various lengths of time. There is in the novel virtually all the 20 century India history - pre and post independence-and also typically India division, dissention, chaos and disillusions, communal tensions, religious fanaticism besides traditional value. All these are 'preserved' in the novel which evokes the truth of India and Saleem and make the novel in Maria Coutos words "an extraordinary saga of epic dimension and resonances".

References

1. Macolm Bradbury; The Guardian Books.
2. Klaus Borner.' The Reception Of Midnight's Children-In West Germany "quoted from Commonwealth Review. Vol, No 2,1990, p. 12-13.
3. Dilip Fernandez: "Such Angst, Such Loneliness, Such Rootlessness" Gentleman (Feb. 1984) p. 100.
4. Gorden Wise: Interview with Salman Rushdie, Gentleman (Feb '84) p. 59.
5. Ibid: p. 57.
6. Reading A Novel (Penguin 1971) pp. 18-19.
7. Kieth Wilson: *Midnight's Children and Reader Responsibility.*
8. Times of India (1 Nov. '81) p. 8.
9. Salman Rushdie: *Midnight's Children* Alfred A. Knopf New York 1980 (all quotes pertain to this edition abt M.C.
10. Book Review, The Sunday Standard 14 June '18. p. 6.
11. Interview: Novelist Salman Rushdie by Chinweizu in Decolonizing the Mind 'South' The Third World Magizine Jan. 83, pp. 22-29.
12. M. Bose 'India's Witching Hour' South' Third World Magizine, March 82 p. 56.
13. Renate Schostack, Frankfurter, Allgemeine, Zeitung, 10 Oct' 73.
14. Hindustan Times Sunday Mag. 23 Oct '88.

6

Shobha De: *Second Thoughts*

Shobha De burst upon the literary scene with her best seller *Socialite Evening* (1988) soon followed by *Starry Nights* (1990) *Sisters and Strange Obsession* (1992) *Sultry Days* (1994) *Snap Shots* (1995) *Second Thoughts* (1996) She began her career as a journalist in 1970 , in the course of which she found and edited three popular magazines *'Star Dust' 'Society'* and *'Celebrity'*, and acted as a consulting editor to *'Sunday'* and *'Megacity'*. Her novels owe their popularity in showing an intimate understanding of the psyche of women-especially urban women- and their problems. She claims to be "a pioneer in the field of popular fiction writing and among the first to explore the world of urban women in India" (1) As a writer she recognizes the displacement and marginalization of women, turns the table upside down. She constantly tries to shatter patriarchal hegemony and raises a voice of protest against male domination.

Shobha De's fictional world has aroused curiosity and interest on the one hand and downright rejection on the other. Her novels evoked hostile reviews, *Socialite Evening* was branded as 'high society potpourri, bland and bursting with orgy....... and voyeuristic serving of souped-up, four wheel drive-sex-in-all-direction "(2) One reviewer found it "choked with listless lust'[1] and criticized its witless dialogues

(3) *Starry Nights* with its brazen portrayal of sex exploitation steals a march over earlier novels. *Strange Obsession* deals with lesbianism. Despite their titillating details, what her novel; indicate is the arrival of a new Indian woman eager to defy rebelliously against the well entrenched moral orthodoxy of the patriarchal social system. As David Davider says they are a serious attempt at 'Discovering India through Indian eyes'.

She created a furor in the world of fiction with her bizarre and murky best sellers. She has been called Jack Collins of India, a label she does relish. Shobha De has thrived on controversies, she has survived controversies. Her critics were surprised and sore to note that *Starry Nights* formed part of the syllabus in Bombay University, which was already on the prescribed reading list of British University.

From *Socialite Evenings* to *Second Thought* De has certainly evolved as a sensitive writer. It has been alleged that in her novels there is little insight into human nature and very little effort made to probe into human nature and feeling. *Second Thoughts*, her seventh novel, set aside these allegations. A departure from her earlier novels, it is a bitter sweet love story of the nineties. The high society, which was the familiar background of her novels, has been replaced by middle class society. Maya, pretty and young, is eager to escape her dull and middle class home in Calcutta and plunge into the whirl of Bombay, where she moves after her marriage. Ranjan, handsome, hard-driving and ambitious, has all the glamour of an American University degree and a wealthy family background. "Marrying Ranjan was like marrying Bombay and she was the luckiest girl in the locality who had bagged a foreign educated Bombay based groom.(4) But soon she finds herself trapped and stifled by the confines of an arranged marriage to a man who, she discovers is rigidly, conservative and indifferent to her desires and does not respect her feelings. She begins to experience utter loneliness. She then strikes a friendship with Nikhil, her charming college going neighbour and the stage is set for an explosive tale of love, betrayal and the paths not taken,

"Maya was an attractive young girl. Maya liked the colour of her skin-tone-a warm rich golden brown, like sunlight dancing on the Hoogly, that setoff the gleaming jet black hair and large eyes to advantage . Maya straightened up threw back her head and concluded she was an attractive young lady. (5)

The novel opens with Maya coming to Bombay to meet Ranjan, her future husband. Maya bored with Calcutta, wanted adventure. Bombay had always fascinated her. While she was growing up when people who had visited Bombay came to their home, she regarded them as wonderful creatures, who had experienced something wonderful. "Like astronauts had come back from the moon trip"; (6) and when her uncle suggested this match, she agreed immediately. Not because Ranjan approved her, but because she was keen to come to Bombay and become part of the city, Hence, when Ranjan approved, it was as if 'she was marrying not Ranjan but Bombay itself and considered herself luckiest in the locality'.

She arrived on a sultry May evening in Bombay- a city about which she had heard so much- a metropolitan the rest of India held in much fascination. But, her first impressions were far from favourable. Bombay smelt - it smelt of desperation and deceit. Maya, took a few steps and recoiled. She had almost tripped on a dead man. What disturbed her was that none of the thousands of people took notice or stopped. It made her to compare it to Calcutta; there would have been a thick, over helpful crowd, a couple of policemen and doctors. But, here in Bombay, it was business as usual. But all this changed once she sees the city throbbing with light, the neon lit shops "South Bombay was different-glittering, menacingly intimidating". It had an entirely different effect on her. Maya found herself falling inexorably in love with this Bombay. She forgets her earlier hostile attitude, and is too eager to become part of Bombay.

Ironically, the desperation and deceit she smelt the moment she set her foot in Bombay, turns out to be a reality, shattering her romantic dream of Bombay. Maya saw that

Mullick household wasn't all that different from her own at Calcutta. She was surprised and disappointed by Rajan's lack of common curtsey-he remained rudely seated and did not bother to get up to pass the tea to her mother. She also soon realized that though they claimed to be modern and living in Bombay, deep down they still cherished the age old norm and tradition, especially in the institution of marriage.

Ranjan's mother, Mrs. Mullick, is rich, seemingly modern and smart. Ranjan too, growing in a big city, educated abroad, and holding a high position in a leading bank, prefers an arranged marriage and a Bengali girl from Bengal and not Bombay for he tells "Oh, no, no. These Bombay Bengalis are different. They've lost their cultural identity. Their roots are not in our own tradition. My mother would not have been able to adjust with someone like that." (6) As individuals, however progressed they may be, but in the institution of marriage the man is still the lord and the woman has to obey him, whether she likes it or not. Mrs. Mullick's reason for choosing her, despite her middle class status was "If you ask me, it's always wiser to get a girl from a socially inferior background. A wealthier wife spells doom. The husband loses all control over her and she ends up having an upper hand. Such marriages can never work, which is why we were so careful while selecting the right candidate for Ranjan". (7)

The same mentality has been inherited by Ranjan. The sarcastic tone and contempt is evidently a trait inherited from his mother. Maya knows the way in which he speaks of her parents- sans respect, is because he feels superior to her and her background. The carefully planned and chosen match ends only in disgust. For, Ranjan, though he has studied abroad and lived in a big city, is as far as his wife is concerned, a virtual dictator. Rajan has a certain mental picture of an ideal wife and Maya, his wife, has to conform to it- whether she loves it or not. "There are certain rules. You have to abide by them whether you like it or not". (8) He imposes restriction on her movements, stops her from mixing with neighbours. She does not even have the freedom to use the telephone freely, us he keeps the STD locked, cannot spend money as she pleases. His responsibility towards her was nothing beyond financial support-not freedom, a decent home and four square meals a day. (9) He is completely indifferent to her emotional needs and responses. The home is always 'his home'. At times he is hardly aware of her presence. She sadly remarks, "It was never a home 'My home,' 'Our home', always 'the home', impersonal distant cold" (10). Sometimes Maya felt like retaliating 'the silent scream stuck somewhere in her throat unable to push its way out'. (11)

Whatever she buys meets with criticism, Basmati (rice) is extravagance. Asks her to ask his mother where she gets supplies from and buy the same brand. On another occasion, she wanted to surprise him with a gift, "an attractive leather bound handcrafted filofax, but the moment he saw it his response was 'it's not my birthday, you shouldn't waste money like this'... Ranjan stared at the filofax and said 'I don't need this ... I prefer an electronic planner which fits into my wallet. Give it to someone else. And...in future, Maya, ask me before you buy something. Every thing costs money, you know, 1 hate waste'." (12)

Lady's finger? At twenty a kilo? Why do we have to eat lady's finger at a price like that?.....wait till the prices come down, all right(10)

Next ....fish....look around carefully you'll be able to find reasonably priced fishes which can be served crisp fried. That way it doesn't matter it is sweet water kind or not"(102)He always lectured on the virtue of eating leafy green -the cheaper and far healthier-and the sins of over indulgence.

Her request to explore Bombay during the weekend is snubbed by Ranjan "Sometimes" you talk like such a kid. Life isn't a picnic. You know .And you aren't in Bombay on a holiday. As a married woman, you have to learn to deal with responsibilities" (27)Her interest in discovering the city was not to attend sun -et-lumiere show at Rajabai Towers or go for a harbour cruise. Neither to visit a film studio nor drink at a five star bar. Rather she wanted the city to seep into her slowly. To absorb, to digest it, make it part of her system, she desperately wanted to become a Bombaywali, to belong to it. But she knew it was futile to say anything.

They never go out together, watch a movie, share an experience. Maya's longing for adventure and romance often suffer a setback. The excitement of the first monsoon shower or the tingling spell of early winter does not arouse Ranjan, rather Maya's excitement and high spirit appears ridiculous He brings down her elevated spirit by sharply rebuking" Why cannot you be still, you know just still you are always so restless-its tiring to watch(39)

Ranjan is never able to relate with Maya because of his mother's (whom he worships)over indulgence in their personal life. She does not resent but is eager to share every bit During their first meeting Maya's mother, Chitra, notes that he is a very dutiful caring, loving son, but he fails to be so as a husband Sex is a complicated issue in their life. The clumsy honeymoon at a depressing hotel at Mahabeleswar, made her feel that perhaps she was inhibited, later she discovers that it was not she but Ranjan. She felt she should take the initiative, shyly she had tried , one night, to snuggle up to him and caress him-but "Ranjan recoiled-jumped back as though he had received an electric shock. He said......stop behaving like a cheap woman. A prostitute, he muttered before turning around arid going to sleep (259)Whenever he loved Maya it was only as a pet dog" It was a gesture devoid of passion. An impersonal friendly soil of gesture which always left me a feeling like a well trained dog being rewarded for his good behaviour"(291)

But this is not what Maya yearned for. She very much wanted Ranjan to confide in her , talk of his inner world , his love , his wishes , his childhood. Being young she always wishes" to step into one of the lively pubs playing jazz" and "sway to the music "Jose themselves in a carefree manner, stroll along stroll along one of the many beaches

.eat at roadside snaky. In fact she expected Ranjan to satisfy her physical and emotional needs, but is sorely disappointed.

Ranjan most of the evenings is immersed in the evening newspaper. He does not discuss his office, his life or anything, which he does so often and for so long with his mother. One day Maya asks him if he did not have faith in her "Of course, I trust you but my mother is my mother, I have known her longer than you. Things take time (205) The emptiness of their relationship is reflected" How week day afternoons were to be suffered silently and stoically with just the whirl of noisy ceiling fan to stir the warm air around"(100)The air conditioner was switched on only after dinner time or when Ranjan was at home. A long lecture would follow on budgeting ending with[1] learn something from mother and follow her' She often wondered who would qualify as a suitable wife to Ranjan and felt it could be no one except his mother.

One day she tried to talk her problem" Ranjan I have been feeling so lonely, all alone in a city .In a home I feel I feel I don't belong to.

He swung around "whose fault is that-huh? Mine? Its in your hands to make yourself at home.......Have you tried to make it more livable I 've told right at the beginning-get Ma involved .She would have helped you to fix up this place better. But did you listen? you stubbornly tried to do things your way. Now look at what has happened I don't know Maya You really have a very negative attitude. All this constant cribbing and cribbing upsets me .1 have to concentrate on my job .How can I....if I have your problems on my head......Remember contentment doesn't come this way learn from my mother (261-62).

Eiven her demand to have a part-time cook so that she could take up a job for she had a degree in textile designing is turned down on the pretext that Bombay is not like New York or London. And moreover ma would not like it. Lack of physical exercise combined with mental lethargy had dulled her life The carefully planned and chosen match ends only in disgust. It was a failure at all levels. They lived like strangers under the same roof. The marriage hardly a year old, sees monotony heavily eroding it. She feels useless and unwanted which gnaws her "Nobody needed me, absolutely nobody. My parents no longer thought I belonged to them. My husband belonged to his mother, it was unlikely I would have children who would belong to me. And I did not have a single true friend to call my own (266-67) There were no one to share her problem, which to Ranjan it was the result of a sick mind.

It was at this point in her life ,when she felt lonely, unwanted, and nobody to call her own that, Nikil Verma, the fourth floor neighbour's son, a collegiate student, a couple of years her junior enters her life. He brings a new meaning to her existence. Her dream and desires once again surface, which she had learned to curb with Ranjan.

At the very first meeting itself he looked straight in her eyes and smiled'(18) Did not want to address her as didi but call he by her first name 'Maya' She did not mind being called by her first name, because she hated being called 'aunty'. After a few meetings on the staircase at her door, offering 'eating idlis' or acting as a hero when Maya is pestered by a salesman or postman, he takes a step further by offering her a cassette sung by him especially for her 'Lonely Lady'. Maya, who was constantly neglected, humiliated and hurt, without a word of praise, now finds for the first time being praised and honoured, she tells Nikil, I loved your song'. After this first success, he becomes bold and visits her in her husband's absence, when Ranjan was on official visit.

Maya does not miss Ranjan. Rather, feels relieved. Feels free from pressure, judged, watched, corrected, scolded, nagged, pushed, instructed (163). He tells her he liked her from the first day he had met her. He coaxes her to go for a ride on his bike. She goes to Malabar Hills, Naaz Cafe, Marine Drive. Nikil does not miss to say she is beautiful "that is so nice you are smiling with your eyes. It suits you Maya ... you are beautiful believe me." (175) Through his soft, slow, skillfully well calculated measure, Nikil succeeds in finding a soft corner in her heart. Ranjan's continued self centered thought and behaviour, and Maya's unfulfilled genuine needs make Maya to give in to Nikil s invitations to go around.

With Nikil in her life, Maya's entire being is sensitized, she feels her spirit lifted ridiculously. Nikil is full of life and caring. He realizes she feels lonely and wants to make her feel good. Like the indoor plants she had brought from Calcutta-ficus and dresnia which was withering due to lack of sun and fresh air and gets a new life when Maya places them in the balcony. In the same way her life too needed fresh air and bright sun which was also withering away. Nikil encourages her to do something natural in life, "stop pretending to be someone you want the world to believe you are(171) He points out at the futility of suffering silently. His constant words of encouragement make her bold. Earlier she too had rebelled but silently I did not lift the phone, though I knew it was he. She heard him ring off finally and I felt triumphant as though I had defied his edit and got away with my first rebellion" She derived a pleasure when she walked into the bedroom when he would be seriously talking with .mother to make them feel uncomfortable.

Nikil's charisma was fast drawing her to him. One day Nikil walked into her house with flowers, saying it was his birthday and surprises her by embracing, kissing and having her. Maya, later describing the act says" it was painless, smooth and gentle Maya feels guilty, since she was conditioned by her tradition and culture. But cunningly she hides the episode. When Ranjan questioned her about the flowers, she says she had brought it for his mother, who was in a nursing home due to chest pain. And to why she had not lilted the phone her answer was that she had gone to buy the flowers.

With a little encouragement she would gladly say goodbye to Ranjan and walk away with Nikil. She had no feeling for Ranjan, she had married him only to satisfy her mother and to get away from Calcutta and come to her dream world Bombay. Sadly, she felt, that she did not get understanding nor love from either her husband or parents. She explains her situation "Now here we were locked together in a relationship that did not satisfy either of us. He obviously longed to be on his own, leading the life he was so accustomed to as a student and then as a promising bank executive living by himself. And I longed for the perfect romantic companion if such a creature existed at all outside my imagination." (252)

After the episode with Nikil, when she had surrendered to him blissfully, she felt "free, lunatic, wonderful".(265) Life had become just worth living, but with Ranjan coming with his mother from the nursing home, she feels that she had become a corpse once again.

With Ranjan's mother, convalescing, for ten days, she had to live only with the memory 'magic of these golden moments and nothing else mattered;' (288) she was just waiting, for a suitable time, to tell her decision to leave. She knew that her decision would as "something of relief to a man who really did not need marriage romance or sex." (283) It is at this moment, Nikil's mother Pushpa, comes to give the news that Nikil was engaged and was at Delhi with his bride to be; and would be soon leaving to Rochester University for higher studies.

While Maya was dreaming of a glorious relationship, Nikil was having another, and was hurt that he did not tell her about his going abroad.

Maya did not know that men like Nikil only took advantage of the weakness of lonely ladies. Being charming, showing concern, caring, loving, helping only to deceive. She did not know that she was one more added to his long list of conquests. For him, such relationships were only stop-gap arrangements before marriage. Nikil has his own preconceived notions of marriage, which is very traditional. He is a product of the modern generation, who do not mind taking one night stand with frustrated married women. But, when it comes to marriage, it has to be an arranged traditional one.

Maya's dream world shatters; she knows that she has

no choice but to live in the stifling atmosphere. She is left to wallow in her misery. So lost is she that Ranjan's angry voice brings her back to the familiar world of sorrow and loneliness. She has allowed the chicken soup to burn. She is a lonely lady; she knows that she has to spend the rest of her life clad in her mother-in-law's discarded sarees and dance to the tune of her rigidly conservative husband. She has to come to terms with her monotonous life The feeling that she had when she first stepped into Bombay, 'one of desperation and deceit' becomes a reality to be lived with. The closing lines of the novel shows what she would do "The more I stared at the spilled soup, the funnier I found it, I knew I would have to make it from the scratch. So what, I had all the time in the world now". (289)

Shobha De has created the characters she has created and treated the themes she has treated in her novels to call attention to the kind of treatment meted out to women in India. She does not present them for any idealistic purpose or aesthetic effect. In *Snapshot* one of the character says that in Bombay, the locale of the novel "Nobody respected ethics" De has touched upon different facets of urban women's life; her plight but no issue has received the same kind of full throated expression as the question of marriage and sex. She lashes at the hypocrisy of arranged marriagesand interference from relatives. What is most conspicuously missing in Indian context is 'communication, full blooded normal relationship 'In *Snapshots* she makes Rita say" we demand communication, attention.

Traditions are so binding and it is difficult to get out. It is the ancient story of sacrifice and adjustment. As there was no alternative, Maya too accepts to remain enveloped in loneliness and sadness. She learns to survive not only the sultriness of Bombay, but her marriage too.

Shobe De wrote, "I did write with a great deal of empathy towards women without waving the feminist flag. I feel very strongly about women's situation." She raises her voice of protest against male domination. Her concern is especially contemporary urban woman and the challenge, she faces, for she explores the world of urban women in India. *Socialite Evening* is essentially a story of "New woman Karuna, who is independent in every way. It is an initiation tale from innocence to experience in the line of Bharati Mukherjee's *Wife* and *Jasmine* in *Starry Nights*. Asha Rani, comes from a small town background to the tinsel world of Bombay, after a great struggle to become a star. To achieve this, she does not hesitate to adopt any means, including semi-nudity to free sex. Asha Rani struggles, survives and achieves. Her third novel, *Sisters* (92) takes us to the fabulous and intriguing world of business tycoons. It deals with the psychic conflict of a liberated woman who is caught between a personal self societal self. *Sultry Days* is in the line of her mainstream new women, but *Strange Obsession* with lesbianism, revolves around two young women, Amrita and Meenakshi. *Snapshots,* a feminist work, unveils the lives of six girls of Santa Maria High School. Like all feminist writers, she is deeply concerned with the alignment of power that exerts physical, political, social and economic central over woman and fragments her. In *Small Betrayals* and *Shooting from the Hip*, take the form of short stories and essays. *Small Betrayals* deal with the betrayal in its infinite variety. Indian English Fiction depicts three kinds of women. First, the poor women belonging mostly to the rural class, portrayed by writers like Kamala Markandaya and. R.K. Narayan; the middle class, especially the educated employed depicted by Nayantara Sahgal and Shashi Deshpande; and thirdly, the neo-rich aristocrat in the writings of Namita Gokhale and Shobha De. One may like or not but De's treatment of the contemporary urban Indian women challenge predicament value and life style is surely significant. Shobha De considers the treatment of the Women's Question as her significant contribution to writing.

References

1. C.P. Surendra "Just Another De, Illustrated Weekly of India, 6 Nov. '92.

2. Madhu Jain" Cat On A Hot T in Roof India Today, 15 October, '89, p. 195.
3. Sunil Sethi:-" De In De Out" Seminar (384), August,' 91 p. 41.
4. Shobha De-*Second Thoughts*, Penguin, Delhi '96(A11 further quotes pertain to this edition).

7

David Davidar's: *House of Blue Mangoes*: A Discourse of the Marginalized and Subalterns

House of Blue Mangoes is a discourse of the marginalized and subalterns. It crystallizes the issue of ostracism against women and the untouchables, all those dispossessed of an identity or a speaking voice. In its setting and its concerns. The *House of Blue Mangoes* reads as a sequel to Arundhati Roy's *God of Small Things*. A sweeping epic of five hundred plus pages David Davldar chronicles three generations of the Doria clan. Covering the period between 1899-1947, a turbulent period that saw the fall of the British Raj, the turmoil of caste war, the rise of Gandhi and the culmination of independence. The story focuses on the Dorai family home. The House of Blue Mangoes of the title in the ocean side village of Chevathar. The novel opens with a description of this beautiful village.

"Across the lower Coromandel Coast, a sprawling village comes into view. The turbulent sky excepted, everything about It is tranquil. 'Away to the West, a great headland, thickly, manned with coconut palms juts into the sea, particularly enclosing a deserted beach on which long slow swells, clear and smooth as glass, break with scarcely a sound. Beyond the beach, the waters of an estuary, reflects the rage of colour overhead. This is where Chevathar, the country's Southern most river and the source of the village name, prepares for its final run into the sea".

Chevathar for all its beauty and deceptive serenity was like any other village in the area rigidly ordered by caste strictures and tradition that had not changed. The paths conformed to the rules of caste. The Paraiyan quarter the 'Cheri' began at the Southern point of the village and ran in a great arc around it, before ending at the bridge. The inhabitants of the 'Cheri' had to walk nearly twice the distance than a Brahmin would to cross the village. Similar rules governed the siting of the houses, areas earmarked for defecation and bathing access to the river and cropland. The highest caste got the best, and the lowest the worst. Even the drinking water they could draw was at the point where the river met the sea.

Even when the 'Pukka' (tar) road was laid it was borne in mind that the road would pass through the Vedhar quarter, Vakil Perumal house and Murugan Temple thereby satisfying the ego of the upper castes. Since it was government road every caste had a right to use it without' breaking the caste rules. But during the Pongal Festival a group of young girls were molested and several young men thrashed for breaking rules Traditional laws forbade untouchables and lower castes from even venturing near the main village path. Paraiyans had been beaten almost to death by Vedhar men for daring to stroll through their quarters, blithely smoking a 'beedi' with the turban firmly on the head.

The paraiyans came to the Thalaivar' (head) Solomon to seek justice. They had no intention of causing trouble, they owed their lives and everything else to their masters but this was unfair. Solomon received the deputation with disfavour. He thought the paraiyans had gone too far. He ruled that everyone could use the road though the polluting classes would have to comply with the rules- their shadows should not fall on the upper caste fellows, they should not approach the village of the highest caste closer than thirty paces, and their lungis, should always be folded above their knees. There was surprisingly no objection to Solomon's ruling and thereafter the road was freely used!

On Ram Navami two members of the Andavar community were caught entering the inner precincts of the Murugan temple and beaten Solomon condemned the beating but he also condemned those who went against the time tested traditions and customs "the polluting classes should know their places" said Swaminathan. Solomon himself respected the customs and tradition. Of the eighty seven families who made the village their home, thirty four were Christian Andavars but he never tried to impose Christian ways on the Hindu villagers, whether they were Brahmins, Andavars, Vedhars or lower caste. He donated generously to the Murugan temple but never entered it, keeping in with caste strictures, when he gave food to the Brahmin priests he was careful to ensure it was uncooked, for it was proscribed to give cooked food to superior castes. There were separate places of worship for Andavars-the Ammankoil, and the Murugan Kail for the Vedhars.

Tradition had ordained that the various members of the caste tree bare their breasts as a deference and subservience to those who perched higher in the branches. At the urging of the missionaries women began to cover their breasts. This threw the upper caste especially the men into a frenzy of insecurity and frustration. Andavar and Nadar women who clothed were abused in public even beaten, "we have a divine right to gaze upon your filthy breasts and you should be flattered we do so. They are ours to enjoy. Whatever benefits your new faith may bestow upon you, this is not one of them, declared a landlord in Travancore in 1858, (p-23) as he wrenched the blouse of a pretty Andavar woman. Riot tore through the entire are resulting in the famous Breast War in 1859.

The caste tree in South India had broadly speaking three levels of caste system-Brahmins, non-Brahmins and those beyond the pail. Initially the skirmishing was principally between the powerful non- Brahmin castes like the Nadars, Andavars, Thevars, Maravans, Vedhars and Vellars. The

Brahmins were concentrated in the cities and the great temple town. *The* two dominant castes in the district of Chevathar were the Andavars, to which Solomon belonged and the Vedhars, who had a long history of strife. Even now Solomon had heard rumours that there might be unrest in the trouble prone areas of the north near Melur, Vakil Perumal as a retaliatory act, after two of the Andavars were beaten had two young' girls attacked and Valli raped and had on a granite outcrop scrawled anonymously.

"Remember the 1859 Breast war. If low caste dogs do not know their place, their wives and sisters will soon remind them of it", (p. 16)

Solomon greatly disturbed had called a meeting to say that the disease of caste and religious violence had struck at the heart of the community and concluded" we must keep away the demon from our village". (p. 39)

When Father Ashworth, the Christian missionary arrived in India he was appalled by the institution of caste. He had tried to understand the viewpoint of those who argued that caste was necessary to give the country's vast and diverse population a sense of identity and belonging, but surely that did not excuse the injustice and barbarity perpetrated in its name. How could any sane and compassionate human being abide in the discrimination sanctioned by caste and religion upon his fellowmen based entirely on self serving interpolations in the great religious texts. He had heard it said that untouchables and the lower caste were forbidden from even hearing the holy Vedic chants and if they did molten lead was poured into their ears.

Father Ashworth soon came to realize that even the birds and animals were sucked into the caste strictures-the most striking raptors were know-as Brahmin kites and the most dowdy the Pariah kites. In Meenakshi Koil a few 'Pariah' dogs barked' 'you' low caste' cur caste had permeated every aspect of their lives.

Just as in God of *Small Things* Arundhat Roy shows that conversion to Christianity did not change anything. They only felt they had fallen from the frying pan into the fire, the master had changed not their misery. Even the blood of Christ could not redeem them. The situation is exactly the same in *House of Blue Mangoes*. Dorai's grandfather who was the 'thalaivar' (head) had been adament that the new converts should not be allowed to worship in the same Church. The worshippers of the Andavar caste sat on the most favoured side. Separate communion tables and cups ensured that the Andavars and Pariyans did not drink from the same cup or eat the same bread. The lower caste left the church immediately after the service through a door set into their side of the building, so that they would not inconvenience the upper caste Christians. Arguments that Christianity did not admit of caste were routinely ignored.

Along with the untouchables and the lower caste, the object of discrimination, exploitation and sexual abuse have been women. Davidar has gone to great lengths to detail the unlucky lot of women, so it seems appropriate that he too relegates his female characters to the background. The only memorable character is Charity Solomon's wife. *House of Blue Mangoes* reads like a feminist novel in the pity and terror it invokes for the condition of women in the given cultural milieu; thus making it a discourse on the marginalized. The novel opens with two girls- thirteen and the other a year younger on the way to the fair. Dressed in their best clothes, jasmine on the hair, adorned with sandalwood, Vibhuti and Kumkum. But their happiness is short lived for they are attacked by strange men from outside the village, though Parvati the younger escapes Valli is raped. The circumstances of their birth and the evolution of their separate lives gave the men and women of the Chevathar village sharply different perspectives on the incident. While the men grew robust in their hate and distrust of each other, and obsessed about the larger consequences of the tragedy. The women identified with the girl's trauma were reminded once more of the misfortune of being born a woman.

When Charity visited Valli's house after the incident, she finds that "There's nothing she can do There was no terrible spill of anger here, none of the fury that drove the mythical

Kannagi to burn up her tormentors, This was different more practical, perhaps the only way left to the women of the village. There was good and evil, and both were necessary to keep the world in balance... you raged against fate only when you didn't understand it. It was best to accept and go on" (40-41).

In Chevathar, Davidar writes the birth of a son was greeted with 'Kuruvai'-a long drawn call from the throats of aunts and sisters Blessed was the mother of a son. Blessed was the family into which a son was born. He would extend the family, bring good luck, dowry and attract the blessing of God. A girl on the other hand was greeted with downcast face. A girl meant nothing but sorrow. One more unproductive mouth to feed, heavy expenses for the family dowry, endless demands of in laws who had done the parents a favour by taking her off their hands. Many despondent mothers quickly extinguished the life of the baby (girl) if she arrived at the tail end of a succession of daughters by smothering her, feeding her the poisonous sap of the calotropis plant or the roots of valli shrubs or encouraging the expectant mother to force sharp edged husk of rice grain which would fatally puncture the alimentary tract of an infant. If the girl was allowed to live the girl was never allowed to forget that through her the family was paying for its sins the previous birth.

Every woman in the village quickly learned her place in life no matter how exalted her situation. When Charity first arrived she was shocked when Solomon hit her for not bringing him his coffee at the right temperature. Tearfully she returned to the kitchen told her mother-in-law about it. Thangammal wiped away the tears and told her something she had not forgotten throughout her life. In these parts, my daughter, a woman must be prepared to be beaten by the husband. If he is good he won't beat you much, and not without reason. We put up with it. It's the way things are when you are newly married you are beaten for not bringing enough dowry, when you give birth to your children, you are beaten for not producing a male heir, or if you have already given a son, for not producing only sons. And then when you have produced enough children, you are beaten for losing your looks and youth", (p.31) The greatest humiliation on women was when they were forced to bare their breasts as a deference and subservience to those perched in the higher branches of the caste tree, because tradition had ordained it. At the urging of the Christian missionaries when they started covering, they were beaten and publically abused. The upper caste held that it was their divine right to gaze upon their filthy breasts. The 'outrage' of covering resulted in the famous 1859 Breast War.

There was a strong prejudice against dark skin, especially women. Charity is greatly worried that her granddaughter is dark and refuses to powder her face 'Let everyone see how dark she is. Who will marry her" Daniel prepares an ayurvedic cream called 'Moonwhite Thylam' which assures brighter colour and there is an unending demand for it.

Discontent, envy and unhappiness swirl through all the castes and communities. Caste violence had been brewing for sometimes. Non-Brahmin caste groups like the Andavars and Nadars, who had acquired wealth and economic clout, demanded enhanced social and religious standing. They had formed a non-Brahmin party-Justice Party. Varadaraja Mudaliar member of the Justice Party said at a Royal Public Service Commission in Madras "The Brahmins have been for thousands of years the custodian and object of all intellectual culture and the other castes have been placed in a very disadvantageous position intellectually". In the past Brahmins had victimized the Non-Brahmins, but the beginning of 20th century saw the brewing of a backlash, they aimed to advance the cause of the repressed communities by siezing political powers.

The novel shows the potentialities of the pariah/non-Brahmin consciousness. The Brahmins and the lower caste who have a long cultural identify refuse to lose It. As Solomon, who belongs to the Andavars say "what a sin had he committed to be born in this ungodly time where a kinsman could ignore his explicit ruling and where every ambapattan (barber) thought he was a Pandyan King" (p.9). On the other hand despite the societies indifference, the casteless outcast aspire to gain their ground- a socio-political cultural identity.

In the concluding chapter of the novel Davidar writes that the differences of caste, community religion have split the society for thousands of years. It has always been India Vs India. But surprisingly we have acquired the wholly undeserved reputation of being a tolerant society, a living example to the world on how to run a plural society. In fact we are happy to adjust when it suits us. If we are not actively tolerant, we are inert. This makes us a fair game for loathsome casteist and communalists (usually priests and politicians) who are always willing to exploit the envy and resentment we nurse against each other. When the Britishers came to India they exploited our fatal flaw, and to- day our politicians too practice the same policy of divide and rule. Though the slogan is caste is and should die, the silent and earnest prayer is long live casteism. *House of Blue Mangoes* in short, is a novel about the rights of men and women condemned to live the life of subjugation simply because the interpolated scriptures and social structure ordained it so.

References

David Davidar: House of Blue Mangoes, Penguin India, 2002. Quotes pertain to this edition.

8

Vikram Seth's: *An Equal Music*—A Symphony of Love and Melody

Even with a career that has spanned two decades and spawned nine books,, Vikram Seth still remains something of a mystery No two books of his have been alike. He is a poet, a novelist, a travel writer and the author of a libretto. Unlike most Indian writers of Indian origin, whose works are obsessed with the sub-continental Seth seems at home everywhere in the world. The *Golden Gate*, the novel in verse that first brought him renown was a witty and inventive story of Californian Yuppiedom; *A Suitable Boy*, one of the longest novels ever written in English is sprawling, multigenerational tale of family, tradition and politics in post independence India. Five years after that epic effort, Seth returned with something completely different again. Gone is the sweep of *A Suitable Boy* Seth's new novel *Equal Music* is an intimate and internalized story of love and music. Set in the exalted world of European classical music circuit, *An Equal Music* is a sensitive novel that has something of the delicacy of a haiku. The book is a gripping and profound meditation on love, music and the irrevocability of time. Narrated in the present tense, in an insistent first person, this meditation is intensely personal, unlike anything Seth has previously written, the novel is distinguished by remarkable psychological portraiture.

An Equal Music is a fraction of the size of *A Suitable Boy,* but is still absorbingly expansive. In under four hundred pages the author offers exquisite complexities- personal and lyrical. In the scope of its canvas, a densely insular work, a man, a woman, a quartet, London, Vienna 'Venice and a violen. Michael Holme, the high-strung narrator, is a violinist in a London string quartet-Maggiore Ouartet. When the Maggiore undertakes a challenging work of Beethoven, Michael is overwhelmed by memories of mastering the piece as a student in Vienna. That's where he had met Julia Nicholl a pianist whose beauty was as mesmerizing as her musical genius, whom he loved with an intensity he never found again, and had also impulsively abandoned her "The last time was when I was a student in Vienna ten years ago. I return there again and again and think: was I in error? was I unseeing? where was the balance of pain between the two of us? what I lost there I have never come near' to retrieving.....I told her I was going, and went. For two months. I could do nothing, not even write to her, I came to London' The smog dispersed but too late. Where are you now Julia, and am I not forgiven? "Michael can't hope to possess Julia, he cannot even dream of owning his beloved Tononi, the violin he has long had only on loan.

Now, years later Michael is living a life devoted to music until one day he is riding a bus, and there in another bus, separated only by a glass window sits Julia Nicholl. This chance encounter with Julia, whom, he had lost in Vienna, brings him sudden bliss. Their passion is reawakened their passion for each other and for each other's music. Although Julia is married and a mother, she is unable to resist the power of their shared history, she agrees to tour Vienna and Venice with Michael's quartet. Against the magical backdrop of concert halls and canals Michael and Julia confront the truth about their love for each other, their love for music that brought them, together and the true consequences for their tangled hearts.

Though the mutual passions flare anew, the love they shared in their younger days is now complicated, by the secrets and silences that have been generated by the passing years, Julia carries with her a heart breaking secret; she is gradually going deaf. While Julia still performs, publicly, she's losing her hearing, her reunion with Michael is idyll that can't last, and the strong down beat ending looms inevitably. *An Equal, Music* is a deeply affecting love story.

The book is about rekindling the narrator's love affair with a musician and his prized Venetion violin. Around the theme of love and possession Seth has woven a saga of heartbreaking intensity. The maudlin, prose tugs at heartstrings especially when Michael meets Julia after years during a concert and writes down his phone number on her palm. (I lean down to kiss her palm,) its life line, its love line". As the love story- ranges from London to Michael's birthplace in the north of London to Vienna, to Venice few readers will remain deaf to its appeal.

Hailed by the critics as a perfect symphony of love, a deeply affecting love story that is destined to capture Seth's wildest audience. Shobha De in an interview to *"Delhi Times"* stated that she had. "never relished a love story as thoroughly as *Equal Music.* It is delicate, poised, elegant and eloquent. The writing is practically flawless, yet the craft is invisible." As the novels progresses it pushes the readers into a lucid silence. There is somber magic, a bracing, energizing after flow that emanates from its pages.

In addition to the pitch of its love story, one of the book's joy lies in Seth's creation of musical extremes. As the Maggiore rehearses, moving from sniping and impatience to perfection, the author expertly notates the joys of collaboration, trust and creation "Its the weirdest thing , a quartet.... I don't know what to compare it to. A marriage? a firm? a platoon under fire? a self regarding, self destructive priesthood? It has many different tensions mixed with its pleasures.

Equal Music places Seth in a tradition of modern fiction' writers who have successfully combined a love story and the love of music as part of the narrative- more particularly Western classical music. A saga of heartbreaking intensity that held the audience spellbound' and remained the talk of London's literary circle for a full week before Salman Rushdie took the centre-stage with *Ground Beneath the Feet* with its overriding theme of love and music. Though both book talk of music the two works are profoundly different. Seth has an all White cast embodied in the world of Western classical music. The choice of Wigmore Hall that "Sacred shoe box of Chamber Music" is symbolic of the upper class British gentry that he caters the music to. It is a well researched book about music and the white washed artifice of London and Vienna.

Talking about the book in a Note at the end of the novel Seth writes" Music to me is dearer even than speech. When I realized I would be writing about it, I was gripped with anxiety , only slowly did I reconcile to the thought of it" Seth's love for music stems from his school when he was part of a choir " I love Western music, but I never learnt it. In England I began to sing in a choir. But my first love is Indian classical music. I learnt some flute and to play tabla".

Sometimes the music vocabulary overwhelms the readers yet the basic narrative survives the terminological prolixity. Indeed such is the strength of the book that in spite of a great part of the book dealing with the 'Art of Fugue' and a host of Western classical music term, somehow the character and the narrative woven around them prevails. To blend the musical theme into the narrative so effortlessly required a great deal of research. The book is a finely researched book at various levels.

In the author's note he acknowledges the gift of those who helped him in learning more of the Western Classical music "Friends and strangers have helped me in the work string players, often those in the quartet themselves......those who aid or help aid the creation or dissemination of music.....teachers' critics, musicians agents, managers, executives of record company, managers of Hall and Festivals" And also Satish Gujral to understand the world of those who cannot hear In his author's note he thanks/ in particular "my lip reading teacher and his class".

The book could not have been written by anybody but a lover of music. The last para of the novel sums up "Music such music its a sufficient gift, Why ask for happiness? Why hope not to grieve? It is enough, it is to be blessed enough, to live from day to day and hear such music- not too much, or the soul could not sustain it- from time to time".

It is a tour de force of poetic impassioned writing, conjuring up brilliantly the world of Beethoven, Bach, Mozart, of individual heartaches and the familial bonds of a guartet. Interweaving with love and music are the themes of loss, longing, loneliness and the strands of passion that runs through all our lives. The book is about loneliness, specially the loneliness of an artist. While reading the book it is impossible not to be moved by the overpowering melancholia and despair that often grasps Michael, Musicians can be a boring lot: they think, talk and breathe music. Who would have thought that a moody, middle aged violinist would be so engaging. But Michael Holme, far all his mood swings, fainting spells, and women cheating is likeable. It is a story about relationships joy of union and the grief of parting, its unpredictabilities of sublime love and passionate possession, ultimate triumph of sanity , a sanity found not only at the pinnacle of artistic fulfillment but also in the solace of such mundane situation as the home and the family.

Described by Shobha De as a genius, who breaks rules with every book he writes. In *Equal Music* too Seth, makes a certain move from his previous book- *Suitable Boy,* which was totally cast in India, now rigorously shuts out any aspect of India. In *Equal Music* the setting is London, nothing to do with India. For the Western reader it has nothing Indian or India except the author's name. One is surprised at his ability to write books which have nothing to do with India, Seth's triumph lies in his ability to create and sustain a central character who has no direct relation to Seth's cultural context. It hopefully marks the beginning of the end of the Indian's perpetual search for roots and endless discourses about the impossibility of home-coming. This novel heralds the ascent of the self possessed Indian who rises above parochialism generated by the modern state, yet is deeply immersed in classical culture.

Vikram Seth deserves the hype he has received. There is a compelling lucidity and simplicity in his writing' which is the hall mark of a great writer. Through the cadence of his words and convincing description of musical ecstasy he presents the characters and how they react and relate to each other through music. He succeeded not only in bringing these characters so fully to 1ife, but the rich ambience of music as well. It is difficult to imagine many contemporary writers who could write a novel that gives so much satisfaction.

This book could not have been written by anybody but a lover of music.

It is certainly true that Seth has undertaken no mean task in trying to distil something original from a subject that is almost by definition generic and sentimental "I'd be bored unless I wrote a book that in some sense was a challenge" he told in an interview. It is to his great credit that despite the occasional lapse, he answers the challenge with a convincing and often beautiful story of passion. Anyone with or without a love for Bach, Mozart, Vivaldi, or the related culture, could still pick up the book and enjoy, it is after all its 'An Equal Music'.

References

1. Vikram Seth : *An Equal Music* Viking, Penguin Book, India 99. p. 5 (All Subsequent reference pertain to this edition).
2. Ibid., p. 94.
3. Shobha De : Times of India, Delhi, April 27 '99.
4. Vikram Seth: *An Equal Music* - p.
5. Ibid., Author's Note - p. 382.
6. Pavan K. Kumar : Hindustan Times Delhi, *May 2nd' 99.*
7. *Vikram seth: An Equal Music : Author's Note* p. 382.
8. *Ibid.,* p. 381.

9

Amitav Ghosh: *Sea of Poppies*

Since the publication of Rushdie's *Midnight Children* in 1981, a new and ancient land has imposed itself on the world's literary consciousness - a land whose language and concerns have stretched the boundaries of the possible in English literature. A generation of post colonial Indian writing has brought a larger world-a teeming myth-infused, gaudy, exuberant many hued and restless worlds-past the immigration inspectors of English literature. Today it seems no year goes by without yet another Indian novel announcing its entry into the global canon, confirming Indian writing as among the most innovative and interesting.

Over the last two decades Amitav Ghosh has established himself as a writer of uncommon talent who combines literary flair with a rare seriousness of purpose. His first novel, *The Circle of Reason,* seemed very much in the Rushdie magical-realist tradition. But, he has evolved considerably since then, notably in works like the *Shadow Lines* and *The Glass Palace* which deal movingly and powerfully in Bengal and Burma. *Sea of Poppies,* his sixth and the first of his projected *Ibis Trilogy,* marks both a departure and an arrival. It sees Ghosh painting upon a larger canvas than ever before, with a multitude of characters and an epic vision, revisits in a new and breathtaking detail and compelling ways some of the concerns of his earlier novels. Among them are the incessant movement of the people, trade and empires which have traversed the Indian Ocean since antiquity, and the lives of men and women with little power, whose stories framed against the grand narrative of history invite other ways of thinking about the past culture and identity.

The year is 1838 and the setting British India, a country immersed in colonial rule, where fertile agricultural lands are swamped by poppies grown to produce opium that the British are exporting to addicts in an increasingly resistant China. In 1838, the opium business was booming and drug money filling the British Empire's coffers offsetting a trade imbalance created by imports of Chinese silk and tea and now the Emperor of China wants the drug trade to be stopped. Hungry Indian peasants are driven of their land and many are recruited to serve as plantation laborers in far off British colonies like Mauritius.

"Along the Gangatic plain Northwest of Calcutta the British East India Company has persuaded peasant farmers to abandon their crops and grow only poppies which are then processed in the Inferno esque Sudder Opium Factory, with the first opium war looming the cash cow now seem to keel over, leaving farming the poverty for the hapless locale".

The British version of history glosses over the time this country was the world's bigger drug pusher. Afghanistan produced the poppies to supply Europe's heroin. But two centuries ago it was British fortune seekers in India who turned the banks of the Ganges into a sea of poppies and tried to force refined opium on reluctant China.

Despite the Emperor's decrees banning the drugs that dulled his subjects and addled his empire, British traders kept shipping jars of opium to Canton, counting on the growing number of addicts to defy his orders. In the end they used force-denouncing Chinese restrictions on free trade and persuading London shamefully to wage the notorious wars.

Against this background, *Sea of Poppies* paints a poignant

picture of the human devastation by this trade. Beyond the brilliant colours of flowers, the realities of the enforced cultivation of the poppies, the ways of collecting sap from the pods, the activities in the processing factory, the medicinary user of opium and its pernicious influence. The fertile farms of the Gangatic planes are blooming only with poppies-beautifully deadly, denying the peasants the crops to sustain them, and indebting them to money lenders and landowners, themselves indebted to the buccaneers of the East India Company.

Set in an era of agricultural scandal burgeoning Western demand for a profitable but inedible crops causing starvation in the subaltern world. The Chinese have been hooked, the Indians have been coerced into cultivating the stuff and Britain is the prosperous dealer. Chinese attempts to curb the trade meant that gunboat diplomacy is on the horizon.

Sea of Poppies opens in a remote village devastated by these circumstances. A young woman Deeti watches her inert husband yield to addiction; he collapses at the opium factory, where glazed workers move "as slow as ants in honey" and even the monkeys are sunk in a 'miasma of lethargy'. Opium has infiltrated into Deeti's family. Around the opium factory, monkeys are stupefied from drinking the waste water. Inside men waist deep in tanks of opium tread it to soften the sludge "a host of dark legless torso...circling around and around, like some enslaved tribe of demon".

Against this background *Sea of Poppies* brings together a colourful array of individuals on a triple-mast schooner named the 'Ibis'. There is Deeti, widow of an opium addict, saved from self immolation on the funeral pyre of her husband by an outcast, Kalua, who signs up for a new life as worker in Mauritus, a free spirited French orphan and Muslim boatman, with whom she has grown up. 'Ibis's' second mate, an American Octoroon sailor, passing for a white, a clerk and mystic possessed by the soul of his female spiritual mentor, a lascar seaman with a piratal past and a dispossessed Raja, who has been stripped of his land and honour and exiled for an innocent act of forgery.

The action begins in March 1838 with the arrival of the 'Ibis" al Ganga Sagar Island and later Calcutta. With the abolition of slave trade, the schooner is scheduled to transport girmitiyas- indentured coolies - to Mauritius. Back in India, it will join the expedition London is putting together "to take on the celestials" with the first opium war, as it is called only months away, what is at risk for the British drug industry in India should the Chinese continue to block the trade.

Caught within the dark web of the Empire's history is a mixed cast of characters for whom the 'Ibis' is a projection of the uncertainties of their lives and the routine at home. On the 'Ibis' a community of sorts begin to form among the migrants. Relationships are forged or broken, hostilities erupt and individual destinies undergo sudden change of direction. Skillfully and seemingly random, Ghosh assembles those who will set sail in his narrative of the 'Ibis'. The novel unfolds with the stories of the event that brings the ship siblings on board and traces the beginning of their voyage from Calcutta to their unknown destination across the Black waters.

'Ibis' is an awesome human cargo. Every passenger has a secret to preserve and a fantasy to pursue- like Deeti married off to a hopeless opium addict, drugged and violated on her wedding night by his brother, bullied into the ritual practice of suttee and rescued from the flames by the loyal massive Kalua, whose cross-caste elopement starts a manhunt the length of the Ganges. There is Paulette, the daughter of a French botanist, brought up with her Indian nurse's son but forced back into European pretension of clothes, class and snobbery in the household of Benjamin Burnham the rich odious and flawed Calcutta merchant and archetype of British rule. There is also Zachary, a mulatoo from Baltimore who guards his emotions with the secret of his birth. Baboo Nob Kissin, the superstitious and bowel obsessed East India Company bureaucrat, Seramy Ali, a willy leader of the itinerant deckhands known as lascars, and Neel, a dreamy cultured Bengali Raja whose honour, extravagancy and financial naivety led him to bankruptcy, trial, shame and sentence of deportation, as the British, who dined at his table seek to grab his land.

The outline of events is barely skeletal, as in his previous novels, Ghosh juggles with a huge cast, weaving in overlapping strands and themes racial porosity, imperialist hypocrisy cultural relativism. It is characteristic of his scope to have an entire vessel of protagonists. They are an interesting lot - migrants, convicts and sailors,others in search of freedom or identity. They are adventurers as well as dreamers, natives and foreigners. We follow then them through the clashes of caste and customs, ruled and rulers, generous sentiments to avaricious deceit, to the fateful ship. They turn the Ibis into a republic of stories-stories mined from the grey remoteness of human mind. Ghosh creates with ample assistance from scholarship and research. He deftly creates a web of beautifully interlocking stories and characters whose fortune cross with Deeti and the former slave ship, 'Ibis', into which she and her fellow exiled are packed. The various tragedies which cause the characters to be sold into bondage successfully brings into life the brutalities of the trade as well as the shrewdness of the colonizer.

The novel is structured around the 'Ibis'. The ship was not like any other ship as Baboo Nob Kissan considers "in her inward reality she was a vehicle of transformation, traveling through the mists of illusion towards the elusive ever receding landfall that was Truth".

In that ship in 1838, sea and land came together as a multitude of Indians from the environs of the Southern shore of Ganges, high and low, such as the Raja in debt to a British businessman, Chinese criminal, fanner and soldier, A Malay crewman and a female French stowaway. It is a voyage that will somehow play a role in the British war to open China to the opium trade.

Like the endless rolling saltwater of the region Ghosh's own beautifully made sentences and paragraphs buoy up ship, plot, character and the setting itself with natural ease and beauty. As in the passage when the 'Ibis' with its crowded crew and indentured passengers, who had never seen the ocean, anchor for one last night in the Indian water, "the last place from which the migrants would be able to view their native shore: this was Saugar Road, a much trafficked anchorage the lee of Ganga Sagar, the island that stands between the sea and the holy river, the very name Ganga Sagar, joining as it did with river and sea, served to remind the migrants of the yawning chasm ahead, it was as if they sitting balanced on the edge of a precipice and the island were an outstretched limb of sacred Jamudvipa, their homeland, reaching out to keep them from tumbling into the void.

Reading the book one gets to feel that the book appeared as a ship, sometimes as an island, and sometimes as a precipice. Like all good books it keeps us from tumbling into the precipice.

At the start of the novel, Ghosh presents two indelible visions-a tall masted ship 400 miles from the Indian coast and voluptuous agricultural crops, a profusion of flowers capable of warping the world. The crop was the livelihood of Deeti and her neighbours at Gazipur, in colonial India. 1830's is a pivotal year in the annals of the opium trade when Ghosh's story so vividly begins. Poppy farming was considered a perfectly legitimate line of agricultural work, especially by the businessmen who consider it so profitable and the 'Ibis[1] transports both drugs and outcasts to far flung corners of the world. Originally a slave ship making raids in the West Africa, the 'Ibis' is not a prized ship. Even in a new improvised incarnation, as Zachary Reid a crew member says, it is "a hell afloat with pinch gist pay". Yet the ship became a home to Ghosh's sparkling array of eccentrics, blow hards, runaway lovers and people seeking new lease of life. One of the memorable characters is the raja seen at the height of his power as the book begins, later humiliated and exiled he sails abroad the ship, past the fife he once ruled. This is a pipe dream, a figment of Deeti's imagination. During the course of the novel, Ghosh turns the ship into something bawdily and imposingly real.

Although none of the people know, their ship appears to be headed towards the battle, which will be central to Ghosh's extended story, the opium war waged between China and Britain over the British India Company's monopolistic drug trade. *Sea of Poppies* is pointed towards the conflict, in a series perhaps headed for the thick of the fray. The opening book concentrates on its oddly matched characters explaining who is abroad the 'ibis' and the curious round about way in which each has wound up adrift in the way.

By the time 'Ibis' sets out she has been transformed from a battered former slave ship into a fateful "vehicle of transformation where rules of caste and empire will either be broken by helpful exiles or enforced with brutality by the ship's guards. Although the pilgrims are all in some way victims of the opium trade, the real theme of *Sea of Poppies* is the alternatively terrifying and liberating prospect of migration across the "Black Waters of Indian Ocean" on a boat of pilgrims where no one can lose caste and every one are equal.

The novel closes with Ibis in mid ocean in a storm. Serang Ali leader of the lascars abandons the ship along with the condemned convicts; the first mate as well as the subedar is dead. Of the key figures only Deete, Paulette, Nob Kissan and Zachary are left, watching from the deck, the disappearance of the boat and those close to them. The principle characters fate are left unresolved, but their stories are compelling. Even though the Ibis journey is incomplete it provides enough dramatic tension to hold interest.

The vessel first occurs as an epiphany to Deeti, the woman on whom anchors his narrative that stretches from the poppy fields of Gazhipur to Calcutta of East India Company to the Indian Ocean that sets the stage for the final act of liberation. The transformation of Deeti from a widow to a lover, to a refugee to the enigmatic leader of the rebellion is as dramatic as the voyage itself.

Ghosh is a living embodiment of what has become one of the principle theme; the journeying and displacement of the Indian Diaspora. Along with Naipaul and Jumpha Lahiri he is one of the three prominent writers who have taken exile, migration and identity as subject. These are the themes that surface over and over again in Ghosh's varied and formidably ambitious body of work, especially mid 1990 onwards.

The narrative of the *Glass Palace* (2000) revolves around the fortunes of Rajkumar, a Bengali serving boy exiled in Burmà, who rises to become a logging magnate. The book follows the fortunes of his family as Britain's East Asian Empire crumbles before the Japanese onslaught in World War II. *The Hungry Tide* is a tale about seas and swamps of the Sunderbans told through Piya Roy, a Non Resident Indian, brought up in the United States. Returning to her Bengal home of her ancestors, she finds a much more foreign country than she had expected. In *An Antique Land* (1993), the plot revolves around the medieval trade network which operated along the Red Sea supplying the Middle East with spices and textiles of Malabar. Bomma Ghashi hero was owned by one Abraham Ben Yiau, the polymath son of a rabbi from Tunisia. During the 12th century as the Mediterranean came increasingly to be controlled by the pirates of Christian Europe, Ben decided to leave the declining market of North Africa and set himself up in India, There he married a Malabar girl, took Bumma as his local agent. Throughout the novel, Ghosh interweaves the slaves adventures with his own experience as a young anthropologist working for his Ph.d. in a village near Cairo.

The same trade route traveled by Bomma and similar question of displacement, power and identity form the frame for the *Sea of Poppies*, a capacious, human and panoramic novel. Rather than an Indian slave traveling to Egypt, Poppies revolve around Deeti, an opium farmer's wife, who escapes Sati, is forced to sell herself into a form of legalized slavery as an indentured labourer bound for the plantation of Mauritius.

Ghosh's anger at the hypocrisy and violence inherent in this trade is justified, which is one of the most shoddy and shocking episode in the whole violent history of the British

Empire. By the late 1830s The European market in spices which had first brought the first East India Company had slumped and the East India Company kept itself solvent by triangular trade which involved growing opium in India and selling to China. In China, the Company then bought tea which it sold to Britain. In order to grow opium needed to buy enough tea to satisfy British appetite, the Company leased havoc across the Gangatic plains, compelling peasants to abandon their traditional food crops and plant poppies instead. The opium went to devastate China, but the trade yielded two million pounds a year and was crucial to its solvency.

If immigration is the movement, that animates history to the rhythm of the outcast's heartbeats, Ghosh is its most elegant choreographer. It is as if the exodus that defies borders-both inherited and imposed-with the dreams and deliriums of the refugees is an idea that Ghosh cannot live without. And the passion is matched by the yearning of his characters, for whom a life scarred of denial and dispossession, is not something to be abandoned but to be reconstructed anew elsewhere far beyond.

In the *Circle of Reason,* Alu the orphan goes abroad a trawler that transports the immigrants to Africa. In the genre defying in *An Antique Land,* the novelist builds his own Alexandrian masterwork of civilizational cross currents with the dexterity of an anthropological detective and the imagination of a time traveler. In *The Glass Palace,* stretching from the Mandalay of 1885 to the Myanmar of Aung San Kyi's resistance in 1996, Asia's biggest exodus is stayed in the backdrop of war exile and the loss of kingdom. In *Hungry Tides,* even as one is being rowed into the riverbank mythologies of the Sunderbans, there is a parallel narrative that brings out the general continuity of the tide country. It has been a journey of astonishing discoveries, in which history takes over when memory fades. It seems there is no pause in the voyage, there are only the possibilities of the unknown "slowly as the vessel's motion made itself felt in the pit of every stomach the noise yielded to a pregnant fearful stillness. Now the migrants began to absorb the finality of what was underway, yes they were moving, they were afloat heading towards the void of the Black waters. Neither birth nor death was as fearsome a passage as this, neither being experienced in full consciousness".

The broad canvas of *Sea of Poppies* displays many features of a sensational novel-a widow rescued from the funeral pyre, a court trial, runaways, disguise, heroic exploits, vengeful acts and murder. A controlling theme running through the many strands of plot is the question of identity.

Cutoff from their roots in transit, and looking ahead to a fresh start, the migrants are prone to invent new names and histories. For some like Paulette, disguised as an Indian coolie to escape her guardian, "the layers of masking do no more than bear within to a human beings multiplicity of selves. For some like Zachary, the second mate, the truth is bleak by far. The son of a slave and her white master, he will always be bound to a brutal history and rhyme of colour. The British unheedingly break up traditional structures, but dislocation need not be experienced as pure loss. The movement of the book is shown by its three sections of 'Land'; 'River[1] and 'Sea' is from fixing to a flux, running together of categories that once seemed absolute. As the novel gathers momentum, having only one identity becomes like having no identity at all. This is reflected in the language of the book.

The tale told engagingly by *Sea of Poppies* is barely a straightforward one. Beyond the clever circuitousness of the narrative is also a language barrier. To overcome *Sea of Poppies* is written in thick, polyglot jargon that is made self explanatory by its context but still gives the book a mischievous linguistic fascination. For instance wasn't a man in town who could put on a burrakhana like he did, Sheeshmull 'blazing with Shannas and candles. Paltan, of bearers, as 'Khidmulgars' Demijohns of French loll-shrub and carboys of iced simkin. And the Karbat.

Sea of Poppies comes equipped with a lexicon of sorts, an addendum that Mr, Ghosh calls "The Ibis Chrestomathy (a selection of literary selection, esp. in a foreign language as an aid to learning)".Ghosh uses this lexicon to provide elaborate amplification of his favourite turn of phrase and to connect those words with the character that use them.

The book deliberately entangles its readers in a thicket of playful language and that language is a virtual character in the elaborate story. The word play abroad the 'Ibis' can be as dizzying as the opium that also abounds, Ghosh's scholarly bent allows him to draw on sources like 19th century articles on Bhojpuri folk songs, a study of Bhojpuri tradition in Mauritius and Hobson Johnson.

The depth of Ghosh's research is staggering. He strives for authenticity not only in his description, but also in the language. If a word in Bhojpuri, Bengali or English exists for a kind of ship on an article of clothing-he uses it. This makes the appended glossary handy and worth the trouble.

The clash and mingling of languages, Bhojpuri, Bengali, Laskari, Hindstani, Anglo-Indian words and phrases, and a spectrum of English including the malapropism of Baboo Nob Kissan, Burnham creates a vivid sense of living voice as well as the linguistic resourcefulness of people in diasporas. The 'motley tongue' is as much a part of the cultural scene at the lower reaches of the Ganga, and of the multilayered history of the sub-continent, as the collision of people on one of the great rivers of the world.

The Sea of Poppies is bathed in rich vernacular, Ghosh is unstinting in his use of lexical obscurities having raided dictionaries of nautical jargon 19th English, French character mix English with Hindi, and upper caste Indians speak like the Queen. There is a glossary, a sensible move, for we are forced to immerse in the melting pot of dialect. The effect is pleasingly intelligible. A merchant's wife commending a girl for having caught the eye of an illustrious magistrate" can you imagine dear what a prodigious stroke of kismet it will be for you to puckrow Mr. Kendalbushe? He's a nabob in his own right, made a mountain of mohars out of the China trade. Ever since he lost his first wife every larkin in town is trying to bando him I can tell you dear there's a palton of mem wh'd give their last anna to be in your jootis. There is a lot to be said for the men of the age. No badmasheo at all hours of the night for one thing. I can tell you dear there is nothing more annoying than to be puck rowed just when you're looking to a sip of laudanum and a nice sleep. That's a respectable woman talking but you'll hardly know it".

The character whose language is least adulterated is Raja Neel Rattan Haldar. The Raja has more familiarity with the 'waves of Windermere and the Cobblestones of Canterbury' than with his own economic position.

Ghosh revels in the unique vocabulary of his British, American, French, Indian lascar providing a Babel of colloquial phrase and obscure novel terms. In *Antique Land,* Ghosh speculated that medical traders communicated "by using a trading argot or an elaborated pidgin language". In *Sea of Poppies,* he has plundered Hobson-Johnson and other contemporary dictionaries of Anglo-Indian slang to imagine such an argot. He tells the story in a modified lingo of the period, when British English mingled with Indian English, and dallied with dozens of other dialects from ship lore to pirate talk of the lascar to the pidgin of the Chinese and all the verbal music of the Arabian Sea.

With this novel, Ghosh, an anthropologist and historian, has come a long way from the magic realism of his earlier novels. *Sea of Poppies* is written in a direct and flowing style, though unadorned, yet on occasion. Ghosh produces a flourish to show that his mastery as with the hills and crags that "sat upon the plains like a bestiary of gargantuan animal that had been frozen in the act of trying to escape from the grip of the earth". The disgraced Raja enters a court room and "the hubbub ceased abruptly leaving few last thread of sound to float gently to the floor like the torn ends of ribbon". The migration of peasants from the Gangetic plains "was as if fate had thrust its fist through the living flesh of the land in order to tear away a piece of its stricken heart'.

The most impressive passages in the book are the closet to tragedy, though it becomes clear that a new life can open up on the far side of disgrace. Raja Haldar, who has always imagined that he only followed caste rules, out of social politeness, must eat food for the first time in his life prepared by unknown hands and override a wave of disgust that he had never anticipated. The Raja's face is tattooed with his crime, the name of the prison and date. The tattooist took pity on him and pushes a little ball of opium between his lips lo relieve him of his pain. The drug, that had destroyed his life, gains admittance to his body and to his picture of reality.

Later, the tattooist whispers that he had watered the ink, out of family loyalty. The mark will fade after a few months. This is an exquisite image of the fancied permanence of the marks the British made in India. But, it has another aspect that what is written on your forehead in traditional Indian term is your fate. However, here fate washes off over time. In teasing several of cultural stereotypes, is the British who are the fatalists trying to condemn others to their own fixity and is their colonial victim who make their own destiny.

Ghosh's purpose is both literary and political. His narrative represents a prodigious feat of research-the wealth of period detail the author commands. His description brings a lost world to life, from the evocatively imagined opium factory, the intricacies of women costume and the lovingly enumerated fare on the opulent dining table of the era; to the richly detailed description of the 'Ibis' and its journey. India, in the 1830s is wonderfully evoked smell, ritual squalor and above all the language brings home the exotic.

Unlike the writers, who placed the white man at the centre of their narrative, Ghosh relegates his British colonists to the margin of the story, giving pride of place to the neglected subjects of the imperial enterprise; colonialism impoverished mostly coloured victims. He writes with great compassion and empathy about members of the underclass, most of all the migrants, "the men and women who were to be torn from the subjugated plain (from) a soil that had to be sown with suffering to yields its crop of story and song".

While on his Ph.d. work at Oxford, Amitav Ghosh, came across a collection of letters written by medieval Jewish traders. In one letter an Egyptian merchant arranges an exchange of silk and cardamom with a friend in Bangalore. He complains that a shipment of Indian pepper has been lost at sea. What really caught his eyes was a mention of the Bangalore traders slave business agent. The man whose origin was uncertain could easily have been forgotten Ghosh spent the next fourteen years tracking down the few references to him in other documents, traveling to Egypt and Judeo-Arabic. What he found is told in his book *In The Antique Land* (1992) Much of Ghoshe's historical fiction has been driven by what he has described in a note to *The Glass Palace* (2000) 'as a near obsessive urge to render the background of my characters lives as closely as I could.'

References

1. Amitav Ghosh: *Sea of Poppies* Penguin Viking, Delhi, India 2008.
2. Interview: 26 May 2008, *Outlook.*
3. William Dalrymple *The Shabby Genteel Apheem Chichis* 26 June 2008, *Outlook.*
4. Umer, Mahadevan and Dasgupta *Splendid Novel* Nov. 22- Dec. 5 2008, Frontline.
5. S. Prasannarajan. A Voyage in Memory 20 June 2008 *Frontline.*

10

Kasturi Sreenivasan: *The Light from Heaven* A Study of Ignored Minority

The caste system was a formative integrating system, bringing about social coherence and helping to ensure in daily life the dependence of each part of the population on the other. But was also a medieval tyranny using religious sanctions and psychological imprinting to preserve the status quo, and abolishing even the essential sense of individual esteem and personal dignity of the lowest class. The hierarchization a major process of civilization gave rise to competition which replaced co-operation, privatization which replaced collective vision, and consolidated social inequality, exploitation and oppression.

Arun Shourie in *Introduction to Indian Controversies* (1993) states" in any tradition there is much that is valuable and also much that is malignant. Hence there is a need for a new religion, a religion which can treat all human being as equal" The value around which the entire edifice of democracy in India was constituted is non discrimination on the basics of religion, race, caste, sex or place of birth (Article 15 of Indian Constitution) To ensure that the existing social prejudice did not become a permanent part of the social landscape resulting in the continued exclusion of some castes and communities from the social and public life of polity, our constitution envisaged a system of reservation on the basis of caste and class, not merely as a remedy for backwardness; seen as an alternative path for social transformation.

Debate on social justice policies of positive discrimination have frequently been seen as compensation for past injury. But the principle of compensatory justice raises two problems. It requires the precise identification of offenders and victims. Even if the entire group has been affected on account of particular practice, it is necessary to identify the offenders who had practiced it. It would be an injustice to penalize the second generation for the crime they did not commit, it could be re-enacting the age old story of the fox and the lamb. Fighting one evil with another is no solution. If social institutions are unjust they should be abolished and not perpetuated in another form. Justice must be done but not at the cost of another class, giving preferential treatment through reservation policy should not create another discrimination which unfortunately has and is towards the upper caste making them an underprivileged ignored minority.

In recent times a number of studies have appeared that detail the downward mobility that has become the chief characteristic of the Brahmin community, particularly since independence, prominent among them being-*A Study of the Brahmin Community of Andhra*-J. Radhakhshnan and *Plight of the Brahmins* by Meenakshi Jain. The popular image of the Brahmin is that of an affluent pampered class, but today the position is not envious.

Financially the Brahmins have been very hard hit. State laws combined with fragmentation of land have had the effect of substantially reducing the size of family holdings so much so that most Brahmins today find it difficult to eke out a living from land. The end of the Princely States has also resulted in the end of Royal patronage. Most of the Agraharams wear a deserted look.

With scientific development and decline of religious faith, the traditional occupation like family and temple priesthood, recitation of Vedas and practice of Natu Vaidyam -country medicine- no longer prove remunerative nor command respect. Their poverty, their traditional style of dress and hair (tuft) have made them the butt of ridicule.

Department of Endowment Statistics figures reveal that there are many families surviving on just Rs. 500 per month. They are under tremendous financial difficulty. They who have spent their lives studying Vedas, Upanishads and other philosophies of traditional stream have been reduced to begging.

Financial constraints, combined with the existing reservation policy, have resulted in the decline in the number of Brahmin students; especially in pursuing higher education.

Appalling poverty has compelled many off them to migrate to towns leading to spatial dispersal and consequent decline in their local influence and institutions. They initially turned to government jobs, but preferential policies for the non-Brahmins have forced the Brahmins to retreat from these spheres as well. Today most of them have to be content being employed as domestic servants, cooks, auto drivers, rickshaw pullers, coolies and workers in Sulab Sauchalayas, for survival.

India undoubtedly needs to do more to uplift the poor and the backward caste and class and to provide equal opportunities for all her citizens. However, the risk in imposing arbitrary quotas on admission in educational institutions is twofold. Any deterioration in the quality of Indian graduates can put India's nascent economic growth story at risk. Open competition is an important aspect of democracy not because it allows the most talented and merited individual to occupy important positions-which itself is in the interest of the society but more importantly it is an expression of non-discrimination And any subsequent slowdown in the economy will only end up hurting the chances of economic upliftment of the people who are at the bottom of the economic order. To quote Pandit Jawaharlal Nehru:

"If we go in for reservation on communal and caste basis we swamp the bright and able people and remain second rate or third rate. I am grieved to learn how far this business of reservation has gone based on communal consideration. I am amazed to learn that even promotions are based on communal and caste considerations. This way lies not only folly but disaster. Let us help the backward group by all means, but never at the cost of efficiency. How are we going to build the public sector or indeed any sector with second rate people?.... I want my country to be a first class country in everything. The moment we encourage the second rate we are lost".(1)

Lack of acquaintance with our tradition fails one to see the commonalities in the life beliefs and practice of people across the country. "The result of seven hundred years to talk of the essence of our tradition was blasphemy, for hundred years it was stupid, for the last forty years to do so has been 'revanchist' ,'chauvinist' and the latest communal".(2) Great men of our country have seen what is common, and where ever there are differences to build bridges. But unfortunately for political mileage politicians see an opportunity in the differences, focus on them and exaggerate, influence the masses, give them a feeling that they have been wronged, of being in peril unless they preserves they identity they will be engulfed. In a word what was the essence of our nationhood has come to be denied and denounced, and the refrain has been that caste, religion and linguistic groups alone are real. "It is all the politicians doing ....They are responsible for all the corruption in the world today and they have brought this anti-Brahmin feeling into every thing" (3)

It was in the wake of this anti-brahmin feeling that the entire politics of Brahmin-Non- Brahmin emerged not only in Northern India but more vehemently in South Indian politics especially in Tamil Nadu. The closing decades of the 19th century witnessed a new anxiety about the power of the Brahmins in Tamil Nadu. K. Subha Rao recalled "the first musing of the Non- Brahmin was heard by me and my colleagues in Madras and Southern districts in the end of the last century" (4)And a long article published in 1895 in *'Sasilekha* 'titled 'an *Impending Calamity*' confirmed a proposal to organize an 'anti Brahmin League' in Madras city , it being claimed also that members of the league would pledge themselves not only to promote the interests of the non-Brahmins, but also from refraining to render any sort of help to Brahmins. It also gave a word of advice to Brahmins "it is also high time that the so called high caste Brahmin took warning from the turn of events" In the slowly evolving atmosphere of non-brahmin defiance the first institutionalized step to address the material consequence of colonial education for non- Brahmins took the form of the Madras Dravidian Association in 1912 by C. Nadesa Mudaliar. With the call for self government in India or Home Rule by Annie Besant in September 1916 things changed. The Movement spoke a language of self government that refused to recognize caste and other differences within the nation in the making presenting a homogenized India. The Home Rule Movement was suffused with reference to India, Indian, the Indian mind, the Indian youth and the people of India, it was bracketed only by references to Muslims and proportionate represented to them ensured Opposing the Home Rulers a number of prominent non- Brahmins met at Madras on 6 November 1916 and decided to 'start a company, publish a newspaper..... to advance , safeguard, and protect the interest of the same community' A joint company named the South Indian People's Association was floated 'to bring out newspapers . The other part was forming political associations, it acquired the shape of South Indian Liberal Federation or Justice Party" This party issued The Non-Brahmin Manifesto in December 1916.

The Justice Party concentrated its efforts towards gaining reservation for Non-Brahmins in the Madras Legislature as well as in government jobs. When the Justice Party was in power in the Madras Presidency from 1921-26 through its G.O. in September 1921 and 15 August 1922 did what it had desired. The party also ensured the passing of the Hindu

Religion Endowment Act according to which committee of elected and partly nominated members from different castes exercised control over temples. It authorized the use of temple funds for public such as sanitation, education, medical and water supply.

The atmosphere of confrontation that the Justice Party spawned resonated in class rooms and streets. The students of Pachayappa College would not allow a Brahmin professor to open his mouth by his non- Brahmin students who wanted only a non-Brahmin teacher. During the 1920 election the cry by girls and boys were 'don't vote for Brahmin .....vote only for non- Brahmins".

It is this atmosphere of anti- Brahmin feeling and reservation policy that forms the background to Kasturi Sreenivusan's explosive novel *The Lights of Heaven* which centres around Balan, alais S. Balasubramaniam , son of Sheshadri lyer, head clerk at the collector's office at Kamalapuram Jiving at the agraharam, the Brahmin part of the town near the temple. In Balan one could see the demoralizing impact on the psyche of a qualified and brilliant student denied admission to a medical college and forced to be content taking a B.A. (History) degree. He tells his mother-

"I am no better than an untouchable .... In some respects we are even worse, for if I had been fortunate to have been born an untouchable I would have been a qualified doctor by now". "What crime have I committed father that I should be denied the opportunity of helping the sick and the suffering" wailed Balan and makes him wish that he was not born an accursed Brahinin. (p.S)

He was bitter against a society that would not let him become a doctor and not even allow him to make an honest living. He was never refused a seat or a job because he was a Brahmin. After all, that would be against the constitution. He was either too tall, too heavy, did not have the personality. Even those who sympathized did not openly say but told him one needed money or connection. When he is rejected by every perspective employer he meets he realizes that this sprung from the fact that he was a Brahmin in an environment that favours the non-Brahmin. In disgust he decides to renounce his Brahmin identity by throwing away the sacred thread in the river.

Shashtri lyer realized how deeply the disappointment of not getting admission in the medical college had affected him, even after five years he could not forget it-

"Look Bala you have studied the Vedas and the Agamas, You know that by merely removing the thread you cannot cease to be a Brahmin. It is not a Lille given by the Government or a degree awarded by any institution that you can renounce. If you transgress the laws of religion you cannot cease to be a Brahmin".(8)

Having failed to find a job, and the 'nagging' question he is subjected to each day, being compared to others he gradually saw hope giving way to frustration and finally to desperation. He saw how love had turned to bitterness-even hatred. Gradually his anger gave way to understanding and sadness. He finally decides to leave his home and find a job-any job. But even a menial job he could not find because people looked at him with suspicion, even a naxalite. Balan is suddenly seized with a mystical fervor to atone for the sins of his ancestors-especially their discriminatory attitude towards the lower which ironically had led to the upper caste being discriminated in contemporary India. As part of his decision-to atone, Balan decides to become an untouchable.

Hunger and heat makes him weak and he faints on a verandah which he later comes to know is the house of a chakkilayan- chamar. He hides his identity and tells Kuppan that he is a Parayan (scavenger). "Parayans are the lowest and we don't have to do anything with them"(51). He is allowed to stay and teaches him the art of making shoes. But, when Balan decides to leave, for his desire is to be a real scavenger, Kuppan is very angry and tells him "I will see that you are exposed as a treacherous Brahmin"(77)

Here Balan had come to realize that Brahmin was not a caste but a way of living. How particular his mother was about cleanliness and how little importance these people gave to cleanliness "He remembered with longing how every morning the space in front of his would be swept clean and sprinkled with a mixture of cowdung and water. Then a kolam would be drawn and flowers would be planted in lumps of cowdung ,as a sign of auspiciousness. A bath was compulsory every morning......Clothes had to be washed and changed everyday.....One was not supposed to eat from .the dish used by other even if it had been washed Food was usually eaten off a banana leaf which was then thrown away. A tumbler was not supposed to touch one's lips while drinking water or coffee. Balan realized now how much he cherished these customs. To see people go without bath and wearing the same clothes day after day , not washing their hands properly befoe taking food , not distinguishing between cooking and eating utensils-all this revolted him" (56) His next journey was to become a scavenger.

He succeeds in getting a job with great difficulty and even marries Lachi of the same clan. This develops a long drawn rivalry between Picchu. the union leader, and Balan: for Picchu feels that he had stolen away Lachi from him. He was always waiting for an opportunity and it does come in the form of an appeal by Balan's friend Ganesh, who had appealed in the newspaper asking Balan to return from wherever he was, for his parents-his mother had died and his father a lonely sick man. Though the name was not mentioned Picchu smells, finds out and starts blackmailing, exposing and finally creating a row that he must leave. Even Lachi's brother is infuriated and tells him "the entire colony will throw you out. You must leave the job and the colony; for you are a Brahmin and not a Chakkiliyan".(126)

The Brahmins Association while deploring Balan's behavior as being against all Hindu tradition and theology, condemned government policies with regard to college admission and job reservation as a result of which Brahmin youths have had to adopt desperate mean (148) Even Muragan a scavenger feels.

"Nowadays it is difficult for Brahmins to get jobs. Half the jobs are supposed to be reserved for people like us though we don't seem to be doing anything but scavenging. So it will not be surprising if some poor Brahmin becomes comes a scavenger out of sheer necessity"(124).

Picchu angrily said.......We can't have a Brahmin take away the rightful job of a Chakkilyan or a Parayan....

Balasubramiam of Kamalapuram has taken on as a sweeper though he has no right to that claim Keeping the town clean has always been the prerogative of the Chakkilyans and the parayans from time immemorial, if we permit one man to take away our job then there will be no end to it. Tomorrow we will have a queue of Brahmin graduates all standing in line to become a scavenger. Then where is our job security?(151)

The novel ends with the murder of Bala by Picchu and his men. Balan had not only been ostracized by his Brahmin community for this act of his , he had not been accepted by the community for whom he was ready to atone for the sins of his ancestors It is a powerful novel that lays bare the pervasive and vitiating effect of caste on Indian society When will this end Has it not already enfeebled the state structure. Has it not already riven our society Has it not subverted parliamentary democracy Has not Nehru's warning come true "This way lies not only folly but disaster".

References

1. Pt. Nehru's Letter to Chief Ministers 27 June 1961:(quoted by Arun Shourie in Falling Backwards, Rupa/ Delhi 2006.
2. Kasturi Sreenivasan: *The Light From Heaven*, Penguin, Delhi 1990(all further quotes pertain to this edition).
3. Gurupreet & Mahajan: *Identities And Rights -Aspects of Liberal Democracy in India*, OUP Delhi 2001.
4. Arun Shourie- *Secular Agenda* Rupa/ Delhi p. 22.
5. Meenakshi Jain: *Plight of The Brahmin*, Indian Express Sept. 18 1990.
6. J. Radhakrishnan -*Study of Brahmin Community in Andra Pradesh* Chugh Pub.
7. M.S.S. Pandian: Brahmin non-Brahmin: Genealogies of Tamil Political Present Permanent Black Delhi 2007.

11

Amit Chaudhari: *Strange and Sublime Address*

Winner of the Betty Trask Award , the Commonwealth Writers Prize for best second novel, Encore Award and L.A Times Book Prize for fiction Amit Chaudhari is prominent among those writers who could not be shaken by the tempest of post-coloniality and post-modernity. With his roots in Sylhet in East Bengal (now Bangladesh) educated at Bombay, University College London and Balliol college, Oxford, possessing the ease of a native speaker in speaking and writing in English. spending a considerable time abroad, he is not a diasporic writer and has a deep attachment to the culture of his country, especially Bengal, its language and literature. Though he was influenced by Catherine Mansfield, D. H. Lawrence, Virginia Woolf and James Joyce and Marcel Proust, he feels no less indebted to Indian writers, especially Bengali, who had molded his literary career and Bishnu Prasad Chakraharty. In an interview to Fernando Galvan:

"I feel in some way closer to Jibanand Das but doesn't mean that 1 don't like Tagore a great writer and poet. But I think Ray's film meant a lot to me and later on the writer Bibhuti Bhusan Bandyopadhyaya from whose novel Ray created his film *Pather Panchali* it's a very modernist novel in a sense"' (1)

He thinks lyricism and fascination with memory are part of Bengali temperament and loves Bengali writers more for them.

Chaudhuri does not follow either of the two distinct existing literary traditions in Indian English Writing one being the tradition of social and metaphysical realism of the 'big three' and the magic realism and the national allegory of the "Children Of Midnight's Children, he considers R.K. Narayan the 'Writer's Writer' and Raja Rao's *The Serpent and the Rope* "a Modernist text ... one of the last Modernist meditation on the limits of language and form and on the disintegration and the redemptive possibilities of 'high' culture. Even then he does not follow any of them. He repudiates the "air-fairy-theory, pot holes in postmodernism and post colonialism and explores an alternative tradition.

"I am not altogether happy with the term 'post-colonial' because it defines everything in connection to the experience of post colonialism which only had a pretty narrow one dimensional meaning"(O.B.48)

His objection to post-colonial theory mainly rests on it treating India ahistorical, or in not realizing "that India had a history quiet independent of coloniality" (48) and on its negation of the presence of the middle class that started growing in the 18th century and has been trying to come to terms with modernity. According to him the writing in Bengali and other Indian languages, are not the result of coloniality"

"It is the condition of modernity and industrialization, coming to India, and the middle class being formed. From that comes a certain sensibility that expresses, itself in the novel, whether through English or Bengali(O.B.48) Chaudhuri himself belongs to the elite upper middle class but he aligns himself with the middle class and is "aware of the peculiar poignancies of a sheltered middle class existence in India (2) He also underlines that "delicacy and nuance are not the prerogative of the rational bourgeois West alone, but are central to and manifest with great skill and beauty in all significant examples of Indian Writing (3)

Aesthetics and emotions are significant for him and he cannot be where they are not. To him the novelist's life is the text and language the source of renewing our perception of reality. He rejects post modernist theory of language which negates presence and as a consequence emotional fullness of the text, which alone can save us from anomies and aporias. Presence and fullness are the soul of Sanskrit and literatures in Indian languages.

Any writer writing in any language including. English cannot escape their impact. Chaudhuri too relates himself to our rich cultural and literary tradition in exploring an alternative tradition for his creative writing he took recourse to syncretism combining the East and the West whose formative influence he never disowns. In fact what he calls 'in between space' is the site of sophistication, refinement and the best Western literary tradition from which he negotiates his Indian rootedness in Bengali and Bengali culture especially the culture of Calcutta. He turns exclusively to modernism in underpinning his creative writing with a focus on physicality and locality. One of the reasons for the delightful reading of his novels even when they are not overlaid with any theory as they often are is the rendering of physicality of space in his novels. Calcutta appears to be more intimate to him than Bombay, Oxford or Claremont. Wherever Chaudhuri might be in the world and whatever period Calcutta is ever present before him. In fact Calcutta is the protagonist of all his novels and could be called 'Calcutta Novels' in the same line as Malgudi or Wessex novels.

A Strange and Sublime Address is about a boy's discovery of Calcutta, *Afternoon Raga* about the narrator-protagonist's estrangement from the metropolis, *Freedom Song* about Calcutta on the brink of change and *A New World* is about Calcutta bereft of childhood magic. Though he writes about Bombay, Oxford, Claremont but noting and no one, not even Amitav Ghosh can compare with the Calcutta he delineates.

The Calcutta Chaudhuri depicts has both physical tangibility as well as specificity. The writer can touch, hear, see and even taste the city. He registers all the sounds of birds, animal, insects and human beings. The sound of different time of the day, can smell and taste various dishes, in fact he relishes the food imagery and suffuses it with poetry and symbolism. Nothing escapes his sensitive observation -a newspaper rolled and flung into a balcony of a multistoried building, how rickshawallas idle away their time sleeping and killing mosquitoes in their sleep, how chotoma sings while taking her bath. The behaviour, and conversations of non-Bengali teenagers and maid-servants. He is like a camera "as a novelist Chaudhuri is a camera, a slow tracking one, observing places and people from continually changing angles"(4)

His love for physicality and specificity is always manifested in his works. However physicality is not located in large space. He is "very uncomfortable with the idea of a nation" (5). Instead he sees the dispersal of a nation into various local spaces and local culture. Calcutta is India, Bombay is India and even any locality in these metropolis is India. He admires those writers who locate their imagination in specific localities without bothering about the particularities of a nation. For Chaudhari a locality does not remain a locality, it becomes the world and the architectural space of the novel can accommodate different, even incompatible worlds of a locality. What Chaudhari actually does is create micro-worlds. Though he may be averse to any pan- Indian culture, he would talk of the culture of Calcutta and by implication suggest the culture of Calcutta and Bengal in *Freedom Song* he writes" I really think of it as an extended poem about the end of a certain phase in Calcutta, in Bengali culture, and in Indian culture (O.B,50)

What makes him unique as a novelist is his focus on local culture, with an ability to distinguish various local cultures-East Bengal from West Bengal in matters of ritual, tradition custom, music and literature, the street culture, suburban and main stream culture very artistically. For Chaudhari places are proper sites of culture-the lanes of Oxford the streets of Calcutta and the suburbs of Bombay.

The localization of culture set him apart from others but also limits his scope.

As a writer he states" Now the kind of India I write about is a lower middle class or middle class India, and not just India because I write about Calcutta in particular and Bengal, a post- independence Bengal reality, lyricising the experience of the middle class and the spaces I which they live(48).

Concomitant with his fascination with local culture is his fascination with minutiae thing especially with everything related to the middle class He has a special liking for the Bengali middle class considers it to be more modernistic, lyrical and literary and less infected by post-coloniality and post-modernity. All his novels offer different vignette of the daily life of this backbone of Bengali culture and society.

In *A Strange and Sublime Address,* his first novel captures middle class Calcutta, a city of industrial and economic stagnation, but with a unique cultural flavor through the eyes of its twelve year protagonist Sandeep. Sandeep comes from Bombay to Calcutta to spend his summer vacation finds the city possessing a quaint magic that is seemingly absent in the fast paced Bombay. When Sandeep goes to a remote suburb of South Calcutta to visit his relative with his uncle "It was off the main road, as the car turned into a narrow lane with cramped shops and rickshawalas smoking dimly incandescent beedis lounging in the corner they moved in space forward and backwards in time simultaneously. Calcutta grew remote and unrecognizable, the city was no longer demarcated from the folk tale Bengal that surrounded it so thickly. Myths and ghosts and Bengal tigers roamed beyond an unclear boundary, the spluttering car passed a temple and a tank where buffaloes and children bathed in the daytime. The place was a little colony or village tied by a network of faint lines, there were few electric lights to iiiuminate the area. One's eyes got reluctantly to moonlight, and one saw houses each some distance from the other, and ponds in which spores settled and multiplied, on which weeds formed an almost firm impalpable surface where the lotus rose and opened with a shy passion in darkness(6)

There is no story, no mystery, no suspense, no heroism, no miracle, still the novel is quiet fascinating and compelling. The novel is about Calcutta and its people like Chhottmama, Sandeep, Abhi, Babla, Mamima Sandeep's mother and others who live in it. Not much happens in the novel unless things like bathing, dancing, gossiping, singing are called happenings. There is nothing unusual about the place or the people. The Calcutta of the novel is not the cosmopolitan Calcutta of the elite, Calcutta of the multinationals, computers, mobiles, cable T.V.. It is the Calcutta of the middle class whose heroism lies in living their daily life. Calcutta of dusts, uncertain power cuts, Calcutta where roads are ever being dug up, where nothing seems to work, where people try to replace a pipe "that does not work with another pipe that does not work (SSA 11). It is a Calcutta where streets are theatres.

"Full of actors and extras reckless digs, insufferable cows lying in the centre of the lane, families arguing, old women gossiping, children chasing cats rickshawwallahs idling, Vaishnav devotees singing religious songs for all to hear" (SSA 104).

The people crisscrossing this fictional space are the people who raise storm only in a tea cup. Chhotomama is "an archetype of that familiar figure that is not often described in literature-the ordinary breadwinner in his moment of unlikely glory, transformed into the centre of his universe".

He is a Marxist thinker in fact, to put it correctly "a water closet thinker" (SSA 45) who ponders on "world affairs" "home affairs" and current situation in his toilet which he uses as a study. Mamima and Sandeep's mother, two main characters in the novel, apart from their daily routine are engrossed in gossips and visits to their relatives: then there are the children Sandeep. Abhijit. Surjit. Babla in the strand with which he weaves his engrossing narration. Chaudhari shows his intimate acquaintance with those aspects of life in Calcutta which usually are denied admittance in the creative works of other writers. The narrator focalizes on

Calcutta and its typical average middle class citizen. He is both concerned and critical at what he sees around him. He registers his protest against the state of affairs and startles by welcoming regressive ideas.

"on bad days like this, when the fans stopped turning because of a power cut, when the telephone went dead because of a cable fault, when the taps became dry because there was no power to pump the water, and finally when the car engine curtly refused to start, it seemed a better idea to return to primitive unpretentious means of subsistence-to buy a horse and a plough, to dig a well in one's backyard, to plant one's own trees and grow one's fruit and vegetables" (SSA 31).

The narrator is amused at the typical often leftist Bengali obsession with Subhas Chandra Bose versus Gandhi. Teaching English by those who do not know English-an example was Abhi's English tutor, who was a typical Bengali teacher.

What ees thee name of thee boy?

Thee name of the boy ees John,
What did John habb for deenar.
John had meelk and bred for deenar.
After the tuition ended

"It was a pleasure to hear his natural eloquence in Bengali after his brave guerilla invasion into the rocky terrain of English, silence descended as he drank his tea and there was a temporary respite from the savage bombardment of those foreign words on this helpless sleepy room "(SSA 85-86).

Chaudhari is both a Romantist and Formalist. He is interested in the perception, the simple joys and sorrows of daily life and also in the aesthetic enjoyment oh these perceptions.

In *Afternoon Raga* the Indian classical music makes the imaginative patterning of tunes not only according to the various seasons, but also as cognate to the different and minute sections of the twenty four hour of the day and night. The association of each of these tunes are distinct and unique, and shared by the ,singer and listener The bulk of the space and time in the novel is occupied by Oxford, But the novel is in no way Oxford raga it is Indian raga and Oxford only resonates with it As the narrator states "his love of music, pride and delight in creation is the gift of his mother land and not Oxford (7). Though the novel is laid in Oxford, there is no fixed border between it and Bombay and Calcutta, the original note or the mother note comes from Calcutta or to be more precise from the ancestral village of the narrator in East Bengal, is finely tuned in Bombay and resonates in Oxford. Chaudhari finds no difficulty in moving from Oxford to Bombay and Calcutta and then back as a raga and can easily float on various planes. Chaudhari's magical raga does not come out of anything heroic or extraordinary. On the contrary he weaves his magic about everyday life. The *Afternoon Raga* is about bits of ordinary things, though emotionally quiet significant about the life of an Indian student at Oxford. Through his beautifully articulated rhythmic prose he tells us how the narrator feels at Oxford, he reminiscences about his parents, about his guru and his homeland. He weaves it into the narrative with his well crafted musical and poetic prose and evolves a raga of his own which suits the fiction as well as the musical composition.

Freedom Song is not about the freedom of the country but what freedom has come to. It is not the song of a nation but part of the nation. Bengal or to be inure precise Kolkota. It is not a hangover of post-colonialism, it sings of Bengal culture and Kolkota Like Bhasker who after reading a book titled *We Are Bengalis* understands "what a wonderful thing it was to be a Bengali and that he was a Bengali himself'(8).

Freedom Song though unusual in the use of words and sliced in form suggests a whole way of life, the life of the urban middle class the urban particularly Calcutta-Bengal. The story time is fifty years before independence till the winter of 1992-93, but the discourse time is just a few months, Chaudhari has successfully rendered the traditional Bengali life with all its superficies and inner realities.

The novel is a chronicle of two families Shib, Khuku and Bhola and Abha, families related to each other. Their stories are mere stories recounting what happened to them in the past and what happens to them in the present there are no climaxes hence no climb down. They tell how children are brought up in large families and how they were looked after, after their father's demise. Their childhood covers a great space and bring out the peculiar qualities of childhood in India especially in a place like Calcutta.

The Freedom Song more importantly touches the deeper rhythm of the political culture in Culcutta and its effect on life at large in the "deep green humid Gangetic delta in Bengal " under " one of the last socialist government in the world (FS 46) where Leftist in Bengal curse foreign investment, pledge support for Cuba and Castro, protest privatization , stage street plays advocating socialism and create the impression that" loud choruses and clenched fists raised together in the air would delay, perhaps even permanently remove the prospect of liberalization, would punish fundamentalists (FS 149) but nothing of that happens.

The Leftist government in West Bengal has created a work culture like the protagonist of the novel, Chaudhari too is highly critical of. After Shiba retires he joins Little Magic Assortment -a company producing sweets and chocolates, as the narrator remarks in Little's History "the history of Calcutta seems to have been written" (FS 89) Shib had earlier worked in a successful private company" where every department whirled and ticked from nine to five thirty like clock work (FS 19) But at Little' he presides over the destinies of "colourful tribes with time tested culture of tea drinking, gossip and procrastination, who had stoutly defended for many years their mode of communion and exchange from being taken over by an alien work ethics(FS 19) The machines were loyal but men were 'dy-functional Since the communist party came into power "The atmosphere had changed to a benign activity, with a cheerful trade unionism, replacing the tensions of the past the representatives of the Chocolate company now also representing the government and the party, and the whole thing became relaxed, ungrudgingly family affair (FS20)

Chaudhari brings out in briefest words how communalism was keeping unsought company with communism in West Bengal, which is supposed to be more secular and committed to common culture than the rest of India. Though there are brief but suggested references to historical events such as partition of Bengal, the rise of Naxialites and its impact on industries, Ayodhya issue sudsequent to Bombay blasts but nothing to beat the novelist picking up tones vibrating in the social fabric of Bengal especially Kolkota. One of the chief notes of *Freedom Song* is 'Azaan' which is very irritating to Khuku, which to her is as disturbing as the humming of mosquitoes near the ear" Is it necessary for the world to hear it?' The natural and common apprehension of non -Muslim especially Hindus is expressed.

"They talk of how by the next century there would be more Muslims than Hindus in the country.....Mini told Khuku that population control was meant for Hindus only, and Khuku listening to Mini began to see Muslims everywhere" (FS 54) They do not consider toppling of the mosque to be bad, will vote for BJP. The novelist is ironical in his treatment of communalism. "The word 'fundamentalism' traveling everywhere and belonging nowhere people tried to understand what it meant (FS 85).

In communicating the typicality of the middle class life in the Bengali metropolis he does not lose sight even of very small and apparently inconsequential detail.

In *A New World,* Kolkata is not the Kolkata *of A Strange and Sublime Address, Afternoon Raga* or *Freedom Song.* To Jayojit, the protagonist of *A New World,* "The City irritated him yet he'd decided that it would give him the space for recoupment" (9). Jayojit came to Kolkata with his son Bonny, he stays with his parents and gets over the blues of his divorce from Amala There is nothing very much new about the world that the novel encloses. However, it is through Jayojit, primarily his consciousness which helps us discover the trajectory of the new in the novel. To him the life in the suburbs of the age old Kolkata where he had now come appears immersed in the new. The life lived in the 1980's and 90's was certainly new- when set against the old world Jayojit had lived by which he "meant the fifties and sixties where everything seemed more sacrosanct than at any other point in Indian history" Given a choice of being born in any time in India's past, would have chosen to be born in the thirties, so that he could have a taste of the first year of post independence (NW 148).

What hurts him is the shrinking space that Bengali culture carries within itself and the changing face of the metropolis. His is a sensitive soul which records everything it perceives with utmost sensitivity. There are things which may appear common place to others for example the presence of the moneyed people "who had guaranteed their own self perpetuating well being, it seemed for generations to come" (NW 54) and the upsurge of consumer culture, which does, not appeal to him. The dominance of the Marwaries and other Hindi speaking people in the city, especially its suburbs, the way the settlers bring with them the space that belong to another culture, the change in the dress code, with the increasing popularity of Salwar Kameez, the craze for foreign things and travel, the institution of adda' giving way to increasing isolation, the "banal nouveau-riche chatter" combining the "new street talk with the immemorial histrionic platitude of tradition" (NW .191) all these appear defamiliarising the life of Kolkata. But, above all it is the increasing encroachment of the Western ways in the traditional familial and societal relationship which perturbed the protagonist as well as the novelist. The major narrative statement of the novel is the breakdown of Jayojit's marriage and the resultant tensions and apprehensions. He is simply intrigued by it and fails lo understand it. Though they could not get along together from the very beginning but "some urge to rehearse what had been done before them had taken a hold of him of her (NW.32). Whereas he clings to it Amala breaks out of it and finds her getting involved with an already married gynecologist "a not unpleasant looking man in his forties who was balding slightly, and surely not charismatic" a person with bad breath. It is impossible for him to understand or interpret "how any woman in her right mind could prefer him to Jayojit" (NW.57). The effect of Jayojit's failed marriage is shattering. Dr. Sen, his upstairs neighbour is astonished he cannot believe "that these things which he'd only remotely heard about actually happens to real people...especially to Jayojit who is eminently desirable, a catch not a divorce (NW.84). Jayojit fails to understand why Amala should choose to go her own way when they "had grown up with the same background". At the back of his mind is the ancient Indian ideal of marriage.

A New World shows Jayojit's alienation and isolation who like many of the affluent arc more familiar with Western ways 'Talk in English, think in English, dress like English, often do not take up their mother tongue as a subject. Jayojit is fed on and later fed up with 'luchis', puts Bonny on a diet of cereal, milk and fruit juice and himself too takes milk, cornflakes, toast and tea. Oily food does not suit them any more. In *A Strange and Sublime Address* we see Sandeep enjoying not only jamun mixed with mustard oil and salt but also relish those tangy berries with others. *In afternoon Raga* the narrator remembers the early years of his parents stay in London, how everyone was curious about the red spot on his mother's forehead. He recalls she was a good cook and such an inspired purchaser of herring and stewing lamb that his father rapidly gained weight and happiness. His mother gradually picked up English like others. Bengali's pronounced 'hurt[1] as 'heart' 'Ship' as 'sheep'. All these have simplicity and charm 'a lovable homely melody that the generation of Jayojit and Amala lack. Sandeep in a *Strange and Sublime Address* craves to extend his stay in his chhotomamas home leading a lazy life "with the flies and the lizards, sound of the conch, the jokes and rhymes in the mother tongue upon the lips (SSA.87). This emphasis on Bengali culture and particularly Bengali language in the earlier novels and the shift to anglicized section of society who shun their mother tongue in the later novels can be seen as a transition in cultural spectrum or an attempt to trace the movement from the middle class attachment to Bengali values to the affluent people flaunting it. The divorce in *A New World* signifies the emergence of the new world.

Jayojit's reaction to places in Kolkata is also ambiguous. Places like Deshpriya Park. Ballygung. Circular Road are O.K. but only with the reservation of one who has seen better places. Amala's attitude when she looked at a Bengali woman was 'ironical'. 'Bengali woman let go so easily' commenting on their old fashionable sarees "a smile would come to her eyes" (N W. 179) This kind of disapproving detachment is hinted throughout the novel. Though Benny is taught to call his parents 'baba' and 'ma' , but he has not been taught the other words that surround these words in our culture.

A New World shows Chaudhari has taken a long journey from *A Strange and Sublime Address.* Contrasted to Jayojit's stay in Calcutta which is brooding barrenness, Sandeep who comes for a vacation to Calcutta to his chottomama is filled with joy and liveliness.

When the novel concludes, Jayojit is returning to Claremont. What sticks to the mind is the poetic rendering of the complex daily life and the personality of Jayojit. He is an economist and writer who had laid an early an important cornerstone of an yet unfinished brickwork of India's new economic order. Who feels disturbed and puzzled by his wife taking a divorce and living with another man who feels bedeviled and beleaguered by the new economic and cultural forces swaying a comparatively becalmed and cultural society of Bengal.

What is new in *A New World* is Chaudhari's poetic rendering of locality, temporality, and humanity. The canvas is small but the reader's vision is led into the beyond by his masterly use of irony, suggestiveness and imagery. In tone and temper it is significantly different and distinguishes itself by its new self assurance in dealing with life language and literariness.

What Chaudhari dwells in his novels are small things yet they are all beautiful and wonderful. The narrative consists of small pieces put together, small chapters with larger like a brief note rolling into a larger and producing a harmonious melody of a gradually unfolding vision of cultural spaces of the middle class families in Calcutta, a metropolis of varied hybrid sound. The stuff of the novel is not the stuff dream are made of, but the dream of which the daily life of Calcutta middle class is made.

What contributes in making the novel poetic is its magic, original offbeat seldom repeated. Chaudhari'sis skill is his capacity his for capturing various sounds and rhythms and the distinct difference each one of them, a quality which is usually marked with song making which his novels usually are: Calcutta is a medley of sound, voices, movement and rhythm. The novelist makes us hear the sound of dawn, afternoon noises and silences of the night. He brings out the rhythm of the speech of the servants, grown-ups, children, the destitute mewing of the cat, the sound of train and various other things which resonate in his novels His description of winter in Calcutta is poetic.

"Winter came only once a year, and it changed the city. It gave its people.......the slight sense of the wonder and dislocation of being in a foreign country.....smoke traveled everywhere, robbing the sunlight of its fire. Afternoon with its gentle orange yellow light was the warmest time of the day, though the wet clothes assisted by a breeze dried more slowly than in summer. And as the orange light fell on the brick work and the sides of the house, it was easier to tell, from the flushed rose centre that now appeared on the terrace and now in parapet that its origin lay in fire (F.S.27)

Chuudhari's novels are discourses on the ordinary and the common place, and he is not contented till he shows how unique the ordinary and commonplace are. In *A New World* Jayojit's mother secretly packs 'gur' hopes the custom don't treat it as a lump of earth' and throw it away but to look it as a sign of love, wish for well being and sweetness. It reveals spontaneous and not laboured Indianness and adds a new flavour to the old one in which Jayojit finds himself. Chaudhari draws images from the experiences of his life, when they are used to vivify life, the ordinary reality, they are charged with poetry with the result that the familiar and the strange go hand in hand. Life mostly comprises the ordinary, the average and common place. Its heroism, beauty its music lies in day to day life. Chaudhari brings out the underlying music and poetry of life and enables one to cope with the monototny of life he charts a new dimension in Indian English novel by pursuing neither the post colonial nor the post modernist trajectory instead sets his vision on what is strikingly fresh and free from the shackles of magic realism and the narration of the nation.

He describes the ordinary things like Wordsworth but castes a magic spell on them like Coleridge. All the banality and triviality of his fictional world is only an arch where through gleams a world of strangeness and sublimity, not the sublimity of Longinus but that of a fine poetry. So *A Strange and Sublime Address* though apparently about ordinary activities and antics of a middle class Bengali tamily living in Calcutta in pre TV days is really a narrative of an alien but fascinating world of wonder and fantasies. The writer does not give any clue to the significance of the title except in the brief passage Sandeep finds the following address written in the first page of Abhi's book:

Abhijeet Das,
17th Vivekanand road, Calcutta South, West Bengal, India, Asia,
The Solar system, The Universe.

The narrator remarks it's a strange and sublime address (SSA.72). The title sets the tone of the novel. Inter mixing of genres-poetry and fiction has been one of his contributions to Indian English Writing though he is not the first to do it, but he is singular for he has done it under the spell of the old tradition of Sanskrit and Bengali literatures. What Chaudhari offers is a poetic rendering of his experiences-not of the bizarre, perverse, sensuous and sexual, the stock in trade of writers with an eye for foreign market. There is the same propriety and decency and delicacy which we find in Sanskrit and Bengali literature All his novels are poetic meditation on the ordinariness and humdrum of daily life of the middle class in Calcutta. He is a lyricist writing about the dispersal of the self and culture in his fiction for the larger space it offers.

Human sensibility for him has little to do with introversion, but very much with extroversion. It is a part of "space, street and sound" (O.B.44), part of life happening everywhere' part of the self dispersing into another who it comes into with. The individual as individual does not charm him. About his first novel he writes I did not wish to write a novel in which the individual was the centre of the novel. I wanted the novel to be about the family or even about the community or even a state, or what it means to be inside and outside, about a house and its relationship to the outside rather than the inner life of a person" (Aalap 165)It is this which makes him opt for the comic mode of his writing as he loves the dispersal of self identity into various things rather than the tragic mode which allows the self to confine itself to itself.

The landscape and its impact on the consciousness of a person appeals to him more than the mental landscape of a person, who is totally immersed in himself and is oblivious of what is happening outside and to others. He seldom probes the depth the psyche of his characters, that is not his forte. Instead

"quiet often to use Isherwood's phrase I just behave like a camera, I just follow them about, evesdrop on their conversation, and see what they are doing. So there's a child like sight that the child who wants to spy, overhear without being noticed (OB.45) He has drawn on memory too, but it is the memory that belongs to the outside, and that the memory that goes turning in and in till it spends.

His sense of humanity is not situated in the "existential sense of the self....which exists in the West because of the closed spaces" In India a person cannot be a single individual" You are a composite of interruptions, smell and sight. What you've overheard of memories ambitions of all kind of things (O B. 46).

Art could mean many things, but to Chaudhari it was primarily poetry In the hands of Chaudhari the novel relives the quotidian reality and seeks metamorphosis through poetry he states "behind the architectural space of the novel where he can talk about lives, and spaces and all kinds of things interacting with each other.....there is a poetic impulse in which I want to let things remain unsaid or want to close up, finish things completely" (O B. 44) His novels are about the things one knows but seldom takes note of, of events that happens daily but seldom holds us back, about people we easily recognize but seldom recognize ourselves in them and about wonders of life that seldom charm us. Chaudhari brings them all in a vivid, fresh lively and charming, and invests them with a new appearance. He does this in a language that is essentially foreign and in a genre originally Western. He uses the form of the novel to express what is typically Bengali and essentially Indian. He uses English words in the context of what even today must appear to the West a new world, Calcutta and its people. He uses Bengali words sometimes, sometimes with translations sometimes without. Chaudhari does not use Indian English, nor does he hybridize. He uses Standard English-English word structure and idioms, in order to encompass the life and landscape of Bengal particularly its heart Calcutta-Kolkota- and out of this he weaves his fascinating tales.

References

1. On Belonging and Not Belonging: A Conversation With Amit Chaudhari" Fernando Galvan Wasafiri, No. 30 Autumn 1900. Susheila Nasta (ed). London 48-49. Abvt. O.B.
2. Pankaj Misra: Blurb of *Freedom Song* Picador, London, 1999.
3. Amit Chaudhari: *The Picador Book* of Modern Indian Literature London XXV.
4. Pankaj Misra: (Quoted from the New Statesman on the blurb of Freedom Song.

5. "Aalap; In Conversation with Amit Chaudhari " by Simian R. Gosh.
6. Amit Chaudhari: *A Strange and Sublime Address,* Minerva, Paperback London '92 p. 59-60.
7. Amit Chaudhari: *Afternoon Raga,* Vintage, London '93, p. 9l.
8. Amit Chaudhari: *Freedom Song,* Picador, London' 99, p. 59.
9. Amit Chaudhari: *New World,* Picador, London, 2001, p. 51.
10. Sheobhusan Shukla & Anu Shukla: *The Novels of Amit Chaudhari An Exploration in Alternative* Tradition, Sarup & Sons Delhi, 2004.

12

Rohinton Mistry: *Family Matters*

With more elderly people than ever before on the planet there is a fundamental change in the attitude towards the old. Though age is a part of life and is a natural process as growth, it is now viewed as a burden-social, financial, draining of energy, a point of tension in the family and destroyer of peace. From old age being celebrated as Hervery Alien said, "Grow up as soon as you can. It pays. The only time you live fully is from 30-60", is now viewed as

The age is best which is first
When youth and blood are warm
But being spent, the worse and worst
Time still succeed the former,

Or to quote Shakespeare's "The Seven Stages of Man"

The sixth stage shifts
Into the lean and slipper'd and pantaloon
With spectacles on nose and pauch as sides
His youthful hose, well saved a world too wide
Last scene of all
That ends this strange eventful history
Is second childishness and mere oblivion
Sans teeth, sans eyes, sans taste, sans everything

The age wave is mounting. With one elderly in every 12, India is poised to become the second largest hub of seniors in the world. According to the study conducted by *'India Today'* there are eight million aged over 80, 29 million 70 plus and 77 million above 66. Life expectancy has shot up from 23 at the turn of the last century to 65 and death rates have fallen from 25 per thousand to eight. The rapid greying is working on an 'astonishingly low' per capita GDP, over 70% elders are fully dependent. A large population of old and unhealthy people is a huge financial and emotional burden to the society this meant a sharper focus on age related problems. In most developed countries, increasing number of Universities and Medical colleges offer courses in Gerontology- the study of old age. The trend has reached India too. AIMS has a Dept. of Gerontology All this has led to the old feeling isolated and uncared for, an agonising life crisis grips families as the younger generation struggle to look after ageing parents, new adjustments and equations are being forced. But the disquiet remains.

Two decades ago caring for the elderly was hardly an issue. Joint family was a good place to be very old or very young. But in a globalized world, lives are busy, women are working. Personal choices and privacy are the buzzword, Joint families are falling by the wayside. The great Indian family-large noisy, with grandparents, parents, children, aunts, cousins all living together under a single roof, squabbling but presenting a united front to the world is history now. There is less tolerance for cramped communal living.

The changing conditions have brought changing scenario and value system. As Manas Ray. a Sociologist points out, "The post globalization hasn't-really experienced a great deal of hardships. They haven't faced the trauma of the Partition or the economic crunch of post-independence era. For most, this is the first really rough patch in their lives." They belong to New India, where Gandhian frugality has no meaning. They shop in malls, patronize private schools and hospitals and relax in gyms and spas. They want to be rich, work hard for it, including women. As life becomes busier and busier there is less time to look after the homes. All this has led to a debate and urgent thinking on the aging parents, a thing that sounds strange and sad in a country renouned for taking care of its elders and holding them in high respect but now being treated as unwanted elements. They are no longer considered.

> As a white candle in a holy place
> So is the beauty of an aged face.

They see no beauty now but as most agonizing life crises, the picture one comes across so often is of an aged man/ woman-'clouded by cataract, staring forlornly, sad, confused, leading a dead life and waiting for death.' Hardly a day goes by without a horror story in the media about the plight of the aged parents-abandoned or abused. The pain of being unwanted, forced to monologues and responded by monosyllables, leaves them silenced, but bursting within them is the desire to be heard, to pour out all their pent up feelings, hence it is not surprising that elders have begun to talk. They talk not only about their lack of access to money, health, mobility leisure but narrate how it feels to 'talk to walls' be a burden to children of disrespect and neglect that makes "old age a disease". They tell tales about the younger generation splitting responsibility by separating their parents, taking care of parents by rotation, pushing parents to smaller rooms. Even if one had money, and a home but circumstances forcing them to live with their son/ daughter family, they are made to feel unwelcome. Getting meals which rarely suits the age, taste or timing, often told to mind one's own business and not 'poke' nose in their personal affairs.

The chairman of the Helpage India Mathew Cherian reports that they get numerous complaints on the helpline of increasing neglect and abuse, and seeking relief from abusive children. Often one also hear that children have turned against them once the property has been signed over.

Families where everyone work lock up Alzheimer parents and leave for the day, well dressed rich people are found living in the park after being turned out by their children.

Health is always linked with wealth. And the aged are generally caught in an unfair financial squeeze. The high level of economic dependence and the cost of treatment often proves a burden on the household. The elderly form one of the most vulnerable groups. Police file show sky rocketing crime rates against them. They fear goons, builders, their servants and even their children. Most of them feel lonely and scared, often reporting 'All sorts of people try to come in and find out if I live alone'.

Adding to the many reasons is the pull of migration with children moving out in search of better prospects caring for the old has become an elusive ideal. Even if they are called to join them, they find it difficult to live there-the weather, missing the familiarity of their neighbourhood the quiet pace of life and friends and feel left out and uncomfortable not knowing English. Baring a few most of the seniors face the same agony. The rich fear-loneliness, lack of work and leisure, insufficient economic resources and dependence on children hurt middle class most, lower classes with poverty, disease, disability. There are very few children who could feel and tell 'Its payback time. I am where I am because of them all, or feeling guilty that they are not able to spend enough time with their parents.' The government's Maintenance and Welfare of Parents and Senior Citizen Bill 2007, makes neglect of parents punishable, it is waiting in the wings, if passed it will slap heavy fines/imprisonment to neglectful children, and will be forced to return inherited property. The reverse Mortgage system an ideal way for parents to extract value out of the property, has come in to the force. But a relationship based society as ours is trying to cope with changes through a rule based-Anglo-Saxon system say Prof. Vaidyanathan, IMA Bangalore. No parents will complain against their children. Family ties and community linkage is still strong in India. This must be enhanced and enriched instead of deriding it in the name of modernization. The truth that parents who nurtured them once are now the ones who need nurturing will not set them free, but recognizing it may open up new possibilities though it can be rough for those who face the dual pressure of the 'Sandwich generation' raising children and caring for the aging parents but would be worth for someone who once did their might for you. Till then for the old and the infirm 'Home' is not where the heart is "Life" is work and worry "Love" children's voice on the telephone, "affection" is their message on the Internet, 'caring' is the nurse they engage when ill, and "responsibility" is the money they pay through the bank.

Old age has always attracted creative writers Indians as well as Western. It has been treated morally, metaphorically and structurally. It has been celebrated as a welcome phase by Robert Browning in his long philosophical poem Rabi Ben Ezra

> Grow old along with me
> The best is yet to be
> The last for which the first was made

or the determination and courage that Santiago the 84 year old fisherman shows in Hemingway's *Old Man and the Sea,* to prove that man may be destroyed but never defeated, or Tennyson's *Ulysses* - who says he cannot rest from travel, he and his mariners are physically old but still young at heart, and sets out to do the impossible 'to follow the sinking star', never to waver, but 'strive to seek to find and never to yield' G.K. Chesterton in his essays *'On the Pleasures of No longer Being Young'* shows paradoxically how it is the old who appreciate modernity rather than the young, and writes 'the older you grow the younger you grow'. Old age has not been welcome to the famous mythological character Yayati, who would want somebody to exchange his youth, for his old age, and the sight of the old age was one of the turning point in Lord Buddha's life.

Among the long array of writing focusing on old age is Rohinton Mistry's *Family Matters* which makes a sensitive study into the psyche of an old man through familial interaction of a Parsi family. Cobwebbed in existential enigma in an uncertain economic state in a traditional society. It deals with the fragile relationship at the micro cosmic level on the one hand and the macro cosmic level of humanity on the other. It revolves around Nariman Vakeel, a 79 year old Parsi widower the patriarch of a small discordant family. A retired Professor of English, Nariman is beset by Parkinson disease, and haunted by the memories of the past, he leads a difficult life, living in a once elegant apartment with his two middle aged step children. One of the notable theme of the novel is the suffering of a man in his old age.

Rohinton Mistry is an Indo-Canadian writer, who migrated to Canada in 1975 and continues to live there. As an Indian who now lives and writes in Canada Rohinton Mistry is a writer of the Indian Diaspora. Like other Parsis, India is his adopted land. A Parsi Zoroastrian, whose ancestors were forced to exile by the Islamic conquest and religious persecution of the community in Iran. He made his mark as a writer with a collection of short stories *Firozshah Baag* (1987) followed by *Such a Long Journey* (1991) which heralded the arrival of a gifted novelist. His novel *Fine Balance* was acclaimed as a landmark in the history of Indian English fiction, and was seriously considered for the *Booker Prize.* It his was followed by *Family Matters* which has been equally appreciated.

The novel deals with one of the major issue in Indo-Canadian writings-the problem related to aging, intergenerational problem of adjustment, communication and the generational gap. The role and the problem of the senior citizens is becoming increasingly important, because the percentage of the aging is on the increase in Canada. This has been partly due to parents being sponsored under the family reunification policy and secondly apart from the immigrants all Canada is getting old it is projected that by 2030 twenty percent of Canada will be over the age of 60.

Rohinton Mistry's *Family Matters* is an enthralling novel of Nariman Vakeel, 79 year old, retired professor suffering from Parkinson disesase, breaks his ankle and finds himself wholly depended on his family. His step- children Coomy and Jal have a spacious apartment- thanks to their father Nariman who signed away the house to them-are squeamish, and resentful to his needs. Cleverly they shift him to his daughter Roxana's house who lives in a two room apartment with her husband Yezad and her two sons Murad and Jehangir. His stay tests not only their material resources, but their tolerance, patience, compassion, integrity and faith. Sweeping and intimate, tragic and mirthful, *Family Matters* is a work of enormous emotional power. A novel of wisdom, beauty and power, it presents a portrait of domestic life in modern Bombay for that matter in India- not a pretty picture but warm hearted and stirring all the time.

The story of *Family Matters* pre-occupied Mistry since 1987 when *Tales from Firoz Shah Baag* was published. The last story of the collection "*Swimming Lessons*" deals with an episode which finds perfect extension in the novel, where a young Indian emigrant to Canada nostalgically describes the care and attention which his sickly mother provided to his grandfather who suffered from Parkinson disease and osteoporosis and ultimately dies. An everyday happening in a family has been meticulously expanded into a novel *Family Matters.* Nariman too besieged by Parkinson disease, osleoporosis, hypertension and further handicapped by fracturing his ankle, which leaves him for the most part bed ridden, lie is constantly haunted and lives in the past. Nariman in his youth had loved and continued to love a Christian girl Lucy Braganza, but was forced to marry a Parsi widow, Yasmin with two children.

Nariman, when he looked back across the wasteland of their lives, despaired at how could he have been so feeble minded, so spineless to have allowed it to happen. And that perhaps was the first big mistake he had made. The day he met his love Lucy, the most beautiful morning, fell in love and continued to love her till his death, for eleven long years before he was forced to marry he had dreamt of a beautiful world for themselves. A cocoon, Lucy used to call it. A cocoon was what they needed, into which they could retreat and after their families had forgotten their existence, they would emerge like two glistening butterflies and fly away together. But he was ground down by their families Nariman's father would not approve of his son marrying a non-Parsi for like many he too was worried about the future of the Parsi community. " The most crucial point is our dwindling birth rate, our man and woman marrying non-Parsi, and the heavy migration to the West", (p . 356) Told by all 'No happiness is more lasting than the happiness that you get fulfilling your parents wishes'. Remember that Nari (13) against his wishes he agrees.

Leave alone lasting happiness, there was no love, no happiness but a long regret for the blunder he had committed into agreeing to the marriage. The only happiness was the birth of Roxana, the little miracle. Added to Parkinson disease, osteoporosis, hypertension he was further handicapped by fracturing his ankle, which leaves him bedridden and totally dependent. Coomy says the strain is killing her, she frankly admits she hates him, though Jal tells 'Even as a step-father he was always kind to us, we mustn't forget that' (71). They can't afford a nurse, hence they decide to send him to Roxana's two room flat fooling him into believing that 'A short visit to *Pleasant Villa*, to help you to recuperate' but Nariman saw it clearly. He wondered if he was seeing the familiar faces (the portrait of his ancestors') for the last time (77). It was not just for three weeks, may be for ever, He was sent out of his own home.

Coomy and Jal lived in his large seven room apartment *Chataae Felicity*, always blaming him for the death of their mother, thirty years ago in a accident along with his love Lucy. Even the days he spent at his home Coomy had made his life miserable with her rules. "There were rules regarding his meals, his clothes, his dentures, his use of the radiogram, even on keeping the door open or locked, she was plaguing him with the rules to govern every aspect of his shrunken life" (4). When he suffered a minor injury while crossing the road, he had to face a tirade which was more painful than the injury. "Tomorrow you'll complete seventy nine years and still you don't act responsibly. No appreciation for me or Jal, or the things we do for you".

Nariman tried to maintain a dignified silence, then spoke "Listen to me, in my youth my parents controlled me and destroyed those years. Thanks to them, I married your mother and wrecked my middle ages. Now you want to torment my old age, I won't allow this (8). The arrival of the handicapped and invalid Nariman creates conflict, constant bickering complaints emotional upheavals and tension. '*The Pleasant Villa*" as Roxana's apartment was called as turns into an '*Unpleasant Villa*'. Yezad does not like it, he feels it is an intrusion, mostly because it is difficult for him to manage with his small incomes Yezad kept thinking to the days ahead. "The morning stress, the over crowding, the smelly front room all would continue. And providing for one person, meant a shortfall of 25% in Roxana's food envelope. Not to mention things like soap and dhobi" (161).

"No he refuses to believe it. His very life the one he had been leading till a few months ago had been kidnapped. Roxana's family had stolen his peace and contentment. And till he could regain, he would have to face the squalor within the four walls, in this place which used to be his sanctum from the brutal city" (269), He shouts at Roxana. "Let me tell you. I didn't marry you for the honour and privilege of nursing your father." (206). "Dry toast again, thanks to your family". But Roxana reminds him, Yezad's family in a way made it clear they would not allow them to stay in their house. Nariman had felt they should not start a new life in quarrel and bitterness, he spent all his money in buying them the flat in which they were living now. Nariman would have been the master with a fat bank balance, if he had not made the big sacrifice to see them happy and settled. To Jal too she says," Nariman may be a problem now, but after your father died, you were fed and clothed thanks to him". (165). More over fifteen years ago when he had brought them their flat, he went to the landlord and put his flat-*Chateau Felicity* jointly in the name of Jal and Coomy.

Nariman had forgotten that he had given away *Chateau Felicity* and had no legal claim on it. " It was many years ago. The poor children, hurt so much already. I think I may have signed something". (167) only to get compliment from Yezad "very foolish of you". Nariman raised his hand "whatever Yezad wants to say, I deserve to hear. You are suffering on account of my short sightedness. It was stupid of me to sign over the flat....,. To so many classes I taught *Lear* learning nothing myself. What kind of teacher is that, as foolish at the end of his life, as at the beginning (169). But Roxana proves the dear Cordelia, who tells Yezad "I'll tell you right now-if you force pappa out you may as well throw me out at the same time". When Yezad angered that Coomy and Jal had conspired not to take Nariman back he says, Nothing doing. If they play this game so will we. They kick him into our house, we will find a way to kick him back into theirs. Roxana says, "Pappa is not a football- I won't behave like that". You don't have to, I'll do it said Yezad (168).

Three weeks had passed, and Jal felt its time they brought their father back to *Chateau Felicity* but Coomy was determined , "I can't have him back, please don't force me".

Finding all excuses about the inconvenience and pain it would cause her father being shifted from here to *Felicity* then to the hospital for X-ray, and again back home, suddenly the plaster from his fractured leg, gave her a brilliant idea, " Is'nt it amazing that the plaster from his own legs gave me the answer to our problem". But it is so deceitful, so destructive, so extreme said Jal trying to dissuade her (.151). He later in anger tells her, " You are kicking him out of his own flat. Coomy watched him in silence, because Jal's anger was a rare thing. "What was the point" he screamed...... "Why did you force me to get Edul's hammer? Why did you destroy the ceilings? You should have told them weeks ago we were kicking Pappa out!"

"I want Pappa to stay away but in a civilized manner" She said quietly "without fighting or ruining family relationships". "Why should you care? Family does not matter to you! You keep nursing your bittemess instead of nursing Pappa. I've begged you for thirty years to let it go to forgive, to look for peace." ..... Look around to see what you have achieved." She looked up saw the dust and plaster everywhere. She raised her eyes and saw the mutilated ceiling. She shuddered. For the first time since the hammer blows her heart sank. "Don't turn away. You said you wanted a ruin, so feast your eyes. Happy ruined house, and ruined relations with our one and only sister "(166).

There is much sadness in the suffering of a man in his old age. Nariman a retired English Professor, the patriarch of a small discordant family, beset by disease is haunted by the memories of the past, and deeply moved to see his love Lucy who had been disowned by her family, working as an Ayah at Arjanis, who knew very well about Lucy and Nariman's relationship. Years ago Mr. Arjani had been sued by Nariman's father for libel, and this was the reprisal. Arjani bragged to everyone in *Chateau Felicity*-"hiring Vakeel's girlfriend as an ayah was a fine revenge".

Nariman asked her if it was money he was ready to help her, or find an office job for her, but her answer flabbergasted Nariman smiling she said, "Don't you understand why I am here? You are on the third floor, I am on the ground floor, and it comforts me". Nariman watched Lucy's struggle in carrying the bags of all the three children under her care. It tore his heart, very soon he joined her to help her carry. Mr Arjani boasted that he had now two servants for the price of one. All this caused tension in the family, to her question his answer was "I care for her only as a human being", he felt it was an honourable way of conducting himself. But soon Yasmin and her children decided to put an end to it by locking all his clothes, left him only with his towel, and finally one day he walked out to meet Lucy with only his towel wrapped. But the whole love episode met a tragic end. Lucy appeared insane, standing on the parapet wall of the terrace of the building. She was singing it was finally when he went there, he joined the singing coaxed her to come down. This continued. Yasmin called this an excuse, she burned every letter, cards, notes of Lucy, but what she could not burn was Lucy in Nariman's memory. One evening when Lucy was once again on the terrace Yasmin forced Nariman to stay back, she would go to the terrace and end the drama. Lucy did not seem to react, Yasmin grabbed Lucy's shoulder but backing away she fell and, Yasmin in trying to pull her, was pulled down- so ended the sad story of Lucy.

Nariman found no peace in his home, nor in his married life, nor with his children where he was often subjected to humiliation. The story takes a slow languorous pace, looking on the troubled family- the whole of India seen in this tiny apartment. Rohinton Mistry has given something absolutely poignant a bitter sweet slice of life in its most ordinary setting.

Though Yezad resents, through Nariman's stay his sons Murad and Jehanger gain much knowledge by their grandfather's presence, and help in taking care of him, even helping him with his bedpan and urinal in their mother's absence. They do their best to keep him entertained. Roxana experiences dire emotional stress looking after her father in a small apartment and limited budget. However at crucial moments of a mental collapse they provide her the necessary strength. Murad and Jehangir make the required adjustment for peaceful co-existence under the same roof. Murad walks to the school to save money, Jehangir takes bribes as homework monitor to help his mother and finally Yezad too ashamed of his behavior succumbs to a overflowing emotion within him and helps in taking care. For the first time he realizes how much Roxana much have endured with no help. How did Roxana do it by herself, wondered Yezad, the lifting, the plastic sheet, the bedpan day after day? And instead of praising her strength what had he done but rage and complain. She had needed his help and all he could spew were his pathetic harangues. The morning, evening and night, his bitter frustrations countered by her patience..... Overcome with shame, he barely noticed the smell of the bedpan, his fastidious nose uncomplaining. "I don't know how you manage alone", said Yezad. "It isn't hard with practice I've got used to it". Not practice, he thought, love and devotion must be some truth in the saying that love could move mountains, it certainly let Roxana lift her fathers (374-75).

Rohinton Mistry shows that there is still lurking in man, a sense of goodness and there is poetic justice too. Jal confesses to Yezad and Roxana, after Coomy's death, "I was the one, I borrowed Edul's hammer climbed on the stool and broke the plaster". But Roxana and Yezad knew Jal too well to believe it, they knew it had to be Coomy. "But why did she want to do that.....to avoid looking after Pappa (383)." Jal's blunt honesty left them mute. But poetic justice was done. Coomy and Edul were killed by the falling beam. To atone, for what they had done Jal invites them to stay at *Chateau Felicity,* which now carried a new brass plate with the owners name in the following order.

Mr. & Mrs Yezad Chenoy
Mr, Jal Contractor
Mr. Nariman Vakeel

Pleasant Villa was sold for forty lakhs, and all the money except the expenditure on renovation and repairs was handed over to Yezad. Nariman the King Lear, as predicted by him returned to his own home, where later he breathes his last.

Family Matters deals with fragile relationships at the microscopic level, but it also has u macroscopic level of humanity. The microscopic Parsi family is miniature. India and macro humanity rendered artistically into a finely woven tale of universal import. Rohinton Mistry shows through the title of the novel the theme family matters, and also stresses that family matters especially in one's old age. Family ties are important in a nuclear state, but it is also the co-existence of the whole society that matters. Survival in the concrete jungle of life is possible only with the support of others-life is give and share. Nariman is touched by the love and affection shown by Roxana, her children Murad and Jehangir and later by Yezad which makes him say "It's truly blessed to have such a family. It makes up for all deficiencies". Even Roxana's neighbour Daisy, who not only is ready to be of help whenever needed, but knowing that Nariman loves music comes to play for him, and promises to play 'One day when we were young', the favourite song of his and his beloved Lucy's when he could be nearing his end.

Mistry's characters are true to life in their ordinariness. The hidden poetry of their lives is beautiful in itself. In their own way they arc the heroes of contemporary India. In an age where heroism has disappeared even the survival battle of the dispossessed and deserted, victims of domestic violence, widows or retired man like Nariman, in an indifferent city/family assume epic proportion Nariman is valorized as a hero, the courage is just staying alive in the changing pattern of life as a result of globalization.

Tormented souls and humans with little social capabilities, their fate is decided by the vagaries of relations within family. Most of the characters appear claustrophobic trapped within the cloister of their unfilled dreams residing in caverns whose walls are decorated with images of hope. Dreams and ambitions are thwarted by the family, the characters are constrained by the affection that the family offers at a price-the price that they are expected to pay is conformity, which renders their dreams null and void and their subsequent lives miserable. Mistry depicts the sort of family love that grounds us to the world. It is wonderfully perceptive in its exploration of the complexities of family life. He has taken in his sweep through the life of Nariman the big question of death, family, the passing of time, the inevitability of loss, God, in a manner and style entirely his own. The greatness of the novel lies in its depiction of the human heart, in all its longing and imperfections and moments of tenderness, repentance and atonement.

The novel embodies a compassionate concern for degenerating human values globally, and how the solution for betterment and survival must be sought within the social framework. He tries to globalize the theme by painting a cosmic picture of humanity in a family, just as T.S. Eliot presents in *Gerontion,* the old man as a symbol of the decaying civilization.

References

India Today, July 16, 2007

Rohinton Mistry: *Family Matters,* Vintage International, New York, 2003. All quotes pertain to this edition.

13

Ameen Merchant: *Silent Raga*: A Silent Saga

Nominated for the Commonwealth Writers First Book Award Ameen Merchant's debut novel uses the raga, a traditional Indian musical form to explore the constraints patterns, improvisation in the plot and in the characters' lives. There is a musicality that permeates this exquisite debut novel. Right from the title, *The Silent Raga* the Tamil Mounaragam is more eloquent-to the way the chapters are structured after the various stages of the ragas performance in recital and the mellifluous prose they contain and in the way certain sentences or words are repeated as refrain, there is an inherent musicality about the enterprise. Ameen has said he does not play any musical instruments, nor was he schooled in the Indian classical music tradition, yet through a happy, almost inexplicable osmosis, he strikes the right chord throughout his tale of a musical prodigy and her sister and the complicated familial past they must put to rest.

Merchant effectively uses the framework of the raga to parallel the expectation and behavioural codes the sisters-Janaki and Mallika- had to follow. Music is the metaphor for the book as suggested in the title. The chapters are named after the various division of a raga, starting with the Alapana and then gliding away to Padam' and 'Varnam' followed by 'Ragam', 'Thallam', 'Pallavi' and finally culminating with 'Tillana' and 'Mangalam'. Though not a trained musician Merchant weaves the story around the musical notes in chapters also sa, re, ga, ma and so forth. While the rhythm of the story is completely in sync with the story, alternating between the past and present as in a 'tala', the Star of this silent raga is the 'Sahityam'.

There is something about books about India. It is as if the images and description of the place are uniquely strong and vivid in the mind of the reader. Light, sound, smell, the touch of India arises from the prose in *The Silent Raga,* It could all be a kind of tourist's indulgence - expect that one is hearing a voice of intimate familiarity with India. And beyond that the pretext and reason for the poetics: the musical scale which informs the whole book. That is inevitable because a major motivation and drive in the story is the making of Indian music.

If raga is a mysterious craft to most English speaking readers. *The Silent Raga's* emotional depth begins to suggest something of it as it moves along and we are touched and seduced by them. It is like being drawn into the ecstasy of musical rhythm, no scholarly knowledge or ability is needed other than knowing how to listen.

Merchant moved to Canada from Chennai in pursuit of a career in creative writing. *Silent Raga* talks about the nuances and flavours of Tamil Brahmin culture with an accuracy and palpability that is as close as real can be. One can smell the fragrance of the jasmine, the fried tingle of a fresh 'appalam' and sense the claustrophobia of a conservative and dominated household. As if in a self imposed exile from his dear Chennai and Southern Indian Tamil Brahmin sensibility, he is able to recollect with such fine eye for detail the entire Tamil Brahmin world view of light, sound and texture is in itself a victory to his creative ability and craftsmanship with words. On the art of 'kolam' Janaki draws, she has interesting explanations to offer.

"On some mornings it was anelaborate welcome to dawn, ambitious and full of snaking grandeur, and my hands would weave a tapestry of blooming flowers, and intertwined stars. I would grab fistful of "kolapodi" ......one, two, three and even four sometime.....and pour my heart into my masterpiece, my sublime welcome mat to the sun. And on other days, it was hurried note of dots and curves-a snappy perfunctory kiss of cordiality.....achieved with half the amount of powder. "The narrative structure is matched by sensual melodic language. Smells-fragrance-taste make the Madras home come alive. One inhales the intoxicating 'parijata' in summer bloom, feels the stickiness of the skin after a siesta, the physical allure of the places and scenes-the description is never overdone, but this seems to be a book which cannot resist the sensuality of India itself.

One is transported to tiny Sripuram and its tinier agraharam -the Brahmin colony where Janaki Venketakrisnan a gifted player on the veena, was brave enough to carve out her own personal identity. Language is the most significant part of the novel, which allowed the writer the ability to experience the book beyond the story. Skillfully evoking feeling and touching one beyond what is often expected in the genre of Indian Writing in English .Liberal use of Tamil words give the book its ethnic flavour. Ameen Merchant has retained many of the Tamil words and locutions of everyday speech, often because they cannot be easily translated. This does not reduce the pleasure of the non-Indian or non-Tamil readers for the meanings are readily apparent from the context. His spot on description of the rhythms and small touches of life and each task that comprises the quotidian routine transcends the humdrum and take them into the realism of the poetic. The remembrance of long forgotten sights, colour, custom, taste and texture is among the many pleasures of the book. Though, the novel is local and setting is culture specific, the story is universal in many ways-love, family loyalty, betrayal reconciliation are part of human culture-from Chennai to Montreal making it not a Silent Raga but an Equal Music. The fact that *The Silent Raga* was published in September 2007 and in October it was chosen as The Book of The Month by the *Canadian Living*

Magazine which itself speaks of its appeal beyond boundaries and beyond culture.

Silent Raga shows Merchant's rare insight into women's plight. Merchant's debut novel takes us into a world of women-a child playing hopscotch, a 'kolam 'drawing young woman , a sister mother, a second wife, an invalid woman, the worker woman caught in a bind, a gypsy-all kinds of women that make up India. The classical ragas are the chapters in a saga of humiliation, of love gone horribly wrong.

The narrative sound slowly and gracefully as Merchant depicts two Tamil Brahmin sisters Janaki and Mallika who are about to reunite after a decade of separation. The novel opens with Janaki revisiting painful memories on her return to Madras, where her sister and her now hospitalized father await. Janaki's return transports the story back to the time when both the sisters suffocated in the family home with their father after the death of their mother.

In confidant prose that resembles the rhythm and progression of an Indian raga. Merchant captures in rich details the world of these Brahmin women-a world restricted by caste and cultural rules. It is a story about the tradition that bind us and the sacrifices that one must make along the road to one's individual destinies. With sometimes too heavy hands, the narrative questions the place of Brahmin women in contemporary society. Like the progression of a raga, the song of the two sister's play out in episodes the way they confront their subjugation. Elegant and atmospheric, the sensitively written novel portrays two sisters trapped in loss and regret. Merchant slowly unfolding tale touchingly narrates the conflicting obligations to self and the family.

The novel takes us on a fictional journey into the world of the middle class Tamil speaking girls in Sripuram. The two sisters Janaki and Mallika live in a closed Brahmin colony. After the death of their mother in a bus accident, their father a puffed up bank functionary, decides to rearrange the family by pulling Janaki a 13 year old, out of school and sentencing her to a life of domestic drudgery Janaki is a talented veena player, her father allows her to continue her veena classes. Apart from music what interests her is the movies.

An early adulthood is thrust on Janaki, plucked from school she is dispatched to the kitchen to become the family cook, cleaning women plus a mother to Mallika her younger sister whom she dotes. As it is with millions of such girls she must live a life of servitude first in her father's home, then in her husbands without a murmur or a question.

Two great qualities of the novel is the vitality of character, smart and passionate ensnared, in a plot, that is full of the play of fate and reality, feeling as familiar as one's own life, however removed that life may be from one's own, A rhythmic current of narrative quickly sets in, a page turning curiosity develops, because the characterization is both rich and strange, yet not exotic. Merchant involves the readers in the narrative for suspense, mystery, complete catharsis-pity and fear. There is an intelligent, incisive scrutiny of multi-generational family relationship-female centered, somehow reminiscent of *Tamarind Men.* A reader gets easily identified whole heartedly with them. It is fascinating that Merchant populates the book predominantly with women. Men-the perpetrators, the oppressors, the aggressors and sometimes saviours-remain shadowy figures. Apart from three sympathetic characters one feels cold contempt for others and return to the women who are uniformly compelling. Women recognize that the world is ordered and run by the patriarchy. They do not rebel and ask their oppressors to go to hell. Feminism as it is known in the West, cannot be transplanted to South Asia and expected to be eagerly accepted, for most of the women themselves will not subscribe to it. Yet a few of them voice the struggle of the silent and most importantly their capacity to claim change like Janaki in the novel who living within a claustrophobic world that offers no opportunities for independence, prospect or hope claims her capacity or her desire to breakaway to realise her dream.

Painfully and repetitively Janaki and Mallika circle around the crescendo of the story. They talk about arranged marriages, their mother's weakness and the tragic fate of unwanted single woman, the haunting suicide of a childhood friend is a brutal reminder of the desperate state of women, whose only hope is matrimony. Meanwhile their aunt's manipulative ways illustrate the danger of becoming wedded to social structure.

The Silent Raga rises to the level of pain and poetry most notably when it tells the story of Janaki's best friend Kamala, who is left devasted at the altar, when the last of her family's dowry fails to clear and the groom's entourage beat a brutal and hasty retreat resulting in Kamala's suicide. Kamala's is the tragic silent raga that Janaki feels impelled to play. Giving voice to untold but common suffering is what Merchant tries to do in the novel. Merchant's sympathy for his two female protagonists is genuine and compelling Janaki realizes that tradition can ensnare only if subscribed to. Janaki uses her wit, uncanny survivor's instinct and the prediction made by the gipsy woman that the veena would be her salvation to forge her destiny. The prediction, the shocking suicide of Kamala, long suffering of interminable wedding negotiations from a long line of horrible but 'suitable suitors galvanize her into putting an escape plan into action She elopes with a Muslim Bollywood star Azgar, becomes his second wife, bears him twins and sinks into a life of luxury in Bombay. Her close confidante is her husband's first wife Zubeda-an infinitely wise, affectionate, understanding and patient wife, living out her life in a wheelchair after a skiing accident in Nepal.

Janaki's life as the second wife to one of the biggest stars in Bollywood is portrayed as staid, calm and mature. Her most compelling interests are still hers-veena performance and teaching. She is famous now in her own rights with a successful classical music academy run by her whose students are on the verge of international recognition. It took her ten years to re-invent herself. There are naturally the psychic scum of abruptly severed ties and the whiff of scandal.

With this act she removes herself from the strictures-social and familial. Her spectacular exit brings the eater-wanting Indian press to the family home for three nightmarish days, and thrusts Mallika into Janaki's previous domestic role of Cinderella. While Janaki dares to rage against arbitrary bondage Mallika becomes acquiescent in her gilded cage. Mallika, Janaki's 'Tangame' was 6 when her mother died, making Janaki 13 years old her surrogate mother. She was as intellectual as Janaki is passionate and artistic. Her idea of fun was reading Dickens, Charlotte Bronte and playing chess with her father hoping to take care of Janaki and her father in their old age. The sisters opposing paths are a reminder that there is room for variation even in the most confining rules. While Janaki revels in the dazzle of celebrity spotlight, Mallika gradually awakens out of her role as a dutiful daughter. She sets to follow her desire for education and an overpowering fulfilling job. Perhaps change was imminent. As the sisters reflect on their journey towards the end, two different yet equally important portraits of resilience emerge, the novel ends on a note of forgiveness and determination.

The skein of the narrative un-pool simultaneously like melody and harmony, while the one relates to the present, the other recounts the past which relies on memory for details. *Silent Raga* takes us on a journey which dips into the landscape of memory. It is in fact an exploration of time gone by and time revealed through a touching story that sounds very true. It is memory recollected in tranquility-in Canada-a nostalgic recollection which worked as a creative trigger. Recounting the genesis of the novel in an interview to Ranvir Shah, Merchant said.

> ".......there is a whole novel in the back of the story. Sometimes in the 1970s a Tamil novel was being serialized in a popular weekly. I read the first few pages of the opening chapter......my proficiency in Tamil was absolutely dismal and it took me hours to read just one page. I never read the novel beyond the first few pages. In 1977 when I returned to India after seven years in Canada those few pages came back in full memory to me. What I remembered of what I had read years ago, there was a character

> named Janaki, the older of the two running away. The author didn't give any explanation why Janaki left her family and I didn't know if she came back in the later part of the story, for I never read beyond those few pages. This bit became a constant nag at the back of my mind, and soon turned into an annoying obsession. I had to find out why Janaki left the family, and what happened to her."

I contacted the author in Chennai and asked her out to dinner. Halfway through the meal I mentioned her serialized novel in 1970s and asked her what happened to that character named Janaki She said she had no clue for the novel was not about Janaki but her younger sister and her struggle to become a writer. I was devastated, I asked her for a copy of her novel, and was told it was out of print. I hit all the second hand shops in the city in the hope of finding a copy. I didn't.

I went back to Canada and started to write what I thought might have happened to Janaki. Ratther naively I thought I would work Janaki out of my system in five pages.....she married an accountant and moved to Delhi, that sort of story was not to be it took me 400 plus pages to fully exorcise her.

The novel is not biographical but definitely remembered elements. I kept going back to all those smells and sights of my childhood in Chennai. I made all these things part of Janaki's life, and the more I lingered the more I discovered. It turned out to be one hell of a journey into the past, and 1 emerged richer for it.

As a writer one is constantly trying to achieve some semblance of authenticity ......my guide was my memory, and my mission was to be as truthful to it as possible......Fiction is what cements the unremembered past...."

The fact that Merchant has lived away and is able to recollect with such a fine eye for detail that the entire Tamilian Brahminic world comes alive with light, sound, color, fragrance and texture is a victory to his creative ability and craftsmanship. The narrative is finely balanced with a rich amount of lyrical imagery. The haste of curiosity is at odds with the desire to linger over the evocation of food, climate, air, the voice of the place, the 'parajata and jasmine' and the beautiful 'kolam' welcoming the dawn. Merchant is from an Agha Khan Muslim background and grown up in such a household deserves all praise for his ability to recount and recreate a reality of which he is not one. At a time when Islamicphobes abound this is a deeply heartening work of a writer who feels and writes, creates a world that *we* can almost touch-a world of the upper caste Tamil Brahmin agraharam which rarely finds expression in Indian English Writing the novel is a testimony to the communal harmony in Tamil Nadu and shows that marriages can be a happy one if there is understanding and mutual respect for each others feelings and talent.

In grafting this epic from Madras to Bombay Merchant draws on countless aspects of South Asia's impossibly rich culture-consumerism, fashion, Bollywood, Hinduism, Islam and especially cooking and music, both seen through the recurring image of a roaring fire, both creators and destroyers. Middle class Tamil Brahmin life of 1970s and 80s with all its celebrations, joys, drudgery and death is depicted so exquisitely that it makes one cry, laugh, clench with anger but one gets intimately acquainted with the sisters Janaki and Mallika two heroines of dignity and enduring love. The story segues in and out of their lives who living with unbearably difficult parents conjoin their fate in a story of sorrow, longing and yet deep in love and a fine gossamer of hope.

Being a silent raga, it speaks in the language of the reader whosoever or where so ever he or she be, making it an *Equal Music* where 'heard melody is sweet but unheard sweeter' and so is *The Silent Ragas*

In the '*Grecian urn*' Keats raises art to divine heights where it is symbolic of beauty. 'Beauty is truth and Truth Beauty' Ameen Merchant *Silent Raga* concludes where every note of Raga is nothing but symbolic of the supreme Siva

– Natraj " *Sa-* sarpa - the serpent round your neck my lord. In its skin we see our world reborn eternally.

Ri - Rundrakasha: The necklace of tears in your chest, my Lord. In every purple bead is our daily breath.

Ga : Ganga; the heavenly river in your wild hair, my Lord, the waters cleanse our world of sin.

Ma: Mriga, the deer you held in your hand, we realise that the world in just an illusion.

Pe-Pushpa- the lotus you dance an my Lord. That is our world at your feet.

Da-Damaru-the rattle drum of creation in your hand, my Lord. It is the music of our inner world.

Ni-Niskara, the crescent crown on your head, my Lord. In it we see the time of our world.

My Raga rises and dips and dances with the dappled gold of the waves

I am my song, and my song is the red of the sun." (p. 446-47).

References

1. Ameen Merchant: The *Silent Raga*: Harper collines, India, 2008.
2. Ranvir Shah: Interivew, Ameen Merchant, The Hindu' Literary Supplement, Sunday, April, 6, 2008.

14

Ayemenem: Arundhati Roy's Literary Stage

From Kanthapura and Malgudi to Ayemenem is traversing from Karnataka to Tamil Nadu to Kerala, just an overnight journey from Tamil Nadu but a passage of more than half a century. The period has undergone seachanges leaving behind the colonial period, entering into the golden era of Independence, moving from Gandhism to Communism to Naxalism, from the sedate Malgudi to turbulent Ayemenem, which, to quote Updike, represents "a vast, violent circling, driving, ridiculous, insane, unfeasible public turmoil of a nation."[1] In one bound Arundhati Roy's *The God of Small Things* ushers India into the "modernity of advanced civilization, the comity of neurosis". The story is about an Indian village, authentic India, but the sensibility is urban, Westernized and modern."[3] This debut novel is set in Ayemenem in the Central Kerala District of Kottayam where "you can feel against your skin the lush vines and grasses, smell the pickle mangoes and sweet banana jam, hear the children singing as their uncle's car carries them home...."[4]

The novel opens with a description of Ayemenem:

> May in Ayemenem *is a hot* brooding month. The days are long and humid. The river shrinks and the black

> crows gorge on bright mangoes, in still dustgreen trees. Red bananas ripen. Jackfruits burst. Dissolute bluebottles hum vacuously in the fruity air. Then they stun themselves against clear windowpanes and die, fatly baffled in the sun.
>
> But by the early June, the south-west monsoon breaks, and there are three months of wind and water with short spells of sharp glittering sunshine that thrilled the children snatch to play with. The countryside turns an immodest green. Boundaries blur as tapioca fences take root and bloom. Brick walls turn mossgreen, Pepper vines snake up electric poles: Wild creepers burst through laterite banks and spill across the flooded roads....[5]

The vivid scent, colour and smell of rural Kerala is conveyed through lines that see-saw in a rhythm of grand nursery rhyme. Ayemenem is the fictional world of *The* God *of Small Things* around which Arundhati Roy has woven the saga of a family which lives in *Ayemenem House*-a saga microscoped in time which irreversibly moves towards its doomed destiny. The novel is memorable not only because of its story of aching love and brutality but also in the way Ayemenem is conjured up into an etherial town when passion and fate collide. Arundhati tells the story by transfixing us to the souls of the characters and making Ayemenem on the banks of Meenachal river, sizzle with life. With the help of her innovative prose she has made the small State which houses the big world the centre stage of her literary universe.

R. Krishna Kumar writes that Arundhati Roy's Ayemenem is actually Aymanam, though its surroundings are all mixed up. Tourists from Germany and Europe have made unsuccessful enquires in Aymanam about *Ayemenem House*. There is no house by that name. Instead one should have asked for Kompanal School for the untouchables built by Arundhati's great grandfather. Across the road from the Kompanal School, along rows of rubber trees on one side and a couple of houses on the other, is a path that leads up to a locked gate. The Yellow house inside is called Pulliyampallil. According to Mary Roy, Arundhati's mother. "Mostly it is Pulliyampallil which the novel describes as Ayemenem House". The family occupying the house were Syrian Christians and were described as 'Anglophile' and upper caste, once feudal now makers of pickle and preserves.

The novel has a tight thematic unity, wonderfully condensed in the few sentences coming at the end of the first chapter. The book is, however, about a certain oppressive social structure that "actually began thousands of years ago in those days when Love Laws were made, the laws that lay down who should be loved. And how. And how much." These laws rest on some taboos. The most ancient and the most universal of them, according to Freud, is the taboo against incest. And in the specific practice of the Indian 'Love Laws' prohibition rests equally on the idea of purity and pollution, lineage and miscegenation that constitutes the caste society. The novel's main claim to transgression is that it ends by violating both these taboos. Velutha is the untouchable carpenter, the maker of little wonders in carved woods-'the God of Small Things" whose tempestuous sexual encounter with Ammu, the upper caste woman, towards the end of the novel violates all the Love Laws laid down by caste boundaries and ideas of propriety. Since the milieu is Syrian Christian, the moral righteousness of a Christian community sweeps through the book.

The novel reflects the social context of the late 60s and 70s at Ayemenem and its surroundings. Despite the fact that it was a Christian conclave, the caste system and problem of untouchability were deep rooted. Communities were sharply defined. Cynicism about religious beliefs were uppermost in the Christian heart even in the midget cook Kochu Maria. She wears her 'Kunukku' earrings, thick and gold, enduring the distension and splitting of her earlobes. How else would people know that despite her lowly job she was a Syrian Christian and not a Pelaya, Pulaya or a Paravan but a touchable upper caste Christian. "Christianity and Marxism," writes Arundhati Roy, have "seeped like tea from a teabag", making casuistic accommodation and never challenging the caste structure. Updike writes:' Occidental readers who imagined that untouchability was banished by Mahatma Gandhi will find the caste onus cruelly operative in 1969." As the novel puts it,

Mammachi remembered a time when Paravans were expected to crawl backwards with a broom sweeping away their footprints, so that Brahmins or Syrian Christians would not defile themselves by accidentally stepping into a Paravan's footprints. Paravans like other untouchables were not allowed to walk on public roads, not allowed to cover their bodies, not allowed to carry umbrellas. They had to put their hands over their mouths when they spoke to divert their polluted breath away from them whom they addressed (p. 74),

Because of the strong Christian presence at Ayemenem there was a feeling that Christianity would not recognize caste distinctions. But many who converted to escape the scourge of untouchability came to realize that they had jumped from the frying pan into the fire. The Syrian Christians were the 'Brahmin Christians'. "But they were made to have separate churches, separate services, and separate' priests. As a special favour they were given their own separate Pariah Bishop" (p. 74). Moreover, after the independence when they found the government benefits going to reserved classes, they felt "It was little like having to sweep your footprint without a broom or worse, not being allowed to leave a footprint at all" (p. 74).

There was a genuine fear of Communism in the Christian community at Ayemenem, which formed twenty percent of the population. "The Syrian Christians were, by and large, the wealthy estate owning feudal lords for whom comnıunism represented a fate worse than death" (p. 66), for the newest most militant faction of CPI (M)-the Naxali ties-had organized peasants into fighting cadres, seized lands, expelled owners, had spread across the country and struck terror. In Kerala "they breathed a plume of excitement and fear into the already frightened air". There was fear, ignorance and dislike. But they did not take any defensive action. They remained too frightened of it. In the novel the family car is stranded in the midst of a Communist demonstration, and the fear felt by the women is vividly described. The anti-Communism of the novel's political ideology is disconcerting but not surprising. It was common among the radical section of the cosmopolitan intelligensia,

Ayemenem and Kottayam and the surrounding regions form the country where the Syrian Christian community was for over a century trying to find a place for itself, the Syrian Christians who populated the region in large numbers, found quite unlikely allies in their quest in the English language and the Empire. Geographically insulated from the larger context of the national movement, the community tried to master the language and send its children to proper English medium colleges at Madras-like the characters in the book. All this finds resonance in the book which caricatures the Western world her characters inhabit. Arundhati lived, recounts Mary Roy in a small home and rather a modern house. Next door was the ancestral house, spooky, huge, too large to maintain, but to Arundhati, it must have been an exciting place full of whispering ancestors, and it forms the backdrop to her tale.

Arundhati mystifies autobiographical elements to evoke simple joys and huge terrors of her own childhood in her beloved maternal grandmother's home, where traditionally a married daughter finds a place only in sufferance-a perception that echoes through the novel like a dirge. Roy's own experience as much as her mother's struggle and combative personality provide the basis for the character of Ammu representing "the infinite tenderness of motherhood and the reckless rage of a suicide bomber". The Rhodes scholar George Isaac-Chacko in the novel,-when questioned, said "Here you are dealing with a writer's perception. Those are her perception. But practically all the characters are real, sometimes she modifies and combines. She has described me (Chacko) very vividly. And Ammu is Mary Roy every bit. There is no Sophie Mol; it is fiction." Arundhati has changed names and details here and there. For example.

Thomas Mathew is based on "somebody we know. He Is not a Police Officer but somebody she does not like."

The *Ayemenem House* lights up and shadows the family. It is a beloved presence, a house aloof with its, contained passions, its well concealed secrets, encircled by natural beauty, its isolation broken by a child's eye view Of varied creatures, animals, insects, fish and life around the Meenachal flowing with "coconut trees that bent into it and watched with coconut eyes, the boats slide by." Though Mammachi presides over the family and Paradise Pickle, the late Pappachi glowers over the family. An Imperial entomologist and wife-beater, he until the day he died, "even in the stifling Ayemenem heat wore a well pressed three-piece suit and his gold pocket watch". He was an embittered man deprived of credit for the discovery of a rare species of moth.

The main action of the book takes place on a day in December 1969, and concerns the drowning of Sophie Mol, the daughter of Ammu's brother, Chacko, and his estranged English wife. On a holiday from England, Sophie Mol spends the fortnight of her stay in a rapture of discovery. Together with her cousins, Estha and Rahel, she explores the lush waterways and meadows of Kerala. She also encounters Velutha, the despised paravan with whom the twins' mother has an intense, doomed and yet ultimately life-enchanting affair. Central to the story is that one 'unchristian' act of Ammu, the divorced daughter of the *Ayemenem House,* who surrenders to the wild allure of Velutha, the dark skinned outcaste. Her two children, Estha and Rahel, are mute witnesses to the tumult in the House and the death of Sophie Mol.

Passion and madness run wild in the *Ayemenem House,* but it is to this home, with the steep, tiled roof grown mossy with age, that they all return to live out their lives: Chacko comes back to his bottling plant for the pickles; Ammu returns with daughter Rahel after the marriage is over, Estha, her son, 'returned' a young man cocooned in silence; and Rahel returns from America. The *Ayemenem House* is the antidote to the diaspora. In putting together the story with tragic grandeur Arundhati Roy rips apart the Christian edifice of morals and values and scoffs at the social norms. In fact, in the *Ayemenem House* every rule is broken.

Although Ayemenem, an expanded village inhabited by the propertied class, in the site of her quest, tradition, family and indeed society are illumined. Roy has stretched language and imagination to recreate the fulfilled yet anguished world at Ayemenem, simple and poignant, alive with terms of endearment, folk songs and snatches of conversation in Malayalam. She is an entirely home-grown writer. Her 'desi' feets are shown not only in her liberal use of Malayalam but also in her description of Kerala. Rushdie seems to err in commenting that Roy's India is any place. "After Menon Marath Kerala gets spectacular representation in Indian fiction In English" through Roy, writes Ranga Rao. Twisting the language to suit her own story telling, she has managed to make the whole world a stage for Ayemenem and its people. She has remarkable talent to invent a new idiom and vocabulary to tell the story of seemingly remote people- Mammachi, Pappachi, Sophie Mol, Kochu Maria, Estha, Rahel, Ammu, Velutha and many others who would keep on popping out once in a while to remind us of some eternal truth. *The God of Small Things* is like the wind that blows across the Meenachal river. It has the sweet fragrance of authenticity, tranquility and triumph.

"A single shelf of good European library is worth the native literature," wrote Macaulay In 1835. The Indian writers like Arundhatl Roy of this century have enacted a thrilling revenge on Macaulay. They have shattered Western prejudices against Indian English Writing and have opened a new world of opportunities.

References

1. John Updike, "Mother Tongue: Subduing the Language of the Colonizer", *The New Yorker,* 23 and 30 June 1997.
2. Ranga Rao, "Book(er) of the Year". The Hindu. Literary Review, 23 and 27 November 1997.

3. *Ibid.*
4. Parveen Swami, "A Tiger Woodsian debut", Frontline, 8 August 1997. p. 101.
5. Arundhati Roy, The God *of Small Things,* New Delhi: Indialnk, 1997, p. 1.
6. R. Krishna Kumar, "Ayemenem and Aymanam". *Frontline,* 8 August 1997. p. 109.
7. Swami, *Frontline,* 8 August 1997, p. 103.
8. Aijaz Ah mad, "Reading Arundhati Roy Politically", *Frontline.* 8 August 1997, p. 107.
9. Swami, *Frontline, 8* August 1997, p. 103.
10. Jason Cowley, "Why We Chose Arundhati," 27 October 1997. p. 28.

15

Jhumpa Lahiri: *Interpreter of Maladies*: A Voice Across the Seas

Jhumpa Lahiri's collection of nine stories, *Interpreter of Maladies* has swept through the United States, winning several admirers and awards, finally arriving at the shores of the prestigious 2000 Pulitzer award. Throughout her academic career, her short stories found recognition. She received the Transatlantic Review Award from the Hens field Foundation Louisiana Review Award for short fiction as well as the O'Henry Award for the best American short stories Following the publication of three of her short stories in 'The New Yorker' in 1998, her reputation was established among critics and readers alike. The 'New Yorker' Summer Fiction issue of 1999 included Lahiri among the "20 best young fiction writers of America" and described her as a writer of uncommon elegance and poise who with *Interpreter of Maladies* has made a precocious debut" When *Interpreter of Maladies* was awarded the Pulitzer prize she spoke about her progression from a scholar to a Pulitzer Prize winning writer that it has given her what "all writers look forward to time money and encouragement. The book had given her just the right amount of all three... Its, wonderful, and its an honour and I feel so humbled and grateful" she stated in an interview with Vibhuti Patel.

Composed of nine stories *Interpreter of Maladies* details the experiences of both first and second generation Indian immigrants. The themes range from emotional struggle of love to immigrants battling new worlds. Born in London in 1967, and raised in Rhodes Island, Lahiri, the daughter of Bengali parents, her heritage and culture are influenced by both India and U.S.A. This multi cultural life style plays a central theme in many of her stories. Using a variety of characters Lahiri gives life in these stories to the feeling of alienation, loneliness and hope that so often mark the immigrants experience. The longing and loss that often comes across the life of immigrants. Its part of what her parents and their friends and she experience. "I always say that I feel that I've inherited a sense of that loss from my parents because it was so palpable all the time while I was growing up, the sense of what my parents had sacrificed in moving to the U.SA, and in so many ways" in an interview with Elizabeth Farnsworth.

Her stories weave into the lives of second generation Indians and their struggle with relationships inter-personal communication and the challenges experienced by immigrants living in a world away from the familiar warmth and constant company of family friends and neighbours in the home they left behind Her stories are emotional chess games focusing largely on the subtleties of the characters internal processing. With their fragile emotional states, hesitant gesture and tight rope walking on the brink of psychological raptures. Characters are coaxed into exploring assorted facets of morality alienation and dysfunction.

The central focus of much of the modern writing is its presentation of society as too remote from or even hostile to the individual for the latter to feel any sense of belonging. In such a situation where the individual is seen as culturally or sometimes linguistically enstranged the whole question of a social cultural and individual identity become unattainable ideals. The strength of the modern literary imagination lies in the evocation of individual predicament in terms of alienation exile or quests for identity. One of the most pertinent statement on the crisis of identity facing the Commonwealth man, which is true of the immigrant as well, as was made by an emancipated negro, Froad, in the West Indian novel *Other Leopards* by Dean Williams "Between Europe and Africa there is this desert. How fitting. Between the white and black this (colour) divide. You cannot cross it, where you, are you remain the same. You change, you becomes in a way, yourself mulato....looking both ways (208-09).

Lahiri addresses the issue of identity and displacement which many struggle with due to their multi cultural upbringing and environment. "The question of identity especially for those who are culturally displaced is a difficult one" She stated in one of her interviews. She belonged to that vast unruly and fascinating metropolis. Calcutta, she visited it frequently but to quote her" I don't experience the country as a tourist, I don't experience as a native either, it is a middle position." (1) *Interpreter of Maladies* is largely about Indians settled abroad negotiating between two cultures, with varying degrees of success, their attitudes, their concern and their life style. Most of them come to the U.S in search of freedom and opportunities. In the story : *Mr. Prizada comes to Dine*" the narrator captures this sentiment she says that her mother knew "she was assured a safe life, and easy life, a fine education and every opportunity in the States. "But what awaits' them and what they experience at every step in life is the other side of midnight. Her characters share a wide range of background. Indians in India, Indians abroad. Indians involved with Americans. The stories can be classified into two groups-those that take place in India and the one's set in America. The stories concern predominantly with social preoccupation-love, marriages, break down of marriages extra marital affairs, old age, illness, poverty and death,

One is impressed by the breath of her scope with studies that vacillates between the motherland and the U.S between the present and not so distant past. One of her strength is her unique socio-cultural positioning as a second generation North American female with enough of South Asian Cultural to reach out to and potentially capture a global audience. It is all the more interesting because it is not common for a young South/Asian female living in U.S. to write about the conflict of culture, modern relationship and memories of a home left behind. The stories were particularly appreciated by South Asians who understood what the stories were about.

Inter-related to the theme of quest for identity, is the problem of alienation in its many forms emotional, sexual, spiritual and physical. There is a constant conflict between the modern liberal, permissive society one goes to and the traditional upbringing where freedom of right and choice have been taken for granted about work and relationship, Lahtri's narratives are about things we are all familiar with and can relate to.

In an interview to *Newsweek International* she states. "The characters I am drawn to all face some barrier of communication. I like to write about people who think in a way they fully cannot express". This idea form the basis of the story *'Interpreter of Maladies'*, - which is the title of the book as well-The story of a tour guide for an Indian American family Apart from being a tourist guide, his main occupation is acting as an interpreter for patient who need to communicate with their doctors. The study was inspired by a person, she knew in real life who was working as an interpreter in a doctor's office in Brooklyne, Massachusetts. He was interpreting for a doctor who had a number of Russian patents, And he was fluent in both English and Russian-four years after this incident, she used it as the plot of a story that corresponded to that phrase. It has more often than not suggested that Lahiris' with her moving tales is in fact herself an interpreter of maladies, and since most of the stories are about Indian American, she has also been called as Interpreter of Indian Americans.

Stories like "*The Blessed House*" "*Sexy*" and "*A Temporary*

Matter" exemplify universal lesson in love and the individual struggle to overcome change and insecurities with relationship stories primarily dwell on relationships and relationship, she maintains preclude no morality. Lahiri shows an astute understanding of human relationships.

Reviewers were entranced not only by her characters but also by the setting and locales of her stories, Many of her stories have a heady Calcutta flavor. Her parents never consciously sat down and told things about India. "They sort of correctly did so, assured that I would learn things just by the virtue of being their child, I think it has always been important to them to maintain strong social ties with Indians, living abroad and visiting India" (2) In an interview to *Newsweek International* she stated "Its easy to set a story anywhere if you get a good book and get some basic street names and some descriptions, but for me, yes I am indebted to my travels to India for several of the stories(3) India is the place where my parents are from a place I visited frequently for extended time and formed relationship with people and with my relationship and felt a tie over time even though it was a sort of parenthesis in my life."(4).

Her stories though set in America are scattered with detail of traditional Indian name, food, cooking and wardrobe giving character and flavour to her stories. One is transfixed by her talent for depicting people and landscape as illustrated in "*The Third Continent* or "*The Treatment of Bibi Haidar*" "At her insistence we showed her our photo album embossed with designs of butterflies she poured over the snapshots that chronicled the ceremony, butter poured in fires, garlands exchanged, vermillion painted fish, trays of shell and silver coins (160).

By incorporating Indian tradition into her work Lahiri created tales of cultural differences, Most of the characters live a simultaneous existence in two cultures. They are Indians living in America, or India or their lover, neighbours or landlords. With informed cultural chilling she shapes them into sharply sculpted personalities. The stories though set abroad are ensured of exquisite attention to exotic details which never appear overbearing or exaggerated but inherent. While the stories draw upon Indian culture and heritage the theme of communication relationship and culture prove to be universal. Though of different ages, nationalities and religion the character demonstrate the universality of experiences. *'The Third Continent'* a descriptive and emotional piece that relays the isolation of immigrants travelling to a foreign country. Through the eyes of an young Indian the readers experience the cultural difference between Indian, London and U.S. Through the interaction between the young man and his aging landlady one comes to learn that despite difference, all people have the same basic need for communication-compassion and understanding. Lahiris recognition is a sign that multi culturalism has truly arrived in the U.S.

Jhumpa Lahiri, was the first South Asian to be awarded the Pulitzer Prize. The Summer fiction issue of *The New Yorker* focusing on the future of American fiction included Lahiri among the "the 20 best under 40 young fiction writers in America", Reviewers, described her narrative voice as elegant and gentle, but the award coming to her so early in her literary career, and that too for her debut work has subjected her to ruthless criticism. Some of the adverse views have been "She may be competent but by no way unique, despite all her gift for story telling, vivid characterization Sensuous description and minute attention to detail, the reader is left with a nagging sense of impoverishment. Thanks to the thin and poverty stricken material that she handles. The range of her experience woefully limited and absence of depth".

There is no special perception or angle of vision that distinguish these stories as a new writer's. The characters are the stereotypes of the diaspora..... None of them have a sense or perception either of their lives or other or of their country of adoption, that gives them an individual existent. Going to extent of adding "Literary awards are literally given away on a platter at regular intervals to authors of questionable merit" and the greatest objection appears to be that the very first publication has received America's highest literary award. Jhumpa Lahiri was not a beginner she did not enter the, literary field with 'forced fingers rude." The lure of writing visited her in Primary school at age of seven. She began co-authoring books" with her classmates. Moreover she was well qualified to be a writer with Master's Degree in English literature, Creative Writing Comparative Literature and a Ph.D, in Renaissance studies. Her talent was long recognized. She had already/won the O'Henry Award, The Best American, Short Stories Transatlantic Review Award and fiction prize from the Louisville Review. The Pulitzer naturally followed, Strangely enough when V.S Naipul was awarded the Nobel prize after a long literary career, it was described as a "curse to creativity" and now the debut one as' to an author of questionable merit.

Jhumpa Lahiris, own reaction was' :I'm still in a bit of a shock, it was so unexpected. It came from nowhere, and its so big and so wonderful and so frtghtening"......its an honour and feel so humbled and grateful."' But Katherine Roth, opines that Lahiri should not be surprised. It turns out her book of short, stories mainly about Indian immigrants in New England gave proof to a trend which editors and publishers have noticed, that short stories are already enjoying new popularity. They point to the run away success of story collections such as Lorrie Moore's Birds of America, Melisa Banks *The Girls' Guide to Hunting and Fishing,* Nathan Englanders *For the Relief of Unbearable Urges* and Annie Proulx's *Close Range.*

Stuart Applebaum spokesman of Random House states that the company is producing more short story collections and added "The short story is enjoying a very real acceptance now both among book sellers, critics, readers and certainly the publisher who serves them[10]. Former Director of publication Paul Bogards at Knoft states that sales have been picking up for story collection and Lahiris prize the genre new prestige. One sees it as a renaissance for short and Lahiri has created a strong foundation for its flowering.

References

1. Hindustan Times: April 14, p. 24.
2. Times of India: April 12, 2000 p. 1.
3. Interview with Arun Agniar for Magazine : July 28, 99.
4. Times of India: April; 12, 2000 p. 1.
5. Jhumpa Lahiri : Interpreter of Maladies " The Treatment of Halder Bibi" p. 60.
6. Ragini Ramachnadran Jhumpa Lahiri's Interpreter of Maladies, " Journal of Indian writing in English: Vol. 29, Jan, 2001, No. 1 p. 50.
7. Vimla Rao: Prognosis: Hopeful Interpreter of Maladies, Journal of Indian Writing in English Vol. 29.: July 2001. No. 2 p. 31.
8. Khathering Roth " A Renaissance for short stores, Hindi.: April 2000.
9. Ibid.
10. Ibid.

16

Jhumpa Lahiri: *Unaccustomed Earth*

Given the sensitiveness that has been awakened in the country since 9/11, thrusting lifelong citizens under suspicion having foreign sounding names and subjecting visitors to the indignity of being fingerprinted. But one cannot forget that America was once conceived in a spirit of openness, as a land where people could build new identities, grounded in the present and future and not in the past. The dream despite current fears has been made real to a great extent. The fact that America is still a place where the rest of the world comes to reinvent itself-accepting with excitement and anxiety and the necessity of leaving behind the constrictions and comforts of distant customs-is the underlying theme of Jhumpa Lahiri's new collection of stories-*Unaccustomed Earth*-which expands upon Lahiri's epigraph, a metaphysical passage from Nathaniel Hawthorne's *The Custom House* which suggests that transplanting people into new soil makes them hardier and more flourishing. Hawthorne argues if men and women "strike their roots into unaccustomed earth "human fortunes may be improved. It is apt and rich metaphor for the transformation that Lahiri oversees in the pages, in which two generations of Bengali immigrants to America-the new comers and their hyphenated children-struggle to build normal secure lives. Lahiri does not accept Hawthorne's notion-as test it.-does transplanting strengthen the plant or does it produce mixed outcome? As in *Interpreter of Maladies* and her novel *Namesake* Lahiri , who is of Bengali descent, born in London, raised in Rhodes Island, living in Brooklyn that the place to which you feel the strongest attachment isn't the country you are tied to by birth or blood, it is the place that allows you to become yourself. This place she indicates may be any place in any map.

Following her thoughtful first novel *The Namesake* (2003) Lahiri returns to the short story form that won her the Pulitzer. The tight arc of the story is perfect for Lahiri's keen sense of life's abrupt and painful changes. This collection of eight superbly grafted powerful stories and haunting triptych of tales covers familiar grounds interpreting the challenges of cultural uncertainties in that quiet meditative way that marked the first book *Interpreter of Maladies.* As in *Interpreter* much of the story is situated in USA flitting to India now and then The exception lies at the end of the book in a trilogy interconnected stories 'Hema and Kaushik', when the geography expands to include Italy and Thailand and the structure expands to take the intriguing form of a novella. The stories in *Unaccustomed Earth* are longer and considerably more complex than *Interpreter*. They allow Lahiri the space to digress, to dwell ever more closely on every day life and experience, and to probe the cultural ambiguities that lie between encounter and assimilation. While *Interpreter* focused on Bengali immigrant in America her novel *Namesake* looked towards the second generation; the young people forced to navigate between two worlds and *Unaccustomed Earth* continues that exploration with greater success.

The stories in the collection don't significantly diverge from her previous writings, either in theme or in tone or style they are but moving renditions of Indian immigrants torn between being American and being Indian. Their American reared children who straddle two cultures and belong to neither, too used to freedom to accept the rituals and customs at home, yet too steeped in tradition to embrace

Americans more fully. The Indian born parents want the American Dream for their children -name brand schools, a prestigious job. a roomy house in the suburb -but they are cautious about the pitfalls of life in this alien land, and isolated by their difficulties with language and custom. Their children too are often emotional outsiders, having grown up translating the mysteries of the US to their relatives they arc fluent navigators of both Bengali and American culture but completely at home in neither They always experience themselves as standing slightly apart given more to melancholic observation than whole hearted participation.

Like the many children of the immigrants Lahiri's characters are acutely aware of their parent's expectations, they get into a good school, medical or engineering degrees, marry somebody from a good Bengali family. Deftly explicating the emotional arithmetic of her character's families she shows how these children learn to sidestep or even defy their parent's wishes. She also shows how haunted they remain by the burden of their families' dream and their awareness of their role in the generational process of Americanization Their parents often seen so exhausted coping with the difficulties of surviving in a strange new world that talk about self-fulfillment or depression or happiness seems utterly irrelevant to them. They are strangely pragmatic and unsentimental about their marriages, their work, and the hardships of daily life. As in her earlier works Lahiri writes about the dislocation of upwardly mobile Bengali Americans, *Unaccustomed Earth* is full of lost old world parents and the shaky modernist marriage that can't quiet replace them and the perplexing hidden forces that pull families asunder. Lahiri's stories of exile, identity, disappointment and maturation evinces a certain mastery that has few contemporary equals

Lahiri delves into the souls of indelible characters struggling with displacement, guilt, and fear as they try to find a balance between the solace and suffocation of tradition, and the terror and excitement of the future into which they are being thrust. Using memory, dialogue, visual detail, sharp and sympathetic observation she captures the family dynamics. The spectrum of people and experience is vast but she has managed to scrape through and unveil the most basic and intrinsic nature of man it is almost like the characters are holding a mirror close to their heart for one to gaze into. Where there are juvenile crushes there is mature love, with a traditional Bengali mother with vermillion and red bordered saris there is her Westernized counterpart appreciating modern architecture and Johnnie Walker. A lonely aged father who tours the world thrives alongside another who chooses to marry a girl half his age. Gleeful nights and warm smiles co-exist with tears and dismal memories. Where there is the promise of companionship there is inevitability of death. Enormous accomplishments and thumping failures, relationships that wither under one roof and inseparable ties form over thousands of miles away, unspoken commitments and startling betrayals all bound together. Each of the stories in her new collection *Unaccustomed Earth* focus on the small moments of human relationship that somehow encapsulates everything that is both right and wrong between husbands and wives, mother and daughters, father and sons. Threaded through the book are themes of mothers and daughters, particularly deceased mothers. In *Unaccustomed Earth* Ruma's mother had died unexpectedly during a gallbladder surgery. In *'Hema and Kaushik'* Kaushik's mother dies of breast cancer -a death that has hallowed the family. In all cases mothers and wives are marginalized figures, often in arranged marriages that are not entirely happy. Daughters are to be watched and worried over, lest they act indecently or end up being unmarried. None of the stories are precisely hopeful, each is underpinned by a strong undercurrent of longing and each seem to focus on fuzzy grey areas where a heart is broken. Although most of the characters are Indians or Indian Americans, that fact seems barely relevant. While adjusting to foreign culture and relating to foreign parents, are important elements of the book, the human relationship it describes is universal.

In *Unaccustomed Earth* Lahiri rethreads her accustomed

territory -the Bengali connection -returns to the familiar fever and fret of NRI - especially Bengalis-lives-lived, realized or apprehended. Lahiri's chronicling of Bengali immigrants stretching and straining between in- cohesive summer holidays in Calcutta and emotionally ragged existence on adopted alien soil, is continually bathed in the wretchedness of being caught between homes and world, memories and desires, parents and selves, roots and routes, past and future. Reading them one seems to agree with Brinda Bose how relentlessly cheerless Lahiri's expatriate Bengalis are? Whatever happened to the famed Bengali joie de vivre that inspires Rabindra Sangeet even under the grey rainy chilly New England? *Unaccustomed Earth* consisting of five long stories and a short novella in three chapters is a predictable variation on Lahiri's now patented melancholic figure of the Bengali diaspora. A Chekhovian sense of loss blows through these new stories and Lahiri's understanding of the missed connections that plague her husbands and wives, parents, children, friends and lovers. *Unaccustomed Earth* the title story of the collection dramatizes the divide between immigrant parents and their American raised children. It is the first of the several scathing inquiry into the lack of deep understanding and trust in marriage between a Bengali and a non-Bengali.

Unaccustomed Earth contains shades of emotions, decisions, choices, dilemmas, values and relationships-lost, forgotten, treasured or cherished- which are all woven together in the most poignant tales about people who are straddled between Calcutta and the US. Yet the stories, their characters, their journeys and their feelings have such a similarity to all our lives that it is impossible to remain objective and estranged. Through these 333 pages one feels everything- elated, crestfallen, cheerful, desolate, compassionate, contemptuous, guilty and blessed. It is a kaleidoscope of emotions and its effect is profound. An eye for detail, car for dialogue and command of family dynamic distinguish this collection.

The last three overlapping tales in the volume *'Once in a Life Time'*, *'Year's End'* and *'Going Ashore'* tell a single story about a Bengali American girl and a Bengali American boy whose crisscrossing lives make a poignant ballad of love, loss and death. The children of Bengali immigrants Hema and Kaushik have known each other since childhood their parents had met in the 60s as homesick graduate students in Massachusetts. Each has experienced the wrenching divisions of Bengali and American cultures, Kaushik's family move back to Calcutta losing contact with Hema's parents, but reappear in America several years later asking Hema's parents if they might stay with them until they find a suitable house. Giving in to both old friendship and Bengali custom they have no hesitation in welcoming them. Hema's parents are shocked by their 'changed' old friends who wear American clothes, smoke freely at home, have an open bottle of Johnnie Walker nearly all time. Kaushik mother Parul has changed dramatically; spending money on perfumes, cosmetics, dresses, fussing over the right house. Hema's parents are perplexed to find that "Bombay had made them more American than Cambridge had." In *'Once in a Lifetime'* the first in the trilogy, Hema recalls the awkward winter when she was 13, and developed a crush both for the teenager Kaushik and his casually glamorous mother. Kaushik is oblivious to her school girl antics and is preoccupied with his mother's deteriorating health and later tells her that his mother was dying of breast cancer. The family had returned to America at Parul's behest, she wanted to die alone far from her hovering Indian family. In the second story *'The Year's End'* Kaushik picks up from Hema, describing his mother's agonizing death from cancer, his grief over her death and his rage at his father's hasty marriage to an old fashioned Indian widow half his age with two daughters and his abrupt departure from their lives. His holiday home is disastrous leaving him permanently distanced from his father. His life long passion for photography becomes his life work traveling to different parts of the globe-to war zones, famine, disaster caused by natural calamities and devastation of all forms. Hema meanwhile becomes a professor, a Latin scholar who after a long unhappy love affair impulsively decides for a traditional arranged marriage to a Hindu Punjabi Navin she likes Navin's traditionalism and the respect he shows to women "It touched her at 37 to be treated like a teenager. Though she is conscious of the 'deadncss' of the proposed partnership, she convinces herself that the relationship will endow her life with a sense of certainly and direction. Then against all odds Hema and Kaushik run into each other in Rome on the eve of her departure for her wedding, in *'Going Ashore'* and thread the stories together. Here after all are two people who truly know one another. Hema is the only person Kaushik knows who knew his mother, who truly understands his life. They embark on an intense passionate affair. And yet it is an affair that conclude not with a happy fairy tale ending but with an operatic denouncement that speak of missed opportunities and avoidable grief, things unsaid keep them apart. The story ends on an elegiac and haunting power of tragedy

Though both are accomplished cosmopolitan adults what brings them together are the memories of the vanished provincial world they once shared. Their relationship closely resembles Gogol Ganguly's misguided marriage to a childhood acquaintance in *Namesake.* Though the characters construct sophisticated new identities for themselves they are irresistibly drawn to the reassuring tradition they've abandoned. The past exerts a wicked pull, even when one is grown up and least expecting it. Though the novella 'Hema and Kaushik' comprises of three stories *'Once in a Lifetime' 'Year's End'* and *'Going Ashore'* they are linked. Hema narrating the first, narrating to Kaushik the second by Kaushik, responding to Hema, and the third bringing them together. Lahiri appears at her best when she surfaces for a brief and tempestuous love among the ruins of Rome in this three part novella which wraps up the collection, ft is as though when she unmoors herself from the safety, boredom and horror of what she knows most intimately discovers the beauty of the unaccustomed earth outside her familiar zone" the most searing of human passion cannot ultimately be borne and can only be tsunami swept into the sea" as Brinda Bose writes.

The stories in the collection while they reflect another culture, they also edge into our lives resulting in universal experience filled with emotional connections that cross borders. The generational conflicts, the waves of admiration, competition and criticism that flow between two families could occur between any Smiths or Taylors, anywhere and the fight for connection between Hema and Kaushik-as children and as adults -replay the tussle that has gone on ever since men and women lived in caves.

References

1. Jumpa Lahiri: *Unaccustomed Earth.*
2. Brinda Bose : 'Life is Else where' India Today May 3 p. 79.
3. Mukund Padmanabhan ;'Roots Migration and Exile "The Hindu, Sunday 23 March, 2008.

17

Kiran Desai: *Inheritance of Loss A Study in Insurgency*

Kiran Desai created literary history by becoming the youngest woman to win the Man Booker Prize 2006. At 35, Desai walked away with the most prestigious award for English fiction. Her father Ashwin Desai had predicted way back in January when the first publication *of Inheritance of Loss* was out "I predict this book will win the Booker Prize. I have read the works of most of the Booker prize winners through the years and this has everything for a Booker Prize". Described as a radiant, funny moving family saga" it is a sprawling novel that runs from the Himalayas to New York city, taking in Mark Spencer knickers, Grand Marnier and Nepalese insurgents and offers an insightful and often humorous commentary on multiculturalism and post colonial society.

Before Kiran Desai won the Man Booker Prize, her first novel *Hullaballo in the Guava Orchard* (1999), had won the Betty Trask award for a first novel, It received an enthusiastic commendation from India's first Booker winner Salman Rushdie for "the first dynasty of modern Indian fiction" with an excerpt finding its way in Rushdie's *Anthology of Indian Writing, Mirror Work* and the *New Yorkers Fiction* issue, though the novel did not really make waves.

The second novel *Inheritance of Loss* comes after a painful seven years apprenticeship, living in Brooklyn, often going off to visit her mother, Anita Desai in upstate New York or travel with her and writing part of it in Kalimpong. Hermione Lee, the chairman of the judges, explained the reason for picking up *Inheritance of Loss* from a list of substantial novel by big names he explained the philosophy behind this unusual but, interesting short-list "A distinctive original voice, an audacious imagination that takes reader to undiscovered countries of the mind, a strong power of story telling and a historical truthfulness. A magnificent novel of human breath and wisdom, comic tenderness and powerful political acuteness" the epigraph from Jorge Luis Borger sets the tone for a novel concerned with the struggles of little people, a novel of troubled times. "They speak of humanity/ my humanity is in feeling we are all voices of that same poverty."

The novel opens with a teenager, Sai, the child of a Guajarati mother and Zoroastrian father who is part of Indo-Russian space collaboration in the last days of the old Soviet State; they are killed in an accident, leaving Sai an orphan. She comes to live with her Cambridge Anglophile grandfather, a retired judge in Kalimpong, on the Indian side of the Himalayas. When Sai comes to live with her embittered grandfather, it is the cook who gives her the warmth that he is unables to give his son, Biju. Biju the cook's son is an illegal immigrant far away in New York, drifting from one temporary job to another in the underworld of restaurant kitchen.

Back in Kalimpong, Sai is romantically involved with her maths tutor, Gyan, the descendant of a Nepali Gurkha mercenary but he eventually recoils from her obvious privilege and falls in with a group of ethnic Nepalese insurgents. Meanwhile in the world outside Cho Oye, a growing insurgency is threatening to explode across the hill.

The novel explores with intimacy and insight, about every contemporary international issues- globalization, multiculturalism, economic inequality, fundamentalism and terrorist violence. It is about the many faces of oppression, the paradoxes of growth and injustices and communities struggling with the violence and pain of change. Though intercut with many overlapping themes the most arresting one is the Gorkhaland movement. Kiran Desai distinguishes herself as one of the few novelists, or perhaps the only one to have deeply and sensitively explored this problem as a theme in Indian English Writing, hence this deserves to be treated exclusively as a distinct feature of the novel. A movement which started as a request to be recognized as a minority, along with the others, like-the Anglo-Indians degenerated into a demand for a separate state of Gorkhaland. Its origin, which gradually shaped into a dangerous, disintegrating virulent, violent nightmarish terrorist movements, akin to the Naxalbari, and how Kiran Desai has successfully woven it into the texture of the novel as an integral part of it makes an interesting study.

The Gorakhaland movement has its roots in the demand of Gorkhas living in Darjeeling district and Duars of West Bengal and the Gorkhas in India and abroad, though they see India as their motherland, want a separate state for themselves within the constitutional frame work of India. The ethnic identity Gorkha comes from the district of Gorkha within Nepal which was the Kingdom of the "hilly billy Napoleon" Prithvi Narayan Shah. The Gorkhaland National liberation Front (GNLF) which led the movement disrupted the district with massive violence between 1986-89. The Gorkhaland movements distinguished Darjeeling Gorkhas form Nepalis residing in* India form Nepali speaking Indian citizen from other parts of the country and Sikkim. Gorkhaland supporters therefore preferred to call the Gorkha language as Gorkhali rather than Nepali. The 1981 census of India, respecting their sentiments called the language Gorkhali/Nepali. However, when the Eighth Schedule of the constitution was amended in 1992, to make it a Scheduled Language, the terms Nepali alone was used. In 1986 the GNFL, having failed to obtain a separate administrative identity from the parliament, again demanded a separate state of Gorkhaland. The party's leader Subash Ghising headed a demonstration that turned violent, which was sternly repressed by the state government. The disturbance almost shut down the districts mainstay of tea, tourism and timber. After two years of fighting and the loss of more than thousand lives, the government of West Bengal and the Centre finally agreed on an autonomous hill district in July 1988. GNFL gave up the demand for a separate state and in August the Darjeeling Gorkha Hill Council came into being with Ghising as chairman. The Council had authority over economic development programs education and culture.

However difficulties arose over the panchayat election. Ghising wanted the Hill Council excluded from the national law on panchayat election. The then Prime Minister Rajiv Gandhi heeding to this request introduced a constitutional amendment in 1989 to exclude Darjeeling Gorkha Hill Council along with several other northeast hill states and region - Nagaland, Mizoram, and the hill regions of Manipur but it was not passed. However in 1992 parliament passed the Seventy Third Amendments which showed a serious commitment to the idea of local self government-by panchayat, the amendment excluded all the hill areas except Darjeeling. Ghising felt this was the doing of West Bengal and threatened to revive militant agitation for a Gorakhland State he also said that GNLF would boycott the village panchayat election. A large portion of his party, refused to accept the boycott and split off under the leadership of Madan Tamang to form the all India Gorkha League which won a sizable number of panchayat seats. In August 1995 Sherpa complained to the state government that Ghising had misused hill council fund and West Bengal Chief Minister Jyoti Basu promised to investigate. In May 2005 the organization organized a huge rally to revive the dormant demand for a separate state but failed to go forward on the issue since then.

Inheritance of Loss opens with a newspaper reporting of February'1986, which sets the tone of the novel.

> In Kalimpong high in the North Eastern Himalayas-where they lived the retired Judge and his cook, Sai and Mutt (the Dog) there was a report of new dissatisfaction in the hills, gathering insurgency, men and guns. It was the Indian Nepalese this time, fed up with being treated like the minority in a place where they were in a majority. They wanted their own country or at least their own state in which to manage their own affairs.... (pg. 9)

A group of young boys under twenty had entered the judge's house. They had come through the forest on foot. Dressed in a universal guerilla fashion - leather jacket, khaki pant, bandana and a gun, they were looking for anything they could find for an impoverished movement with a raging army, Kukri, sickles, axes, kitchen, knives spade any kind of firearm. They had come for the judge's hunting rifles. But took every thing that they could lay hand on-drinks cigarettes, ordered tea and snacks, defecated in the toilets, left it stinking and forced the judge and other to say "Jai Gorakha" "Gorkhaland for Gorkhas"

In the beginning nobody had paid much attention to the events in the hill side. The new posters in the market were referring to old discontent the slogans scratched and painted on the side of government offices and shops. "We are stateless" "it is better to die than live like slaves" "We are constitutionally tortured. Return our land from Bengal" (p-126) the call was repeated along the road at the top of Ringkingpong Hill one saw LIBERATION scrawled across the water works.

For a while nobody knew which way it would go, it was dismissed as nothing more serious than the usual handful of student agitators but then one day fifty member of the youth wing of GNLF gathered to swear on oath at Mahakaldara to fight to death for the formation of a homeland-Gorkhaland. They marched down the streets of Darjeeling took a turn round the market and the mall. They shouted "Gorkhaland for Gorkhas we are the Liberation

Army" they waved their unsheathed kukris, sliced the fierce blades, though the tender mist under the watery sun Quiet suddenly; everyone was using the word INSURGENCY.

There were some like Noni (Nomita) who lived with her sister Lola (Lolita) in a rose covered cottage named 'Mon Ami'. When Lola's husband died, Noni who was spinster came to live with her sister. Noni felt the Nepalese had a point "First they were thrown out of Assam and then Meghalaya, and then there's the King of Bhutan growling against ...." They have been here, most of them, several generations why shouldn't Nepali be taught in Schools.

> Lola: Because on that basis they can start statehood demands... the Neps have been encouraged by the Sikhs and their Khalistan by ULFA, NEFA, PLA, Jharkhand, Bodoland Gorkhaland, Tripura, Mizoram, Manipal, Kashmir, Punjab, Assam..... You saw the letter they sent to the Queen of England Gorbachev and Reagan? Apartheid genocide colonial subjugation, vivisected Nepal. When did Darjeeling and Kalimpong belong to Nepal Darjeeling, in fact was annexed from Sikkim and Kalimpong from Bhutan" (128-29)

Historically, Darjeeling and its surrounding terai areas formed a part of the then Kirat Kingdom called Bijaypur, after the disintegration of Bijaypur kingdom it fell to Sikkim and Bhutan. From 1790-1816, Darjeeling and its immediate contiguous area were overrun by the Gorkhas of Nepal After the Anglo-Nepalese War (1814-1815) the Treaty of Sigauli was signed between the Gorkhas and the East India company, Darjeeling was wrestled back from the Gorkhas of Nepal by the Britishers and handed back to Sikkim, after the Treaty of Tataliya. Col, Llyod became the representative of the East India Company to Darjeeling, during his time Darjeeling was annexed into the British India Empire. The map of Darjeeling came into existence after the induction of Kalimpong and Duars area after the Anglo-Bhutanese War 1864. And Indira Gandhi as Noni says had maneuvered a plebiscite and all the Nepalese who had flooded Sikkim voted against the King. Indiahad swallowed the jewel colored kingdom.

Noni, Lola and Mr. Sen feel it was all due to Nehru, the biggest mistake he made was "this state making" under this rule any group of idiots could stand up demanding a new state and get it "Mrs. Sen to whom Pakistan and Muslim were favorites topics continued" Pakistan, there is the problem first heart attack to our county, no, that has never been healed"

Lola: Illegal immigration it's an issue of a porous border is what' you can't tell one from the other. Indian Nepali from Nepali Nepal, and then the way these Neps multiply.

Mrs. Sen: Like Muslims (129)

Meanwhile Gyan and Sai's romance flourished and the political trouble continued to remain in the background for them. Gyan asked Sai about her family, but she felt uncertain about what she should say, because she thought if she told him about the Space Program, he might feel inferior and ashamed hence she said "My parents eloped and nobody spoke to them again they died in Russia where my father was a scientist (141). But his own family story also led overseas, he told Sai quite proudly. They had more in common than they thought.

In 1800, Gyan's ancestors had left their village in Nepal and arrived in Darjeeling, lured by promises of a work in a tea plantation. By and by came the Imperial Army measuring potential soldiers in village all over the hills. Gyan's great grand father had been chosen, they were attracted by the comfort and money provided by the army. So they swore allegiance to the crown, and off he went the beginning of over a hundred year of family commitment to the wars of the English.

The family had since invested their money in school teaching and Gyan's father taught in a tea plantation school beyond Darjeeling but for all they had done, what did they get?

"In 1947, when the British left granting India her freedom,

granting the Muslims Pakistan granting special provisions for the scheduled castes and tribes leaving everything taken care of, brothers and sisters-

Except us EXCEPT US- The Nepalese of India, we are laborers on the tea plantation, coolies dragging heavy loads, soldiers. Are we allowed to become doctors and government workers, owners of the tea plantation? No! We are kept at the level of servants we fought on behalf of the British for two hundred years. We fought in World War I we went to East Africa to Egypt to the Persian Gulf. We were moved from here to there as it suited them. We fought in the World War II in Europe, Syria Persia, Malaya and Burma. Where would they be without the courage of our people. We are still fighting for them... we are soldiers, loyal, brave. India or England they never had cause to doubt our loyalty. In the war with Pakistan we fought our former comrades on other side of the border. How our spirits cried. But we are Gorkhas. We are soldiers... And have we been rewarded. Have we been given compensation? Are we given respect? No. They spit on us".

In our country, the country we fight for, we are treated like slaves. Everyday the lorries' leave bearing away our forests sold by foreigners-to fill the pocket of foreigners. Our stones are carried to build their houses and cities we are laborers, working barefoot in all weather, thin as sticks, as they sit fat in the manager's houses with their fat wives, with their fat bank account, and their fat children going abroad we must fight brothers and sisters to manage our own affairs. We must unite under the banner of the GNLF GORKHA NATIONAL LIBERATION FRONT... This is our motherland where we were born, where our parents were born. We will run our own affairs in our own language. If necessary, we will wash our bloody kukris in the mother waters of the Teesta. Jai Gorkhas. Some drew blood from their thumb with their kukris to write a poster demanding Gorkhaland in blood. Brave Gorkha soldiers protecting Indian please quit the army at once. For when you retire you will be treated as a foreigner" (159-60)

The men were shouting they meant what they were saying; they felt a lack of justice. Gyan who had listened to it felt a moment of shame remembering his tea parties with Sai, the cheese toast, queen cakes from the baker. He voiced an adamant opinion that the Gorkha movement take the harshest possible route. So in the excitement of the moment, he told of the guns, the well stocked kitchen, the liquors in the cabinet, the lack of phone and there being nobody to call for help, all about the judges house Cho Oyu.

A few weeks after the robbery at Cho Oyu, a program of action was drawn.

Roads blocks to bring economic activities to a stand still and to prevent the trees of the hills, the boulders of the rivers valley's from leaving the plains. All vehicles would be stopped.

Black Flag day on April 13

A seventy two hours strike in May. No national celebration. No republic day. Independence Day or Gandhi's Birthday.

Boycott election with the slogan "We will not stay in other people's state of West Bengal.

Burning of Indo-Nepal treaty of 1950

Nepal! or not, everyone was required to contribute funds, to purchase calendars and cassettes tapes of speeches made by Ghising, the top GNLF in Darjeeling and Pradhan the top man in Kalimpong. It was requested that every family send a representative to every procession and also to show up at the burning of the Indo-Nepal Treaty. If they did not they would know... (191 -93)

The Gymkhana club taken over by the GNLF who camped in the ballroom and the skating ring

As Lola, Noni Father Booty, Uncle Potty was leaving Glenary after a lunch, they met the procession, and in it they saw Gyan, who refused to recognize Sai.

During their visit to the Teesta Valley renowned for its butterflies Fr. Booty caught a snap of butterfly on a cable of bridge but since photography was strictly prohibited on the bridge and Fr. Booty was caught by the guard. The police did not take his words of butterfly; he was taken to task, booked. He was found to be residing in India illegally, his property snatched, and he was asked to leave Kalimpong were he had lived for 45 years.

A series of strike kept business closed, every one were terrorized to keep their shutters down. The conditions were worsening. No tourist arrived from Calcutta, no visitor with their riches, nobody came to the hotels, nor the company guest houses, children were withdrawn from boarding schools as parents reads with horror of the hills being disturbed by separatist rebels and guerilla tactics. No gas, or kerosene, no water, no electricity because the electricity department had been burned down.

Apart from looting, the worse was yet to come, forcibly occupying the land as Lola's and Noni's was- going to the Pradhan was useless, because you would only be ridiculed and humiliated as Lola was. It made her feel that Gorkha's were not good people, were mercenaries that's what they were. Pay them and they are loyal to whatever.

The incidents of horror grew, through the changing season, through winter and flowery spring, summer then rain and winter again. Roads were closed, there was curfew every night and Kalimpong was trapped in its own madness. The GNLF boys had burnt down government rest houses, Circuit house. Men trembled at home for fear of being picked up, being tortured on any kind of flimsy excuse.

Kalimpong was transformed into a ghost town, the wind tumbling around the melancholy streets, garbage flying by unhindered.

What sounded like an ethnic nationalist, movement became largely as an opportunity to vent one's rage and frustration "Old hatreds are endlessly retrievable because they are pure because the grief of the past was gone. Just the fury remained distilled librating" "The half educated uprooted men like Gyan gravitate to the first available political cause in search for a better way. He recoils from Sai's obvious privilege and falls in with the ethnic Nepalese insurgent.

At "Cho-Oye" Mutt was kidnapped, and Biju, who had returned from America, was looted - his baggage, his savings, even the dress he was wearing, worst of all his pride.

In the meanwhile in the aftermath of the parade, the police had been reinforced and were hunting down the GNFL boys, combing remote hamlets, trying to weed out Gorkhaland supporter from the Marxist from the Congress supporters, from those who didn't care either way. They raided tea gardens which were closing down after the attacks by rebels. While the residents were shocked by violence, they were also surprised by the mundaneness of it all. Discovered the extent of perversity that the heart is capable of as they sat at home with nothing to do, and found that it was possible faced with the stench of unimaginable evil, for a human beings to be absorbed by the problem of a missing socks, return, once again to the pressing matter of what to eat. There they were, the most common place of them, these quite mismatched with the larger than life question , caught up in the mythic battles of pasts vs present justice vs injustice - the most ordinary swept up in extraordinary hatred, because extraordinary hatred was after all a common place event

Although the novel is set in 1980s a time of turbulence and change, the judge came from a generation for whom identities are fixed, he is referred through most of the novel as 'the judge', his cook as 'the cook' It is only in the judges memories of his painful students years, in a racist colonial England, that he is referred to by his name Jemubhai Patel

The novel originally was 1,500 pages but in its final shape cut down to 300 page Even in its present form there is an overflowing richness in its description- a leak in the toilet, playing hanky to a the cook hissing softly to himself as he takes in the soup tureen, the hiccupping back drain at the Queen of Tarts bakery-as they vividly evoke both the misty mountains atmosphere of Kalimpong and the rat infested underbelly of New York.

Kiran Desai's has not been an inheritance of loss but an inheritance of literary gain, She has been lucky inheriting form V.S. Naipaul and Rushdie especially in her exploration of post colonial chaos and despair and R. K. Narayan. Her winning on 10th October coincide with the birth centenary of R. K. Narayana. Her first book *Hullabaloo in a Guava Orchard* set in a small town features a likeable cast of characters who could have wandered' down South into Narayana's territory and felt entirely at home. But in her second novel also with ordinary eccentric character muddling along in a small hill station in North Eastern Himalayan town beside a struggling immigrant trying to make his way in the kitchen of New York restaurant that really pays homage to Narayan's traditions of gentle and humane story telling. More than anything there is a common Chekhovian sensibility running through the novel of both writers- delicate stories that unfold in evocative natural setting that are imbued with a gentle concern for ordinary people caught in a changing world. The greatest literary inheritance came from her mother Anita Desai about whom she writes "was written in her company and in her wisdom and kindness" especially during the writing of *Inheritance of Loss* "She was not only there to support me, but she was the only one who understood me and my turmoil" and befittingly the book is dedicated "to my mother with so much love"

Anita Desai's novel *Fire on the Mountain* (1977) has a close resemblance to *Inheritance of Loss.* Anita Desai in her novel dwells into the mind of an embittered old woman who retreats into an ancient house in Kasauli, deliberately disconnected from a world she despises, till a great grand daughter shows up In Kiran Desai's novel too a crusty old judge retires to a home in Kalimpong preferring the company of his dog Mutt and his cook to the exclusion of all other till a grand daughter arrives and disturbs this carefully constructed isolation.

Too close for comfort and comparison it must have been delicate and different for Kiran Desai to maintain safe distance from her mother's work, while cherishing security and intimacy it must also have provided her. When asked if Kiran's material were different from hers Anita Desai replied

"No we mostly used the same material". And it is natural given their shared lives, it must be tough for two gifted persons to carve out their own identities and individual voices It must be terrible-the inevitable comparisons and the avoidable rivalries-seen from Kiran's perspective and her's Occupying the same space with a living legend working in silence knowing too that the other is hard at it, right above you. Kiran has been a witness to her mother creative impulse all her life she has lived and breathed the loneliness that is a writer's fate but now that Kiran's Desai has won, she is bound to be the toast of the literary world and she will have her future carved out in the hullabaloo.

Though Kiran Desai has the fortune of and is aware of her literacy inheritance specially her mother Anita Desai,V. S. Naipaul Salman Rushdie and the foundling father of Indian English fiction R. K. Narayan she has her original way of taking it forward as Hermione Lee said "she seems to jump on these tradition and create something which is absolutely of its own. The book is movingly strong in its humanity and I thing that in the end is why it won.

There is an accumulation of wisdom in its sweet half stories and fragments, composed of broken paragraph and sighing musical sentences the novel hints at a lot but never says everything- forcing us to reflect on the aching turns of sub-continental history, the painful, creation and recreation of borders and the endless cycles of oppression endured by the poor and dispossessed. While the future shines brightly for those who are more privileged.

Reference

Kiran Desai: Inheritance of Loss, Penguin Delhi, 2006 (all quotes from the book pertain to this edition.

18

Arvind Adiga: *White Tiger*— Another Slumdog Millionaire

The Booker for 35 year old Chennai born Arvind Adiga's novel *White Tiger* is yet another big win for India's literary writing. It is the biggest and most visible literary prize the British bestow on a writer from any of the Commonwealth countries every year. In little over a three decade three Indians have prevailed over the competition to bring home the award. But the year's award has been the most controversial; the choice seems to have run into passionate opposition. It was felt that the book was selected and won all round praise not for it's literary but mostly for its political and economic documentation. Adiga too considers this book as his political mission "The book is an attempt to relegate India in a political and economic context ....traveling along the Ganges, this fabled river, and seeing conditions along It for the first time, it got me thinking about India in a new way".

The chairman of the panel of judges called it an 'angry book' praised it for the way it gives expression to the underclass anger which the privileged ignore. *White Tiger* takes the form of a series of letters addressed to the Chinese Prime Minister Wen Jiabo, by Balram Halwai the Bangalore business man, who is the self styled 'white tiger' of the title. Bangalore is the Silicon Valley of the sub-continent, and on the eve of a state visit by the Chinese Prime Minister. Halwai -the entrepreneur wishes to impart some truths about the New India "out of respect for the love of liberty shown by the Chinese people, and also in the belief that the future of the world lies with the yellow man and the brown man, that our erstwhile master, the white has wasted himself through buggery, mobile usage and abuse"(6)And also that he may not be fooled by any false picture painted by the politicians he may meet about India

"India is two countries in one: an India of Light and an India of Darkness

The ocean brings light to my country. Every place on the map of India near to the ocean is well off. But the river brings darkness to India -the black river

The black river is the Ganges beloved of the sarees and spices tourist image of India. No; Mr. Jiabao, I urge you not to dip in the Ganges, unless you want your mouth to be full of faeces, straw, soggy parts of human bodies buffalo carrion and several kinds of industrial acid (14-15)

White Tiger paints a vivid and disturbing picture of life in the strikingly different culture that comprises modern India. The country is growing to be a great economic power, yet a vast number of its inhabitants have little to show for prosperity. The conflict created by that reality propels this riveting tale.

Balram is the narrator and anti-hero. We learn of Balram's life through the letters he writes sitting in his 150 square feet office in Bangalore. Balram begins at the very bottom without so much as a name. His family called him Munna. Later, it was his school master who gave him his name 'Balram' and the local official his date of birth, to steal his vote. His mother died of T.B. even before she could name him. His father, a rickshaw-puller, too died of T.B.

Balram is born in grinding poverty in that portion of India which he calls the 'Darkness'. He is a bright student nicknamed the 'White Tiger' for an animal that appears only once in a generation, still by the accident of his birth it appears he's sentenced to a near subsistence level in his native village, where raw sewage courses through the streets and the residents are at the mercy of venal landlords. Balram describes his family life in the darkness a region deep in the heartland marked by medieval hardships, where brutal landlords hold sway. Children are pulled out of school into indentured servitude and elections are routinely bought and sold. In his village, everybody is beholden to one of the four landlords. If you want to grow anything, you have to pay money to one person; if you want to graze you have to pay money to another. If you want to use the roads, to make money as a rickshaw-puller, you paid 10% of the earning to the third. Finally, the fourth owns the water. If you want to fish or use the water for ferrying goods you pay him.

Balram's family is forced to borrow money to pay for his cousin's dowry; so he had to leave school and work in a teashop. But, he is destined for greater things and his grandmother came up with six hundred rupees so that he may learn driving. And, when he seeks to be employed as a driver, luckily he happened to be in the landlord's compound, where the youngest son, Ashok, had returned from America, and he needed a driver, he found Balram just the person who would fulfill his needs.

Balram is expected to be more than a driver. It turns out that he has also to cook, clean and, in short, do whatever his master desired him to do. When his master moves to Delhi, he also accompanies him. And while he drives him around the capital, he observes his master bribing parliamentarians and various political fixers to ensure that his family business survives. Balram in his driver's seat sees nothing, but witnesses it all. His long climb out of the darkness of poverty begins then. Though bullied, uneducated, underprivileged, coming after shocking deprivation from the vast rural hinterland in which 70% of our national population still lives, which Aadiga calls 'Darkness'. Balram with his grit, cunningness, resourcefulness and driven by a consuming ambition to escape into the bright light of the big city, in which all that he has been denied exists, finds his dreams fulfilled when he is taken by his master to Delhi. The city is a revelation. As he drives his master to shopping malls and call-centers, he becomes increasingly aware of the immense wealth and opportunity around him. At first, the novel appears to be a straight forward tale, though given a dazzling twist by the narrator's sharp and satirical eye for the realities of life and the changes that "See this country, in its days of greatness, when it was the richest nation on earth, was like a zoo. A clean, well kept, orderly zoo. Everyone in his place, everyone happy. Goldsmiths here, cowherds here, land lords there. The man called a Halwai made sweets. The man called a cowherd tended cows. The untouchables cleaned faeces. To sum up in the old days there was one thousand castes and destinies in India. These days there are just two castes. Men with big bellies and men with small bellies. And only two destinies, eat or get eaten up". (65) But as the narrative draws it darkens. For the 'White Tiger' stands at the opposite end of the spectrum of representation of poverty from these images of doe-eyed children that dominate the electronic media - that sentimentalize poverty and even suggest that there may be something ennobling about it. Halwais lesson in *White Tiger* is that poverty creates monsters and he himself is just such a monster.

Adiga with an imagery brings the theme into focus, as Balram arrives in the city as a driver says, "with their tinted windows up, the car of the rich go like dark eggs down the roads of Delhi. Every now and then, the egg will crack open- wherein a woman's hand, dazzling with gold bangles stretches out of the open window, flings an empty mineral water bottle on to the road-and then the window goes up and the egg is resealed.

The life of the poor, however, is very different. "Go to old Delhi ... and look at the way they keep in the market place. Hundreds of pale hens and bright roosters stuffed tightly into wire mesh cages. They see the organ of their brothers lying around them. Yet they do not rebel. They do not get out of the coop. The very same thing is done with the human beings in the country". (85)

Balram" s voice is seductive and his observations are

acute, laced both with a sardonic wit and a trace of sadness as he expresses the inescapable truth that the benefit of India's remarkable economic success are not dispersed fairly. His depiction of life is what he calls 'The Rooster Coop' in which millions of Indians arc destined to live short, miserable lives, hardened by poverty and disease, is shocking in its brutal frankness.

White Tiger is a penetrating piece of social commentary attuned to the inequalities that persist despite India's new prosperity over the past couple of years. In the current free market love fest to which India has been invited, the country boasted a GDP growth of 9%. inequality is a word that has been successfully air-brushed out of existence. Yet what docs an economic miracle mean when even a casual acquaintance with India shows that a large number live in abject shocking poverty-Who exactly is benefiting from this growth"? the Telegraph wrote in its review. Everywhere, everyday India (old) limps, coughs, splutters, one of every six Indian continues to live in the shadow of insurgency, farmers with little access to irrigation and devastated by failing crops continue to commit suicide. Further, 300 million remain unsure of where their next meal would come from.

Adiga presents an indomitable central character, Balram, and an India bristling with economic possibilities, competing loyalties and class struggle. It echoes a saga of resistance and oppression. Adiga presents the unique modern Indian dilemma. Intense family loyalties and a culture of servitude clash with the unfulfilled promise of democracy. The rich live like kings in a shiny new world where servants are expected to serve even prison sentence for crimes committed by their masters. Through Balram, Adiga shows the absolute devotion of the servant class. "Never before in human history have so few owned so much to so many-you can put the key of his emancipation in a man's hand and he will throw it back at you with a curse". (95) At one point, Balram asks the Prime Minister why he thinks the servants arc so loyal to their masters. Why don't they demand a raise, threaten them with the police or at least stand up to the masters when they outnumber by at least a thousand to one. Balram calls it the 'Rooster Coop Syndrome" In the market in New Delhi, hens and roosters are stuffed into a wire cage where they spend their days pecking and fighting with each other just to breathe. According to Balram, it's the same for the poor in India. They are too busy fighting among each other for the chance to breathe, that they will never be able to escape the cage.

The threat of violence against their families if they go against them is a big factor. Balram recounts how a servant of one of the landlords in his home village did some thing wrong and the landlord had the entire family killed. Balram suffers humiliation after humiliation and is expected to take it. His employer's wife gels drunk one night and forces Balram to let her drive and crushes a child. They make him sign a confession saying that he was driving, just in case they press the police for action. They take it as a matter of course that as their servant he would be glad to go to jail. After all one cannot expect their rich master to go to jail. (166-67)

Balram's letter to the Prime Minister is like the confession of a Christian penitent to his priest, save for one detail. He is not seeking absolution for any crime he has committed- he is just using himself as an example, to let the Prime Minister know the facts of life in India. Bribery and corruption are what greases the wheels of the great economic miracle of India; wheels that are still turned by slave labour. Underneath the statue of Gandhi and behind the walls of beautiful temples is corruption so ingrained that it's taken for granted as being the way things are and always will be.

The picture Adiga paints of India in *White Tiger* is of a nearly feudal society disguised as democracy. The country might have gained independence from the British but the majority of people are still trapped in servitude. Balram is a perfect servant. He worries whether his master is eating enough, takes pride in him when he behaves honourably and is disappointed with him when he is weak. For all his protestation of the system he is part of it as anybody else and it takes an enormous amount of strength and luck for him to live up to his name of "White Tiger".

He learned his lesson well and knows how to grease the wheels with the best of them. He's not some reformer advocating changes, although he dreams of opening a school where children get a real education so that they too can be 'White Tiger'. There is no room for mercy in this jungle that is Balram's India and the more tiger he has in his side the better.

Balram evolves to see the injustice of having to choose between family and self, slavish devotion to the master and autonomy. There seem to be two futures available "in the old days there were one thousand castes and destinies in India. These days there are just two castes. Men with Big Bellies and men with small Bellies. And only two destinies eat or get eaten up". (64). Balram seeks a third option to break free from the class of eaters.

The novel explores with wit and insight the realities of two India, reveals what happens when the inhabitants of one collide with those of other.

The secret of India is that its extreme inequality is stabilized by its strong family structure. His advancement can be achieved only by patronage and corruption-if you make friends with the local political setup you might can get a job as a bus conductor or by Balram's eventful method-stepping outside the [4]coop' of conventional morality.

The *White Tiger* traverses the familiar territory class and caste divide, poverty and exploitation and the triumph of the human spirit that one expects in a book that unfolds from a place called 'Darkness' in Bihar and draws its protagonist from an impoverished family of rickshaw puller who were Halwais before fate intervened. Balram, the hero as well as the narrator is a 'self taught entrepreneur; the story of whose upbringing is the story of "'how a half baked fellow is produced" "I am not an original thinker, but I am an original listener" (47). From the day the school Inspector singled him out as being the 'White Tiger' - the rarest creature in a jungle - the only boy who could read and write in the village school, and promised a scholarship to further his potential, Balram had his dreams, though fate intervened, his education discontinued, but ends up being a driver to a rich man, who takes him to Delhi. As he drives his master to shopping malls and call centers he becomes increasingly aware of immense wealth and opportunity around him, while knowing he will never be able to gain access to that world. As Balram broods over his situation, he realizes that there is only one way he can become part of the glamour that was new India by murdering his master. Balram confesses in the first person narrative, how he murdered his master, how the plan to commit that crime gradually and yet inevitably took form. How, on a rainy day in Delhi, he crushed the skull of his employer and stole a bag containing a large amount of money, capital that financed his Bangalore Call Centre for business. That business- ferrying technology workers to and from their job- in turn depended in keeping the police happy with occasional bribe. Balram says it would take a unique individual, a White Tiger, to be depraved enough to risk the lives of his entire family to steal the seventy thousand rupees his employer was carrying in a red leather bag to bribe a politician. As a startling denouement Balram describes how he capitalizes on his crime to recreate himself as an entrepreneur in the blooming Indian economy.

In page after page Adiga teases the readers with facts that the reader is familiar with but does not acknowledge. From common or petty parochial regional prejudices Balram learnt, "kill enough people and they will put up bronze statues near Parliament House in Delhi. What is glory or not. What am I, after all. All I wanted was the chance to be a man and for that one murder was enough". Balram's tale takes a macabre twist. He is not an entrepreneur but a criminal with a skill for self justification. The background against which he operates is not just resurgent economy and nation, but a landscape of corruption, inequality and poverty. He begins in rural darkness of a world of landlords and peasants; and, when he escapes to the Light[1] of cities, it is a world of servants and masters. Through Balram's personal story of murder and uncertain success we are drawn into the vortex of India's underbelly where as the narrator says. "The story of a poor man's life is written in his body with a sharp pen". (10-11)

In *White Tiger,* Adiga not only feels the gloss of the economic miracle to expose the rot beneath, he also shows the means by which a small minority subjugate the majority. It is a furious, brutally effective attack on India is shining advertisement and its hypocrisy.

Adiga presents an indomitable central character. Throughout the novel what sets him apart from his family, follow servants and even employer is that he never gives up his fight and ambition to reach high.

Towards the end of the novel, Balram, walking through the Delhi zoo thinks, "The moment you recognize the beautiful in the world, you stop being a slave". The *White Tiger* adheres to this revelation-beauty always exposes injustice, rather than mutely serving it.

The White Tiger contains passages of startling beauty-from reflection on the exquisite luxury of a chandelier in every room to a description of skinny drivers huddled around fires fueled by plastic bags. Adiga never lets the precision of his language overshadow the realities. No matter how potent his language, one never loses sight of the men and women fighting impossible odds to survive.

In a country inebriated by its new found economic prowess, Balram is a successful entrepreneur, a self made man who rises in the back of India's much vaunted technological industry. In a country proudly shedding a history of poverty and underdevelopment, he represents, as he himself says, tomorrow.

Adiga said the book was born of conversations with the servants and rickshaw pullers of India. "It is an attempt to capture the voice of the man you meet as you travel across India - people at a train station or a liquor shop. What struck me how funny a lot these people were, how similar their voice was, their sense of humour, their cynical intelligence, how similar they were to black America and this was a voice that had never been captured, and it was important for me to get that voice down. And to do so without sentimentality", The merit of the book lies in getting that point of view across.

The Time Literary Supplement said *White Tiger's* lack of subtlety can be weary, as can its cynicism. But it is a useful counter to optimistic tales of India's roaring economy'. *The Independent* wrote 'Arch defenders of India's claim to be truly democratic and there must be found few outside of the Indian cabinet-might balk at the *While Tiger.* Everyone else would be seduced by it.

From the beginning the *White Tiger* received an uncomfortable reception. Adiga if not a foreigner-a foreign returned. Regardless of his ethnicity he was a writer for *'Times Magazine'* and therefore guilty of writing bad stuff about India that the people here are poor, they suffer from diseases like polio, T.B. and the like.

There is much to comment on the novel, yet there is much to ponder. The scales have fallen from the eyes of some Indian writers, many either living abroad or educated there like Adiga. "The home country is invariably presented as a place of brutal injustice and sordid corruption .... My hunch is that this is fundamentally an outsider's view and a superficial one".[2]

The reaction to the *White Tiger* has not altogether been hostile, it has had varied responses Michael Portillo, Chairman of the five member panel of judges praised it for its 'originality'. The book was chosen because 'it shocked and entertained in equal measure' successfully engaging the reader with a 'thorough going villain' and dealing with social issues with 'astonishing humour'.

The reaction is not, because he holds a mirror to the ugly reality as Vijay Nair holds, but perhaps there is nothing new for the reader at home. A writer's job is not only to present reality, but as John Steinbeck said, the writing has to celebrate man's capacity for greatness...for courage, companion and love. The book must contain some redeeming quality. Like *Crime and Punishment,* a book of overwhelming darkness, is redeemed by the love and compassion in it; or, Hemingway's *Old Man and the Sea* which holds the nobility of man to prevail against all odds - man may be destroyed, but he cannot be defeated .... which *White Tiger* fails to impress.[3]

For a novel that is supposed to be a portrait of real India *White Tiger* comes across as curiously inauthentic, especially his presentation of ordinary people who are not only trite but offensive. His description of the Bihari migrant workers returning to their village after hard labour, "a month after the rain, the men come back from Dhanbad, Delhi and Calcutta leaner, darker, angrier but money in their pockets. The women were waiting for them. They hid behind the doors, and as soon as the men walked in, they pounced like wildcats on a flesh. They were fighting waiting and shrieking. My uncle would resist and keep some of the money but my father got peeled and skinned every time. I survived the city, but I couldn't survive the women in my home", he would say sunk into a corner of the room. The women would feed him "after they had led the buffaloe The novelist seems to know nothing about either the love or the despair of the people he was writing about. All the varied views only show what Shashi Deshpande aptly said, 'Being ignored is definitely worse than hostility, it is like your work falling into the abyss. A bad review is better than no review'.[4]

Adiga was seen as something of a dark horse, in a race in which Philip Hensher's, *The Clothes on Their Back,* Sebastin Barry's, *The Secret Scripture* and Amitav Ghosh's, *Sea of Poppies,* were fancied. Adiga beat the odds with his unusual voice and unsparing vision of India, that one may prefer to ignore, but perhaps the only part noticed and appreciated and recognized by the literary critics, especially the West-to whom this is reality, this is 'The Truth', though it may be half Truth or Ardhasatya, for it is the vogue of 'Slumdogs' which can bring million. Unequal distribution of wealth characterizes not only India, but the world over as George Orwell said, 'All men are equal but some are more equal than other and industrial revolution, as Carlyle commented had made England not one nation but two-the haves and have-nots and Dickens was considered the best guide to the 'Underworld of London' while Thackeray to the 'Upper', it was this disparity that had resulted in the French Revolution and the Bolshevik, and Oliver Goldsmith's observation in the *Traveller* still holds good" The rich men rule the law/ the law grinds the poor"

Reference

1. Arvind Adiga -.*White Tiger* Harper Collins Delhi 2008(all quotes pertain to this edition)
2. The Guardian: '*Outlook*', 27 Oct., 2008.
3. Vijay Nair: '*Hindu*', Feb. 2009.
4. Shashi Deshpande: '*Hindu*', 1 Feb. 2009.

Conclusion

Apart from being a part of a tradition that is now broad based and sturdy the creative writers in English are today more fortunate than their predecessors were as far as publishers and readership is concerned. Publishers are now ready to invest in books by Indian authors, not only because of the sizable market, but also because the depth and range of Indian authorship is very much larger than decades before. This is related to an enormous widening in the size of the middle class, our educational system, the general vibrancy which has emerged in our intellectual and cultural life over the past few decades. Our creative writing can now draw on a body of ideas which modern Indian scholars and thinkers have developed. Our scholars in several disciplines are second to none in the world. The level of academic writing and publications has undergone sea changes beginning roughly in the 1960s. The intellectual seeding that has occurred through some of the universities since independence has nourished the general level of debate and performance in innumerable areas including creative writing. It has provided a receptive audience for books, particularly to worthwhile material emerging from our own backyard. The interest is not only in printed matters but also visual and performing arts including cinema. In the world of scholarship, frameworks of analyses concerning India were laid down by the West and research dominated by English and American authors. The growing independence of the Indian mind has led to a rebirth in our arts and a confidence in our English writers which was lacking halfway through the century. They are also subject to fewer obstacles both within and outside the country as reflected in their attitude to their use of English. The Sahitya Akademi which was reluctant to recognize with an award to books written in English, with the only exception of R.K. Narayan, has since 1975 has been honouring Indian English Writing which reflects the fact that Indian Writing in English is no longer under siege, it can now look forward not only to dismal survival but regular acclaim. All this has contributed to the quickening pace of their emergence.

The hostility of Indian language chauvinists and the periodic ridicule of the West deterred many from believing that they could achieve anything worthwhile in English. It took the courage of a handful of writers, the vision of a few publishers-principally P. Lal and The Writers Workshop, and a new found interest outside India in Commonwealth Literature to free Indian Writing in English from charge of cultural sterility Though slow in coming once achieved it has given a sudden spurt to writing from 1980 onwards that it seems to celebrates the fact that it has done it A new generation of readers have come to age who do not carry the colonial freight which tags that every thing West is great. There is a kind of India today that is young and is interested in discovering India.-through Indian eyes as opposed to India being interpreted by an outsider .The contemporary capacious mind of India is today being nourished by the growing English reading public who read and buy them. It is heartening to see that many Indians have taken to writing in English as a profession, not as a past time or part time only, and are receiving wide attention and acclaim.

Index

D

E

G